3.25

UNDER THE EDITORSHIP OF

LUCIUS GARVIN

MACALESTER COLLEGE

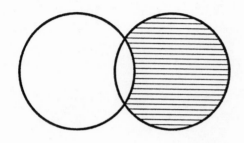

The Art
of Critical Thinking

TROY WILSON ORGAN
OHIO UNIVERSITY

HOUGHTON MIFFLIN COMPANY · BOSTON

05093

ACKNOWLEDGEMENTS

The author wishes to thank those who have contributed in diverse ways to the publication of this book: his students, who have made clear what will and what will not work in introductory logic courses; his colleagues, who have shared ideas philosophical and pedagogical, especially Robert M. Wieman who cooperated in the composition of the first five chapters; Richard N. Clark of the Houghton Mifflin editorial staff and Lucius Garvin, Editorial Adviser to Houghton Mifflin Company, whose encouragement and helpful advice have enhanced the satisfactions of this creative endeavor.

CONTENTS

INTRODUCTION

Critical Thinking and Education

A large American business corporation a few years ago posted signs marked THINK in conspicuous places in its offices. Shortly thereafter an artist drew a cartoon of a large office in which each person sat without movement at his desk in the familiar furrowed-brow, chin-in-hand posture of Rodin's "The Thinker," and a card manufacturer made and sold thousands of signs marked THIMK. This ridicule was deserved, for to command a person to think is much like commanding him to breathe. Of course man thinks — he thinks during every waking moment, although his thoughts are often rambling and undirected. Undoubtedly what the managers of the corporation had in mind was that their employees should think better than they were thinking, but even this command involves the dubious assumption that by taking pains people can improve their thinking. Is good thinking an ability which some possess, but others do not? Or can everyone learn to think better? And, if improvement is possible, is it teachable? A study sponsored by the American Council on Education indicates that college courses in logic bring about some improvement in thinking, but the number of students tested was admittedly too small to justify reliable generalizations.[1] Improvement in thinking is akin to improvement in writing. Do English composition courses help students to write well? Probably most teachers of English would contend that they teach the mechanics of good grammar and call attention to well-written essays, but whether they actually improve the students' writing depends largely upon the students. Those students who wish to write well will very likely improve, but students content with a telegraphic style of composition probably won't improve. Similarly, this book, which focuses attention on the process of good thinking, may be able to improve one's thinking if one wishes to think better. It is a question of leading a horse to water. Without thirst, nothing

[1] Paul L. Dressel and Lewis B. Mayhew, *General Education: Explorations in Evaluation* (Washington, D. C.: American Council on Education, 1954), pp. 202–206.

xi

happens. If a student is not aware of the possibility of improvement in thinking, no one can promise him very much from the reading of this or any book on thinking. While this is a negative way to begin, the author does not wish to mislead anyone into believing that the reading of this book will automatically turn him into a good thinker.

There are various kinds of thinking: ritual, random, appreciative, and critical. One thinks ritually when one devotes only the bare minimum of attention to following through a familiar succession of acts. Dressing in the morning, walking to class, talking about the weather, saying please and thank you—these are activities which require little attention. Random thinking is sometimes called reverie, wool-gathering, or free association. This type of thinking is often so unconscious that when someone offers a penny for our thoughts, we find ourselves unable to close the deal since we can't recall just what our thoughts were. Appreciative thinking is the enjoyment of nature, music, human love, etc. Critical thinking is the use of intelligence in making decisions. Improvement in this kind of thinking is the aim of this book.

Critical thinking does not occur unless a problem has blocked customary patterns. It is the process by which we overcome that block and move on. Of course, there are degrees of excellence in critical thinking, depending in part upon whether the problem is understood clearly and accurately, or dimly and indistinctly. To "solve" a problem before identifying it is a foolhardy way of acting which sometimes ends tragically. However, we may understand a problem and arrive at a happy solution (by accident or by following the lead of others) and still not think critically, since our solution did not consider the evidence which bore upon the problem. Evidence may consist of either our own observations, present or remembered, or the results found by other people in earlier situations.

In critical thinking we solve problems and settle doubts by exploring possible answers. These are called hypotheses. One of the most baffling steps in critical thinking is how to arrive at more and better hypotheses. This is a creative process about which we know very little. Frequently these suggestions come to a person when he is least expecting them: while taking a bath, upon waking from sound sleep, while dozing in the shade of a tree.[2] After hypotheses have arisen, the critical thinker selects among them. He understands the connection between the hypotheses he selects and the problem before him; he sees how they remove the uncertainty of the puzzling situation in which the thinking process started. He also recognizes why the rejected hypotheses would not clear up the difficulty.

[2] See Radoslav A. Tsanoff, *The Ways of Genius* (New York: Harper and Brothers, 1949), for many delightful accounts of the origin of hypotheses.

The critical thinker tests his hypotheses by imaginatively working out their implications and also by observing the results when the hypotheses are experimentally tested. After one of the hypotheses is accepted as a solution to his problem, the critical thinker must state his solution clearly, determine the degree of confidence it merits, find out how other beliefs are affected by this decision, and apply the solution to the disturbing situation out of which the problem arose.

This study of critical thinking is a discipline for improving the ability to solve problems. It is also a study of the process by which knowledge grows. By critical thinking man has risen from savagery to civilization. But critical thinking is more than this. It is the means through which civilizations improve. René Dubos has written, "The persons most likely to become creative and to act as leaders are not those who enter life with the largest amount of detailed, specialized information, but rather those who have enough theoretical knowledge, critical judgment, and discipline of learning to adapt rapidly to the new situations and problems which constantly arise in the modern world.[3] Man's knowledge is not a static inventory which can be divided into courses to be offered in college, transmitted to students, and then held as stock from which to draw dividends for life. The body of knowledge is a living organism. If, as some have claimed, the total of human knowledge in the twentieth century is doubling every ten years, and if, as others have claimed, the tempo of change in the second half of the twentieth century is ten times that of the first half and one hundred times faster than that of the immediately preceding centuries, even the notion that colleges can equip young men and women with "detailed, specialized information" adequate for their lives is absurd. According to Dubos, man in the modern world needs theoretical knowledge, critical judgment, and the discipline of learning. This volume is limited to the second of these educational goals.

[3] *The Torch of Life* (New York: Simon and Schuster, 1962), p. 65.

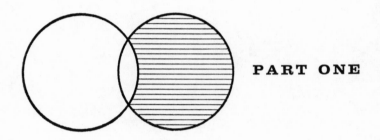

PART ONE

The Analysis
of Problems

1

Recognizing a Problem

1. *What is a problem?*

Much of life is routine. Routine is commonly thought to be a dull, monotonous way of acting, but James P. Thomas, a typical New York City commuter, is untroubled by the regularity of his life; indeed, usually he is unaware of the routine. He rises at 6:45 each morning; dresses in the current fashion; shaves with Soft-as-Velvet Brushless Cream; eats breakfast — orange juice, eggs, toast, and coffee; kisses his wife, and is off to catch the 7:30 train into the city. In the most important aspects of these acts he makes no decisions; his course is settled for him by habit. He may choose whether to get up immediately when the alarm rings or to stay in bed for five more minutes, but under normal circumstances he does not choose whether to get up or to lie in bed all morning. Getting up is an unquestioned routine. He may choose his tie, but usually he does not decide whether to wear a tie. Wearing a tie is settled by standards of appropriateness that he accepted long ago. He does not decide each morning whether he wants to work for a living. He may never think there is a decision to be made, since the grooves down which he moves are worn deeply by the actions of others who have preceded him. His job requires him to make many decisions, but, since his business is conducted efficiently, there is routine in the way he makes decisions and in the types of decisions he makes. His work for the most part is the adaptation of routine to new situations. The main outlines of his activities on most days are settled according to pattern, which means without thought, since in the words of John Dewey, "Men do not, in their natural estate,

3

think when they have no troubles to cope with, no difficulties to overcome."[1]

The actions of most men are largely routine. Some are well aware of the habits by which they live; probably most are contented with this regularity. They are well adjusted to their patterns. They live in their usual way without difficulty. It is true that things keep changing and people must adjust their courses of action in response to these changes, but most changes are not bewildering, and the adjustments become habitual. People do not have to make up their minds anew in every situation or re-examine their assumptions and intentions. Motorists do not have to think "Press foot on the brake pedal" when the traffic light shows red. Their adjustment has become thoroughly routinized; it has been embedded in habit.

William James once described habit as "the enormous flywheel of society, its most precious conservative agent."[2] The value of habit lies in the organization which it provides, making manageable the multitude of minor acts which must all fit together in some orderly way if they are not to cancel each other. A man acting without the aid of habit would resemble the centipede in the fable, who, trying to think which leg to move next, became unable to walk. The grooves that habit provides ease us without conscious attention from one action to the next. A life without well-established habits would be unthinkable. Imagine the absurdity of finding ourselves in a new situation every time we tied our shoes! It is well that much of life from day to day can be turned over to habit.

Especially it is important that social life follow strict routine. Custom enables us to predict what others are likely to do. Consider the chaos that would result if motorists drove their cars on either side of the street according to their whims. Knowing what others are likely to do is not only a help in avoiding mutual obstruction but also a necessary condition for any sort of intelligent interaction. Unless we have some idea of how

[1] *Reconstruction in Philosophy* (New York: Henry Holt and Co., 1920), pp. 138–9. Albert Camus has expressed man's routine — and break from routine — as follows: "Rising, streetcar, four hours in the office or the factory, meal, streetcar, four hours of work, meal, sleep, and Monday Tuesday Wednesday Thursday Friday and Saturday according to the same rhythm — this path is easily followed most of the time. But one day the 'why' arises and everything begins in that weariness tinged with amazement. 'Begins' — this is important. Weariness comes at the end of the acts of a mechanical life, but at the same time it inaugurates the impulse of consciousness. It awakens consciousness and provokes what follows. What follows is the gradual return into the chain or it is the definite awakening. At the end of the awakening comes, in time, the consequence: suicide or recovery." *The Myth of Sisyphus*, trans. Justin O'Brien (New York: Random House, Vintage Books, 1955), p. 10.

[2] *The Principles of Psychology* (New York: Henry Holt and Co., 1890), Vol. I, p. 121.

people will respond, we do not know what to say or do in our dealing with them. Cooperation and mutual support depend on successfully anticipating what will come next. For this reason the development of more perfect routines is one of the aims of any society. A. N. Whitehead says that "Routine is dominant in any society that is not collapsing."[3] "Routine," he adds, "is the god of every social system; it is the seventh heaven of business, the essential component in the success of every factory, the ideal of every statesman. The social machine should run like clockwork. Every crime should be followed by an arrest, every arrest by a judicial trial, every trial by a conviction, every conviction by a punishment, every punishment by a reformed character."[4] But we do not live in such an ordered society, and — Whitehead notwithstanding — when we consider what is involved, we would not wish to if we could. A life totally controlled by routine would be insect-like. A society of perfect routine would not require intelligence; it would not need to be understood. It might be a society ruled by instinct, as is the society of ants. Routine tends to produce routine-minded people — people who are so rigid in their pattern of thought and action that they cannot adjust to change. When railroads were first introduced in Germany, it was deemed advisable to explain the construction of the steam engine to the peasants. A group of men spent many months demonstrating the locomotive at hamlets along the railway. On one occasion after the engine had been thoroughly explained in terms of the pressure of steam in the steam chests which pushed the pistons and finally moved the wheels, the speaker asked if anyone in the audience had a question. A peasant spoke out, "We thank you for explaining the engine to us. We understand it very well now, except for one thing: where's the horse that makes it go?" Routine-minded persons find it difficult to take a fresh view of a situation. They attempt to interpret the new completely in terms of the old. Such people become obsolete quickly; the world passes them by.

Situations in which something needs changing and settled routines are not adequate to provide the needed change are problem situations. They demand decisions which are not entirely provided by existing habits. The change that is called for may be in ways of reacting, that is, in habits, attitudes, and beliefs; or the needed change may be in what we are reacting to, that is, in the externalities in the situation. A motorist who has difficulty with his car on cold mornings may need to develop the patience to allow the motor to idle several minutes before putting the car into

---

[3] *Adventures of Ideas* (New York: The Macmillan Company, 1933), p. 118.
[4] *Ibid.*, p. 113.

gear, or he may need to install new spark plugs — or he may need to do both. Disturbances in routines are probably increasing as modern living becomes more complex. Perhaps as routines become more varied and elaborate their application becomes less automatic.

What can we do when routine thinking is challenged? How ought we to deal with the indecisions and uncertainties that occur when routine thinking is inadequate? As long as the days move smoothly in their familiar order, we have few doubts and hesitations. But what happens when we face a problem situation? There are at least three ways in which a problem situation can be handled. One way is to play the ostrich: just ignore the disturbing situation by refusing to face the facts that would upset routine. Pretend the problem does not exist. Occasionally this may be the best way to deal with a problem. For example, idle gossip is best ignored. But a person who solves all his problems by the ostrich method is in need of psychiatric help.

Another way to handle a problem situation is to escape the unpleasantness of indecision (and also the unpleasantness of decision) by following the lead of someone else. A college freshman may try to get his counselor to take the entire responsibility for selecting his college courses. Or a young person may select someone as his hero and then try to copy him in everything he does. He talks like his hero; dresses like his hero; thinks like his hero. This use of an authority as guide frees him from a troubled mind — but at a high price. Being a blind follower results in an impoverished life, a life without the depth of experience that comes only from the contrast of alternatives both glimpsed and lived.

There is a third way to overcome the indecision and uncertainty which accompany a problem situation. This is to consider what alternatives there are to habitual ways of thinking and acting, and to shop around among these possible approaches for a solution. Considering other ways of organizing a situation and weighing these possible patterns against one another according to what difference they would make is the third way of meeting problems. Critical thinking is the process which brings about changes in habitual ways of thinking and acting in order to be more responsive to realities.

2. Causes of doubt and uncertainty

A problem which disturbs routine thinking and generates critical thinking is usually first detected as a vague feeling that something is not right. It is felt as a disturbance in the on-going pattern of life. The order of living ceases to be smooth; no longer is there an effective, comfortable adjustment between the train of events that are happening and the feelings, actions, and thoughts that these events provoke. The channels of orderly succession in responses become confused and uncertain.

People differ widely in their sensitivity to the signs of problems. Some drivers of cars are overly aware of strange noises in the engine and body. They are constantly taking the car to the garage to have every faint squeak and rattle diagnosed. Others drive their cars until they break down on the highway; they are completely unaware of the signs of trouble. The same contrast is found in abstract intellectual problems. Some people are very much agitated by everything which they cannot explain completely with their present beliefs, while others show a wide tolerance for things that do not fit their beliefs, sometimes expressing this tolerance by saying, "The exception proves the rule." In its usual use, such a saying means only that the speaker is content with considerable imprecision in his thoughts. Since we must live with our routines until better ones are developed, some degree of tolerance for confusion and disturbance is a practical necessity. But this insensitivity to problems can easily be overdone.

The feeling that all is not right does not arise out of the blue. Something has happened to destroy or weaken confidence in previous beliefs and habits. We shall consider five sorts of occasions for doubt and uncertainty.

(1) *When expectations of what will happen do not work out.* A small boy lights a firecracker on the Fourth of July, runs away, and then waits for the explosion. But nothing happens. So he is tempted to go back to investigate this unexpected development. A businessman stocks heavily in a certain popular commodity, but for some reason the goods do not sell. A physicist develops an apparatus to measure the difference in the speed of light as the beam of light is sent out with or at right angles to the earth's movement. To his astonishment he finds that the speed of light is constant in all directions — a fact that doesn't fit what he had assumed about the nature of light. These are cases in which a person is puzzled because events did not turn out in the manner expected.

(2) *When others do not think as we do.* Many young people find their college experiences disturbing, since during these years they hear for the first time ideas presented and defended which are quite different from the ones they met in their home communities. The broadening experience of exposure to new ideas is often first regarded as a threat to "true" ideas, meaning of course the ideas which were acquired in home and church. The German philosopher, Immanuel Kant, said he was aroused from

"dogmatic slumber" upon reading the works of David Hume; Karl Marx saw a completely different way to interpret the movement of history upon reading the works of Hegel. It is often supposed the awakening of theoretical studies in ancient Greece was a result of increasing contact with people in other parts of the world whose ways of thinking were strange to the Greeks. All of these are examples of how that which was assumed to be a natural way of thinking ceases to seem natural, and becomes problematic instead.

(3) *When different lines of thinking lead to contrary conclusions.* A problem sometimes arises in this way in the mind of a young person who has not yet decided upon his vocation. He is motivated both by the highly commendable desire to enter a profession in which he can make a significant contribution to the lives of other people and by another commendable desire, the desire to earn enough money to provide his wife and children with moderate luxuries. In his idealistic moods he would like to be a minister; in his realistic moods he would like to be an advertising man. Another example of this cause of doubt and uncertainty is the effort of archeologists to account for the prehistoric paintings of animals on the walls of deep caves in southern France. When the archeologists had in mind early man's superstition, they were inclined to interpret these paintings as part of a primitive magic to insure good hunting; but when the archeologists had in mind early man's love of decoration, these paintings seemed to be the efforts of prehistoric men to create something of artistic value. These are cases in which following out routine ways of thinking leads to conflicting conclusions, making the routines themselves problematic.

(4) *When someone asks an unexpected question that interests us but which we cannot handle.* Not every question presents a problem — but some do. If a question can be answered without effort by applying an accepted procedure, there is no problem. For example, someone asks the time of day, and referring to a watch, we reply "Three o'clock." No problem is involved in answering the question. But, if upon looking at the watch, we discover it is not running, then we have a problem. If a question is not provocative, even if we have no answer for it, it presents no problem to us. Probably the question "Where is Samarkand?" would exemplify this. Most people, although unable to answer this question, are unconcerned, and just dismiss it. But if the question presents a live issue and cannot be answered automatically, then it gives rise to a problem. The asking of such questions is one of the chief sources of critical thinking. There is an old adage that any fool can ask questions that the wisest man cannot answer. This saying has a sour tone, for it sounds as if it were

the observation of a wise man who couldn't answer a particular question put to him. Often the fool's question may be one which embarrasses the learned man because it approaches a subject from a new angle. But approaching a subject from a new angle usually makes our decisions more pertinent to the facts. In the Renaissance period of European history asking such questions was recognized as a service of the professional court fools. A favorite "fool's" question of college deans is "Why are you here?" The average college student, ill at ease in his first appearance before the dean, realizes that he has no ready answer. He is bothered by this question because he has probably never really considered it, although he would admit that it is highly relevant. These examples show how problems arise from interesting questions coming from a fresh point of view for which our routine responses are not sufficient.

(5) *When events are felt to be threats.* Sometimes events cause an unsettled feeling. Smoke pouring from under a car, strange rumbling in the plumbing, a black cloud rapidly rising in the western skies, a man approaching on a dimly lighted street with his right hand in his pocket — these are occasions which may cause a feeling of fear, confusion, and impotence. The situation calls for action, or for a readiness to act should the unsettling events develop further, but we may not be ready with any particular action. The response called for is outside the run of our settled adjustment patterns. In such circumstances we are unsettled and shaken. Customary patterns of accommodating to what happens do not provide a guide for what to do next. But there is a mounting pressure to do something. There is need to settle on a course of action that will meet the threat in such a way as to derange the overall structure of our environment as little as possible. But in serious threats the emotional strains are often so strong that we cannot act at all for a time, or we may act wildly with no rational control. The most difficult thing is to get over the paralysis of indecision or the equally useless uncontrolled action and get started adjusting our pattern of thought and action to the demands of the situation.

Not all threats are physical. Problems arise from threatening events when production patterns indicate that many farmers will have to learn to do different work from what they are now doing, when large numbers of children threaten to swamp present educational facilities, when judicial rulings undermine traditional practices in the Southern way of life, and when automatic machine controls give evidence of sharply changing roles for foremen. All these are problems arising from change which threatens to do away with the conditions upon which the even course of someone's life is based.

3. *Misunderstood problems*

Critical thinking takes its direction from the problem situation in which it arises. When mistaken about the nature of the problem, our thinking becomes fruitless and frustrating. Sometimes there is a feeling that something is wrong, but no change is demanded — at least no change is demanded in the external environment. A tired person may feel that everything is going wrong. A person who is ill, angry, worried, sleepy, or hungry may have feelings which he interprets as indications that his world needs changing, when actually there is no problem that a good meal and a sound sleep would not solve. In his situation, something is wrong, something does need changing, but the source of the trouble is not where he thinks it is. A settled, smoothly functioning personal world depends on patterns of reaction that are appropriate to the chain of circumstances. When there is a disturbance, the break between circumstances and reaction patterns may be caused by a temporary distortion in habits of judgment and behavior. If this is the cause, the obvious solution is to give ourselves a chance to get back to normal. At conferences of the United Nations in New York City the aides are trained to bring in refreshments at moments when tempers start to fly. They have learned that many problems dissolve during a coffee break.

Sometimes the presence of flying saucers is thought to demand an immediate change in our ways of thinking. A few years ago many people were giving quite varied reports of such objects. Some of the reports undoubtedly did not represent situations that constituted problems, except insofar as someone's jangled nerves demanded soothing. A great many of the entirely subjective conditions that give rise to problems can be known for what they are by asking others to confirm the existence of what seems to us to be a problem. Individual peculiarities are cancelled out by use of such a social check. Usually it is a good idea to check our awareness of a problem with someone else. This prevents concern over the wrong things in troubling situations. Sometimes it makes the solution so obvious that the problems vanish. Sometimes there was no problem at all. Every physician knows that a large number of the people who come to his office are not sick; or, if they are sick, it may not be a physical illness. Medical practice in ancient India held that the first job of the physician was to determine whether the reported illness was real or non-real. If the physician determined that it was real, he next diagnosed its cause. His third step was to determine if the illness was curable. If he thought it curable, the fourth step was to prescribe the cure. These four steps were used by the Buddha as the schema for his Four Noble Truths: suffering is an element in all of life; suffering is caused by desire; desire is caused, and therefore can be eliminated; the Eightfold Path is the way to eliminate desire, and therefore is the way to eliminate suffering.

Problems are sometimes misinterpreted in other ways. A plumber who used to be called frequently to a certain house always greeted the family upon his arrival with a curious question: "What seems to be the trouble?" At first they were annoyed by this question. What the trouble was seemed obvious enough. If a pipe drips, there must be some way to repair the leak. But they learned to appreciate the plumber's question. Perhaps it was not a leaking pipe that needed to be repaired. Perhaps the drip was caused by condensation, in which case the problem was quite different from what they had thought. It is as important to ask the right questions in a problematic situation as it is to know the answers to the questions.

Other examples of misunderstood problems can be found in the history of science. For example, scientists had asked for centuries why the heavenly bodies move. Ingenious answers were proposed, but it was not until Copernicus asked a different question that modern astronomy began. He asked what makes the heavenly bodies appear to be in the places where we see them. When he asked this revolutionary question, he was able to produce the revolutionary answer that the apparent changes of position are in part the difference of man's perspective due to the movements of the earth.

In all the above cases, the problem was ill conceived because the symptoms were not correctly interpreted. It is not enough to know that there is a problem; the problem must also be understood. It is the problem with which we are dealing that gives direction to our thinking. If the problem is not understood, we lack a sense of the direction our thinking should take to attain the most effective answer.

4. Is all critical thinking problem solving?

So far we have suggested that all critical thinking is directed by the feeling that something is wrong and needs to be changed. We have been discussing critical thinking as reflective adjustment to troubling situations, including confusions in our thinking. Not all experts agree that critical thinking is always an attempt to solve problems that were there before the thinking started, although it can be assumed that all experts believe critical thinking starts with questions. As R. G. Collingwood says, "You can't collect your evidence before you begin thinking . . . because thinking means asking questions . . . and nothing is evidence except in relation to some definite question."[5]

Sometimes the question arises from something external to the person: a job that must be done, a policy that must be settled, a technique that must be worked out. Externals that cry for solution certainly are often the starting point of an act of critical thinking. Herodotus claimed that mathematics arose in Egypt out of the necessity of resurveying the land after the annual inundation of the Nile River. Aristotle, on the other hand, thought that mathematics was founded by Egyptian priests in their leisure after the arts which aim at pleasure and utility had been discovered.[6] The problem which originates critical thinking does not necessarily have to be an external situation which arrests the even flow of one's life; it may be a thought problem which one has proposed to himself. Critical thinking which solves a problem presented by external conditions is said to have instrumental value. But critical thinking may also yield intrinsic values. The joy of achievement in orderly reasoning and the satisfaction in neat and precise results are not to be overlooked. Indeed, people often set problems for themselves for the sheer pleasure to be derived from the solving process. How else account for the popularity of jigsaw puzzles?

The task of recognizing the problem to be solved cannot be entirely separated from the other stages of critical thinking. Progress toward a solution of a problem provides a better understanding of the situation with which we are dealing and consequently leads to a sharper delimitation of the problematical aspects of that situation. A sharper delimitation in turn enables us to make more progress toward an adequate solution. It is a spiraling process in which each part of critical thinking contributes to every other part.

[5] *The Idea of History* (Oxford: Clarendon Press, 1945), p. 281.
[6] *Metaphysics*, 981 b 20–25.

Recognizing What Kind of a Problem It Is

After recognizing that he has a problem the critical thinker seeks to identify his problem by classifying it according to some meaningful order. One useful way is to attempt to fit the problem into one or more of the following possible classes of problems: (1) problems of identification, (2) problems of causation, (3) problems of means, (4) problems of ends. We shall examine the special characteristics of each of these kinds separately.

1. *Problems of identification*

These are problems that can be expressed by asking, "What is that?" To ask the question at all we must have something in mind for the word "that" to represent. "That" must stand for something distinguishable, such as a word, or a noise, or a patch of color, or a movement, or a taste, or an odor, or a touched thing. The problem of identification cannot arise unless we already know, in a sense, what the thing in question is. We must have some sort of acquaintance with it to be able to talk about it.

Furthermore, the question "What is that?" is asked in a context. Our hearer, if we are communicating well, knows in general what sort of an answer we are seeking. For example, if in a museum we stand before an article new to us and ask, "What is that?" it would be absurd for the

13

guide to reply, "That is an article displayed in the museum." This we know already. When we ask, "What is that?" in this context we are asking for information of a different kind. The problem will not be settled by being told that the article is a metal object, or an ancient relic, or a black thing, or a stimulus to the optic nerve. Under these circumstances, these facts about the object are almost certainly not problematic. The problem has not been met by any of these answers. Where we are and what we are doing makes the question "What is that?" an expression of uncertainty about the function or origin of the article in question. If the guide says it is a candle mold used by the early settlers in New England, our problem has been solved — if we know what a candle mold is.

If we have never heard of a candle mold, we may then quite properly ask the same question again, or at least use the same words. "What is that?" now expresses interest and uncertainty about what people do with the kind of objects the guide just referred to as a candle mold. The guide answered the question about the object by saying it belonged to a group called candle molds. We are now asking a question about the group to which the object belongs. The point is that the meaning of what is asked is in part determined by the circumstances and background and not solely by the words used to express the question. Also, a question that does not shape the sort of answer we are seeking — if such a question is possible — would be too indefinite to be of any use.

The problem of identification arises when we feel a need to characterize a thing more explicitly. What is meant by characterization can be illustrated by a little metal statue bought in a curio shop in Casablanca during World War II. The little statue, a vivid representation of a man in a pointed hat playing a musical instrument, is done in a primitive style which shows great skill. We know very well what it is in one sense; it is an object that can be called to mind at will with all the richness of its mood, form, and texture. But in another sense there is still a mystery about what it is. To ask, "What do we have here?" calls for something more than familiarity with the statue as an object to be looked at. The question calls for specifying the relations between the statue and other things.

An attempt was made to solve the problem of identification at the same time the statue was bought. The shopkeeper who sold it said it was dug from the ground, that these little statues were not rare, that they kept turning up all over that part of Africa, and that he thought they were made by the Romans. The reliability of his answers was doubtful, but his answers reveal what sort of information is asked for in a problem of identification. He stated an opinion on how the statue had been obtained, he gave some indication about how people would react to it, he stated where else he thought objects of this kind were found, and he placed the makers of the statue in relation to a historical period. Note that each of his comments related the little metal object to other things — to digging in the ground, to other objects similar to it, to a geographical area, and to an age.

Recently more expert advice was obtained to solve the problem of the statue. It was shown to an expert in art history. He was told what the shopkeeper had said, and then was asked, "What do you think it is?" He replied roughly as follows: "Oh, that is clearly modern; that is, no older than two or three hundred years. It is made of brass. And it was cast, not forged or filed, apparently with the use of a wax mold." He went on to say, "The little man's musical instrument has just one string. The loop around the neck of the instrument is slipped up and down to control the pitch. I don't recognize the instrument. His bracelets and features are African all right, but that conical hat seems Portuguese. His shirt has thick ornamented seams where it is closed down the back — that is African, as is the distortion of the body by elongation. But it doesn't follow the conventional patterns of traditional Central and West African art. I would guess it was made in Benin, in Nigeria, where they did a lot of this sort of casting and where the Portuguese influence was strong. If it was made there, it was probably cast between 1700 and 1750."

This answer shows what is involved in identification. The identification given is a list of statements that relate the object in question to our understanding of history, geography, metal-working processes, music, fashion, and style. "What is it?" calls for locating the object with regard to its significance and place in the complicated structure of related ideas that is our mental world.

A part of the identification given consisted of naming — and little more. Benin, for example, the name of the place where the expert thought the statue was made, meant little or nothing to his listeners, yet it satisfied our curiosity somewhat to know the place name. Although he was able to describe adequately how the musical instrument worked, the expert clearly would have felt he had given a more complete answer if he could have named the instrument. When we can give a name to a thing, in a sense it is no longer a strange unknown. If a thing does not have a label, we have trouble keeping it distinctly in mind so that the same kind of thing will be recognized when we come across it again. Labels are handles for catching hold of things and keeping them distinct from other things to which we give attention.

It has often been noted that people have a tendency to find a name for things they know nothing about. Then, having a name for their ignorance, they can answer questions with this name and their lack of information is no longer unsettling to them. For example, the question, "Why does opium put people to sleep?" has been answered, "Because opium has a dormitive virtue!" It is true that naming does not in itself add any information, but we should never overlook its importance in identification. Names do represent the fixing of attention on a given cluster of distinguishing characteristics so that we can recall them at will.

Problems of identification have their own peculiar sources of confusion and entanglement: (1) Any given thing ties into the web of other things in many different ways, so many as to make a complete statement of the connections of any given thing with all the others a hopelessly unmanageable task. We cannot identify a thing by all its qualities and relations, but must make some selection. There is no fixed guide as to which qualities or relations should be selected. A thing is identified by the characteristics which one assumes are most significant. What is most significant depends upon our concerns and activities. Our identifications thus reflect our interests and prejudices. For example, a brick may be identified as a part of a wall, or as a door stop, or as something to prevent a car from rolling downhill, or as a weapon, or as a flash of red color for an oil painting, or as that **##!! thing that fell on my foot. A complete identification would be one that correctly anticipates the future concerns and problems of everyone who will be related to the thing identified. This, of course, is impossible. (2) In making an identification there is always some tendency toward wishful thinking. If we desire strongly that something should be related to our activities and knowledge in a certain way, a very slight suggestion will bring about belief that these relations are fulfilled. In deer hunting season some hunters are so eager to see a deer that with great conviction they identify movements in the underbrush as deer. This wishful thinking sometimes results in disaster for other hunters. In making identifications one's wishes must be held in check or desire will lead to false conclusions.

2. *Problems of causation*

"What caused that?" or "What will that cause?" are questions that express the second kind of problem with which we are concerned. Problems of this kind arise when we need to find some pattern in occurrences so that we can trace backward to determine what led to the present state of affairs, or we can trace forward to predict what will follow from them.

Our concern in problems of causation is how different events are connected in a regular succession. Man's ability to control his environment is dependent on knowledge of such patterns in the succession of events. Other ways to express problems of causation are: "Why did that happen that way? How did that come about? What will be the effect of that?"

An example of a problem of causation is provided by the development of psychosomatic medicine, the study of bodily disorders induced by mental or emotional disturbances. One aspect of this interesting development in medicine is the change in beliefs about the causes of some skin diseases. It was once believed that all skin diseases resulted from either bacteria, fungi, and other growths or from chemical and physical irritations of the surface of the skin. In both cases it had been assumed that curing the disease was a matter of changing the physical conditions and chemical environment of the skin. It was assumed that change would remove the irritation or would create an unfavorable condition for the growth of harmful bacteria and fungi. Internal body chemistry was taken into account only insofar as nutrition and internal medicine had been found to affect the course of the disease.

The problem arose when it was noticed that a good many cases did not respond to treatment as expected. The use of medicines, changes in nutrition, and removal of chemical or physical irritations were not followed by disappearance of the symptoms. Also there were cases of rather dramatic healing when none of the supposed causes of skin disease had been altered in any way. The existing notions of the succession of events in bringing on skin diseases and in curing them were inadequate. Things did not happen as expected.

As has been said, perhaps with some exaggeration, there is nothing new under the sun, and these exceptions to the usual theories of the causes of skin diseases were not being noticed for the first time. The story of Job, reported in the Bible, includes an interesting case history of skin trouble appearing under unusual circumstances. Job, a man of position and substance, regarded his wealth as the just reward for his having always walked in the ways of the Lord. But then everything went wrong. His oxen and asses were stolen, his sheep were destroyed by fire, his camels were seized by his enemies, his servants were slain by the sword, and his children were killed in a whirlwind. Job could not understand why God had forsaken him. As God's perfect servant he had merited the wealth which had been showered on him. But now it was gone. He could not understand, and his body began to itch and ooze intolerably.

It was something of a surprise to modern observers to note cases similar to Job's. G. G. Robertson, for example, described a girl who developed a skin disease of the hands after working for five years in a tobacco factory. She was given medical attention, but the skin irritation did not respond to treatment. This raised a problem. Further investigation showed, among other things, that the illness began when the girl's supervisor had taken an unreasonable dislike to her and had made her life miserable. After the girl was transferred to the same sort of job under another supervisor, her hands improved in a few days.

The problem occurred because the succession of events over a period of time did not follow the expected pattern. Variations in expected patterns occur all the time, for no knowledge is perfect in every detail; but these variations give rise to critical thinking when there is some reason to expect or hope for more exact patterns of what will follow from what. In the case just outlined, the problem took shape because the vague outline of regularity in a whole class of occurrences was beginning to stand out. A sense of unjust suffering was noted as a common condition in many cases. This is an instance in which some suggestion of an answer preceded the isolation of the problem for systematic investigation. Not all critical thinking follows in step-by-step progression. Sometimes the elements of critical thinking occur in an intertwining order, as in this case.

Perhaps the special characteristics of problems of causation would be clearer if they were illustrated by a second problem — one that has not been solved. Penicillin is widely used to treat disease. It does not affect most micro-organisms, but it is known to kill a certain group of disease bacteria known as Gram-positive organisms. But no one knows how it kills these bacteria. The problem is how does penicillin bring about the death of Gram-positive bacteria. In this case the beginning and the ending in the chain of cause and effect is known. Penicillin is the cause which results in the death of the bacteria, but the succession of events which links the beginning with the end is unknown. The problem is to trace the connection in finer detail.

The first step in investigation was obvious, but it made the problem only more baffling. A bacterial cell can be treated with penicillin while it is being watched under a microscope. The usual life processes can be measured both before and after treatment with the drug. It was discovered that cells that are not increasing in numbers are unharmed by the drug. Their respiration and digestion of food continue unchanged. If cells are just marking time, they can go on living indefinitely even though dosed with penicillin, but as soon as conditions become favorable enough for the cells to reproduce the penicillin takes effect.

Bacteria reproduce by a process of division. A cell splits, becoming two cells that are just alike, each of which can split in turn after a period of growth. And here the mystery deepens. For even if the penicillin is washed away immediately after the cell division, the cells will eventually die. These affected cells look and act like healthy cells, growing, digesting, and respiring. But later on they cease to function and eventually dissolve. What the penicillin did to change the cells that divided in its presence was not observable.

The first hint of an answer to this problem came, as is often the case, from research done for an entirely different purpose. Work was being done on the part bacteria play in the formation of protein, the chief substance of living tissue. Proteins are formed by the union of compounds known as amino-acids. The researchers had picked one particular amino-acid, glutamic acid, for study because it was the easiest to measure. They soon discovered that some, but not all, bacteria store glutamic acid, drawing on it later to digest it into protein. Of all bacteria, it is only the group called Gram-positive organisms which have this trait of storing away glutamic acid for future use. As we saw before, only the Gram-positive organisms are killed by penicillin.

This coincidence suggested a connection between the results of the study of protein formation and the study of penicillin. This provided the break that was needed, and difference in penicillin-treated bacteria from those not treated by penicillin was found. The treated bacteria no longer stored up glutamic acid. Once they had divided in the presence of penicillin, no more glutamic acid came in, and they had to live on the accumulated store that was brought with them in the cell division. When this supply had run out, the cell died. In a way, this is the answer to the problem. Penicillin works by stopping the absorption of glutamic acid by cells that divided in its presence. This is the connecting link between the administration of penicillin and the death of the disease-producing bacteria. But in another sense this is not a solution to the problem. What piece of the cell is changed by the penicillin so that the cell can no longer store up glutamic acid? From further investigation a good deal has been learned about the way these cells accumulate glutamic acid. But the discovery of connecting links of ever finer detail in the succession of events between the administering of penicillin and the death of the micro-organisms goes on with no final end. As long as our interest in the possible results continues, the problem remains. Problems of causation can be pursued until present concerns are relieved, but our knowledge of the order by which events in a series are connected is never complete.

The special characteristics of the problems of causation may be indicated in three questions which the critical thinker must ask in connection with this kind of problem: (1) Is X (the "cause") always followed by Y (the "effect"), or may there be some instances in which X is followed by Y and some instances in which X is not followed by Y? (2) Is Y always preceded by X, or may there be some cases in which Y is preceded by X and some cases in which Y is not preceded by X? (3) Are there conditions of the appearance of X such that it is not X that accounts for the appearance of Y but rather these conditions of X that account for the appearance of Y? Causality as a relationship of events will be analyzed later in this volume.

3. *Problems of means*

Now we turn to the third class of problems. These are the problems that have to do with the means of bringing about a result which the critical thinker has decided is a desirable state of affairs. "How can I accomplish that?" expresses this kind of problem. As in problems of causation, the concern is with the connection between earlier events and the consequences that follow from them.

A problem of what to do is only a problem of means if goals are already set. "What should I do?" is an ambiguous question. It can express a questioning of the aims; in which case it expresses a problem of ends. Or instead it can express a questioning of the way to accomplish aims that are already established. In the latter case the question expresses a problem of means. If an apprentice mechanic working on a car in a garage asks the shop foreman, "What should I do?" he expresses a problem of means. So would a young man who writes to an advice-to-the-lovelorn column in the newspaper asking what to do about his shyness in getting acquainted with the young lady of his fancy.

Some of the distinctive characteristics of problems of means can be brought out by an example from international affairs. The nationalist movement in Egypt forced the British to abandon their military bases in that area in 1954, including their bases along the Suez Canal. The canal continued, however, to be an essential channel for obtaining oil for England and other countries upon whose economic well-being British security depended. In violation of a convention that had long regulated the use of the canal, the Egyptian government closed the canal to ships bound for Israel, with whom Egypt was technically in a state of war. As relations between Great Britain and Egypt worsened, there was danger that a time might come when Egypt would threaten to close the canal to British shipping, which made up a majority of all ships using the canal. In July, 1956, Egypt nationalized the Suez Canal Company, an international corporation which had built the canal and operated it under a 99-year concession that was to run until 1968. This action increased the threat that access to the canal would be used as a weapon of Egyptian diplomacy.

The problem for Great Britain was to make sure that the canal would never be closed to the trade that was so essential to her, nor be used as a threat to force her to give up other vital interests. After suffering severe setbacks in her dealings with the Egyptian government, Great Britain was also concerned to re-establish her prestige and influence in the Middle East. The possible solutions were limited by several facts. The British had found ground for mistrusting the permanence of negotiated agreements with the existing government of Egypt. Furthermore, the British government had little confidence that international organizations dominated by the United States would solve this problem, since the American State Department was more concerned with maintaining the Arab nations' favor in the struggle between the Russian bloc and the Western alliance than she was in the ends that were so important to the British. What was needed to accomplish the ends the British had set for themselves was some international agency to regulate the operation of the canal. Obviously the existing routines for dealing with foreign affairs were not safeguarding what the British regarded as their essential needs.

Under these conditions, there were several possible ways to get Egypt to accept some international control so that canal users would have greater security in their right of passage. Financial pressure could have been exerted by tying up Egyptian funds in England. Nations upon which Egypt depended heavily might have been persuaded to express disapproval so strongly that the Egyptians would not push their canal claims because of the unfavorable consequences that would follow. There was also the possibility that British aid to the political groups opposing the present Egyptian leaders would bring about a change of leadership more favorable to England. Another possible course of action to attain the aims that Great Britain had set for herself was forcibly to seize the canal and then insist that her demands be met as a condition for the withdrawal of British military forces.

Probably all of these possibilities were explored. Attempts to organize an effective boycott broke down because of lack of interest on the part of some of the nations which used the canal. Financial pressures were attempted but did not seem to be effective, partly because international exchange funds tied up in England were not needed for Egypt's growing trade with Communist nations. Getting the effective disapproval of nations with which Egypt had indispensable dealings was thwarted by a wait-and-see attitude in the American State Department and by agreements made between Egypt and Russia which would provide commercial and military ties to replace those lost with the countries that Great Britain could influence. No information is available concerning intervention in Egyptian domestic politics, since this course would have violated fairly widely held principles of international morality and would have been kept secret, but the personal popularity of President Nasser of Egypt almost certainly would have made this course impractical. The remaining course of action, forcible seizure, became more promising as time passed, for it was learned that the French would join such a venture and that military action by Israel against Egypt was also imminent.

The British government apparently thought forcible seizure would have the greatest chance of accomplishing the desired goals if it were accomplished quickly. Ending the fighting quickly would also have minimized the danger of provoking a war between the major powers, a war which certainly would have been contrary to British aims of much greater importance than those involved in the canal dispute.

On October 31, 1956, with as little previous notice to other nations as possible, the British and French landed at the north end of the canal and the operation was under way. It did not succeed in accomplishing the British aims. Before the occupation of the canal zone could be completed, the Russian government threatened to send volunteers and equipment to aid the Egyptians. The American government declared it would not aid the British and French in the event of local Russian intervention. In the face of such a prospect and without unanimous support at home the British and French forces were withdrawn.

The distinctive characteristics of problems of means illustrated in this rather lengthy example are these: (1) Settling a problem of means is making a choice between the various ways in which aims might be attained. The choice is between courses of action which would theoretically solve the problem, but the circumstances in which the problem arises limit practical consideration to a narrower field. In the example just given certain potential solutions were ruled out in advance because of knowledge of the concerns of the American State Department and because of past experience with the impermanence of Egyptian policy declarations obtained through negotiation. (2) Even when a general course of action is settled upon, the problem of means repeats itself in question of detail. In this case the decision on speed and the decision not to consult with other powers were again choices between alternatives. A problem of means becomes a series of interrelated questions as the details of a possible course of action are worked out. (3) Decision on the best way to attain a particular aim cannot be isolated from a consideration of the influence of this decision on the attainment of other aims. In the case cited, a part of the British-French decision was determined by their concern with maintaining peace between the great powers. Actions undertaken for the attainment of one goal obviously also have effects on the pursuit of other goals; so they cannot be dealt with in isolation from one another. (4) Another characteristic of problems of means appears in their relation to other kinds of problems. The elements of the situation to be considered are known through identification, the process of finding out how each element fits into the web of facts known to us. The effectiveness of various possible actions in bringing about the desired result is estimated on the basis of knowledge of causation. (5) Lastly, success or failure in attaining aims that have been accepted is one of the most important influences leading to a modification of ends. In this case, the British failure to find any successful means to attain what had been their settled aims led to a considerable contraction of their aims in this area. Thus, problems of means are closely related to the pursuit of problems of other kinds.

4. *Problems of ends*

Sometimes people become uncertain of their goals. An eager "young man in the grey flannel suit" occasionally wonders if he really wants to become president of the company; a struggling actress has moments when she doubts that becoming the star of the show would be the finest of all achievements. They doubt that what they want is entirely adequate, and they suspect there are other things more worthy of pursuit. Their aims become unsettled. This kind of problem is expressed by asking, "What should we want?" or "Is such-and-such a worth-while goal?" Uncertainty about ends may arise because people find that their experiences on attaining a goal are not what they had expected them to be, or they suspect that the pursuit of some goal (or the failure to pursue some goal) alters their sensitivity to the values of other possible goals, or they find that the goals they have accepted are not attainable. Each of these sources of problems suggests one basis for critical thinking in re-examining ends — an appeal to the qualities of experience that accompany the attainment of a goal, an appeal to changes in sensitivity or responsiveness that result from the sort of ends pursued, and an appeal to practical attainability.

One of the clearest examples of a people facing the problem of ends is the struggle of Russia in this century. In 1917 the Russian people made a sharp break with their traditional principles of government. Late in 1917 the Bolshevik party obtained control and declared a dictatorship by a committee which intended to plan a completely new social order. The next nine years were chiefly occupied in consolidating control over the state. Then on October 1, 1928, Russia embarked on the pursuit of one of the most comprehensive sets of goals any nation has ever explicitly formulated. These goals, called the "Five-Year Plan," were published in volumes containing more than 1600 pages. While these national ends were primarily directed to the industrialization of Russia and the creation of a society with more centralized planning and control, the ultimate declared goal was a higher standard of living for all the people. No longer, said Stalin in 1931, will Russia be derided by other nations "for her backwardness, for military backwardness, for cultural backwardness, for governmental backwardness, for industrial backwardness, for agricultural backwardness." Some of the goals set were tremendous increases in production under the Plan: coal, 259 per cent; cotton yarn, 229 per cent; pig iron, 238 per cent; cattle, 134 per cent; grain, 129 per cent; agricultural machinery, 743 per cent.

At the end of the First Five-Year Plan the Soviets discovered that their industrial output had increased about 20 per cent, but the quality was inferior, and agriculture had lagged seriously behind other activities. The Seventeenth All-Russian Conference of the Communist Party examined the successes and failures of the First Five-Year Plan and prepared a Second Five-Year Plan in which the development of electricity was a major item. Subsequent Five-Year Plans — the Third (1938–1942) stressed the development of the eastern part of the vast Soviet Union, and the Fourth (1946–1950) stressed heavy industry, transportation, and scientific research — are further illustrations of a large nation struggling with the problem of what goals it should set for itself. Some of the goals had to be changed because of widespread dissatisfaction. The First Five-Year Plan had placed too much emphasis on heavy industry and not enough on essentials like soap, food, and clothing. Propaganda about the glories of industrial production did not fill empty stomachs nor warm ill-clad bodies; hence, in the next Five-Year Plan more attention was given to the improvement of the unsatisfactory living conditions that were causing unrest and disorganization. Allowances also had to be made at the end of the First Five-Year Plan for two unforeseen international complications, the Japanese invasion of Manchuria and the reluctance of nations to sell on credit to the Soviets.

No plan was in effect during the war years of 1942–1945. The experience of the war years was evident in subsequent plans where there was a shift of emphasis between the goal of industrialization and that of improvement in the standard of living. A better standard of living continued to be desired by the planners, but attempts to achieve this end had to wait on the attainment of more pressing goals. A large increase in material comforts for all the people was pushed into the never-never land of remote future hopes. This goal did not actively guide the practical decisions of the moment. Industrialization was pressed harder than ever, but the focus shifted from the competitive desire to avoid backwardness to a desire for international influence by a more direct means than ideological agitation and persuasion. Industrialization was not now regarded merely as a means to international influence, just as it had not before been sought solely as a means to attain respect. Industrialization was sought as an end in both plans, although the qualities associated with this end shifted. But a lack of industrialization now suggested weakness and ineffectuality. Even though an end may be pursued for its own sake, its suggestive associations enter heavily into the valuing attitudes with which that end is regarded. Of course it could be said that all these goals were means to attain the ultimate goal of progress. But to say this does not help matters, for progress is such a vague term that although it represents something that approaches our aims, it does not indicate in any way what these aims are.

From this example of the problem of ends, these distinctive characteristics may be noted:

(1) Goals tend to keep shifting. Even when the same ends are pursued, after a time they come to have different associations. To control these shifts by critically re-examining ends is to solve problems of ends by critical thinking. In the case of the Russian planners, the goals sought were modified as a result of experience in pursuing them and as a result of new attitudes and concerns that came into existence because of difficulties with other nations.

(2) Some ends come into view only after a satisfactory level of progress toward other goals has been achieved. For example, development of the eastern part of the Soviet Union became a goal after reasonable progress was made toward industrialization and centralization of authority. But with an unfavorable change of conditions this process can be reversed; aims that have been consciously pursued may be replaced, even though not attained, by more fundamental ends which had formerly been taken care of by nonreflective routine. The ends which enter into critical thinking are not a final exhaustive representation of the aims of man, but a selection of those ends that lie between the aims that are assured by automatic routine and those that are impossible of attainment under present condi-

tions. We can only wonder what ends men would be aware of if the possibilities of controlling their environment were either greatly increased or disastrously decreased.

(3) The distinction between what is sought as a means to something else and what is sought as an end is not a hard and fast one. The original declared aim of Communism was to speed the progress of social evolution, progress in this case being identified with the development of the classless society and a higher standard of living to be shared in proportion to need. The later Five-Year Plans showed what happened to the second ultimate aim: a higher standard of living remained as an ultimate end in the thought of Communists, but it became so exclusively associated with a world of perfection in the distant future that its connection with the decisions made in an imperfect present world became more and more vague. When an end becomes so separated from practical decision-making, it may be called a mythical goal. Every society and probably every individual has some mythical goals.

The other ultimate end declared by the early Communists was the development of a classless society. This end also shifted. A classless society was envisioned as one in which the manner of one's participation in the order of society would not set his interests apart from those of other people. To accomplish this end, a centralized dictatorship was established in the U.S.S.R. to plan, coordinate, and enforce the necessary changes in the existing social order. But when a classless society did not come into being, the totalitarian dictatorship that had once been regarded as a means to bring about a classless society came to be thought of in practice as the classless society itself. What had been a means to something else was now sought as an end in itself.

The division into problems of identification, problems of causation, problems of means, and problems of ends is not the only way of classifying problems. Problems might be classified according to the number of people involved. Some problems are largely personal, others largely social. They might be classified into economic, social, political, scientific, and religious problems. They might be classified according to their urgency. Some problems must be solved at once; others are problems in which the solution is not urgent. There are doubtless many other ways of classification. Our classification is only a suggested way of dividing problems. The purpose of identifying the problem in some scheme of classification is to provide a starting point for settling the disturbing situation, to make the problem definite enough so that something can be done to solve it. After the problem is identified, the next step is to state it clearly and usefully.

Stating the Problem Clearly

1. *Importance of a clear statement of the problem*

In a problem situation something needs changing, and the change is not forthcoming from routine behavior. Every day we come upon many situations that need to be altered. Most of them are not problems, since we usually have no hesitation in making the required adjustments. If our hands itch, we scratch; if we come across an unfamiliar word, we look it up in the dictionary; if the telephone rings, we answer it. These are situations requiring change, but they are not problems, since we have ready-made responses for them. If the bodily sensation is not a simple itch but rather a dull persistent pain in the abdomen, or if the dictionary does not contain the word, or if the noise is not the ring of the telephone but a loud report high in the cloudless sky, then we may have a problem.

One of the first steps toward a solution is to state the problem clearly. Clearness refers to communication, and communication usually means a relationship between two or more persons. Our statement provides symbols which keep thoughts fixed in the mind for later use. It is only by the use of symbols that many considerations can be kept in mind and kept in any manageable order. Robinson Crusoe probably made his predicament clearer by forming statements in his mind during those first tragic days when he found that only he had survived the shipwreck. In less solitary circumstances the statement of a problem does double duty, marking out the problem for others as well as for oneself.

There are three reasons why it is important to state a problem clearly: (1) to enlist the help of others; (2) to get clues for action; (3) to know when the initial problem is solved. Let us begin with the first reason.

27

There are some problems that cannot be solved without the help of other people. Even if a person can handle a problem alone, he may want to discuss it with others to supplement his insight and experience. Sometimes it is difficult to state a problem to another so that he understands it. Two of the most common causes of lack of clarity in the statement of a problem are unfamiliarity with the subject and a limited vocabulary. Let us consider an example in which both these difficulties are present.

A young woman drove into a filling station one evening and announced in panic that the battery of her car had "blown up." The attendant was at a loss to know what to make of the trouble. He began by assuring her that batteries may go dead, may become dry, may corrode the wiring, and may even drop off the car, but they do not blow up. The attendant assured her that since the motor of the car was idling, the battery was supplying electricity to the spark plugs while they were talking. The woman then explained that her husband had always told her not to start the motor when the lights were on. But, forgetting his caution, she had started the engine this time without turning off the lights; and when she turned the corner a block from the filling station, IT had happened — "the battery blew up!" After more questioning, she admitted that what had happened was that the lights of her car had gone out. When the filling station attendant examined the car, he discovered that the lights were out because the light switch was turned off. Evidently the excitable young woman had unknowingly hit the switch as she turned the corner.

The filling station attendant was unable to help solve the problem presented to him until it was stated more clearly. He would have been spared considerable confusion and could have given assistance at once, if the question put to him had been "How can I get my headlights to work again?" The young woman's use of words that have no generally accepted meaning in this situation obscured her predicament instead of communicating it. More seriously, her misinformation about the electrical system in an automobile had so confused the problem that her thinking gave the attendant no practical point from which to start his investigation.

The second reason for stating a problem clearly is that the representation of the problem gives direction about what to do. Until we state the problem clearly, we have few clues for action, and we have no way of knowing whether the clues we have are adequate. Frustrations do not carry with them their own remedies. Until problems are made clear, efforts to solve them are haphazard and may even block a satisfactory solution. For example, a homeowner upon arising in the morning finds there is a slight smell of gas all through the house and no hot water. If he does not think of the problem in some definite way, he will probably act aimlessly for some time. Meanwhile the problem very likely will become more serious. He may realize that the flame in the hot water heater has gone out in the night, and say to himself, "How does one light that thing?" This way of expressing the problem has not clearly represented many of the problematic aspects of the situation. The immediate clue to action that is provided by the question asked may lead to far worse troubles than the present ones.

Sometimes we do not get good clues for action because our statement of the problem does not take into account all the relevant factors. A statement that only partially represents a problem is inaccurate, and the action based on such a statement is often unwise. Consider two married couples assigned to live for one year in identical student housing. Both couples disliked the dull gray color of their living room walls and decided to do something about it. Both were living on very small budgets. The Smiths thought of the problem as "We don't like the gray paint in our living room." As a problem of paint, the action that was suggested was a trip to a paint store. In time they bought some brighter paint and spread it on the walls themselves. The Browns represented the same problem to themselves as "We don't like the dull impression this gray-painted living room makes." This statement of the problem suggested some slightly different courses of investigation. The Browns bought some bright material for curtains which extended beyond the windows and also devised a modernistic wall hanging out of colored strips. When the students received their degrees and left the university, the Browns took their curtains and wall hanging with them, while the Smiths had nothing to show for their investment in paint. The Smiths had not stated their problem clearly because their statement limited the clues for action to painting, although in fact several other lines of action would have taken care of the problem situation as well or better. The problem was not really one of paint but of the visual impression produced by their living rooms. To state the difficulty as one of paint was to jump to a conclusion about what could best be changed under the circumstances. The Smiths conceived their problem too narrowly; they were not clear about all the aspects of the problem.

Suppose either of the above couples had failed to keep in mind their limited financial resources. The range of possible solutions would seem much broader. A good professional interior decorator might have been called in. In that case the living room would probably look fine, but with unmanageable bills there would still be a disturbed situation. The absence of funds was one of the elements in the problem. This element was included in the way both couples thought of their situation, although not put in words in their statement of the problem. It may be impossible to state explicitly all the things that enter into a problem situation. An adequate statement is one that guides attention to all the factors that might otherwise be overlooked. The statement need not point out that which is obvious to all concerned, although people sometimes take too much for granted on this point. Occasionally elements such as a limitation of funds are overlooked. In that case people have not stated their problem clearly enough to give adequate direction to their efforts in looking for a solution.

The third reason for stating a problem clearly is to provide a standard for determining how much progress is being made toward a solution. The statement of a problem singles out certain characteristics of the unsettling situation as needing change. The sense of progress in the solution of a problem is guided by a comparison of results with the changes indicated in the statement of the problem. Unless we have correctly located the problem, we may be quite mistaken about the progress and may think our task is over, even though the troubling aspects of the situation remain. This is often observed in a person who has trouble in telling a story well. He sometimes thinks he has made his point, although he has not in fact communicated the essential point to his listeners. Sometimes it works the other way. He tells his story well; but, not realizing he has done so, he continues to talk until the effect is ruined. In both cases the trouble is that he is mistaken about what prevents his telling a story well; consequently, accomplishment of the task as he has represented it to himself does not correspond to accomplishment in the objective sense.

2. *The necessity of signs*

We have indicated that one of the steps toward the solution of a problem is a clear formulation of it. While this is a sound procedure, a solution is not excluded if the problem is not clearly expressed in words. Sometimes problems are solved without the use of words at all. Two friends traveling in France a few summers ago needed new soles on their shoes. One of the two spoke French. He took both pairs of shoes to a cobbler, but the cobbler, carefully explaining that he had more work than he could do, refused to repair them. Then the second traveler, who spoke no French, took the shoes to the same cobbler and conveyed by gestures that he needed them fixed. For lack of words that his customer could understand, the cobbler could not explain his objections to more work. The problem was solved — the shoes were resoled within the hour. But this illustration of getting along in a foreign country without knowing the native tongue does not destroy the claim that it is important to state a problem clearly. Although no words were used, a statement was conveyed by other signs. Words are just one of several forms of signs which may be used in stating a problem. An understanding of the use of signs is helpful in stating problems clearly and is useful in other stages of critical thinking as well.

A sign is something that is directly sensed that calls attention to something other than itself. Signs are like fingers that point to things. There are three kinds of signs: (1) *iconic* signs, which direct attention to some object because they are similar to it, e.g., a cartoon represents a person because it looks like him; (2) *indexical* signs, which point to something because they are associated with it either as cause or as effect, e.g., smoke is a sign of fire; (3) *conventional* signs, which stand for things by virtue of custom alone, e.g., red stands for stop, yellow for caution, and green for go, although there is no reason why red could not mean go, and yellow mean stop, and green caution. Most words are conventional signs. Of course some words are iconic; words such as "hiss," "buzz," "purr," and "murmur" sound like that to which they point, and so their meaning is not dependent on customary associations alone. But these words are exceptions. In the more common case of conventional signs, it is important to remember that customs change from time to time and vary from group to group. As a result, conventional words do not have single, fixed meanings. They mean whatever people use them to mean when both speaker and hearer agree in their interpretation. Rules of usage are ways of finding such agreement and avoiding confusion; they are not laws that say what words must mean.

There are natural signs and artificial signs. Natural signs are not devised by one who is trying to communicate, although an observer does find meanings in them. The example of smoke being a sign of fire is a natural indexical sign. There are also natural iconic signs, as is evident from the many mountains that have represented sleeping giants or bald men to some people. Conventional signs, however, are always artificial; the sign is intentionally produced by some person to whom the meaning is known. For each case in which an artificial sign is used, there is a sender, a receiver, and a referent. (The referent is the object, action, or idea to which the sign directs attention.) The use of the sign indicates something about all three. That the sign was used reveals something about the sender — he must have had the feelings that give rise to the behavior that culminates in expressing the sign. This indication of what is being experienced by the sender is what the sign expresses. The sign also indicates something about the referent. What the sign directs attention to is its descriptive meaning, what the sign describes. In addition, the sign provokes some response in the receiver. This is what the sign motivates. A man in deep water yells "Help!" to express his alarm, to describe the fact that he cannot swim to safety, and to motivate the lifeguard to give assistance. "Help!" under these conditions is all that is needed to state his problem clearly. But if he were to walk out on his front porch on a quiet Sunday afternoon and yell "Help!" he would mystify his neighbors rather than reveal a problem to them. The customs that establish the meaning of a conventional sign depend on the presence of appropriate circumstances. Outside these circumstances the sign's meaning becomes indefinite, and clarity is lost.

As we have just seen, the functions of words are expression, description, and motivation. These three functions do not always fit together smoothly. A sophisticated user, aware of the effect of his words, may choose his words to express his feelings exactly, although the words chosen are somewhat misleading descriptively or motivationally. This is commonly the case, for example, in poetry. On another occasion the same person may sacrifice something in expressive and descriptive clarity for the sake of exact motivational communication, as in persuasion or in giving orders. Or he may permit expressive and motivational vagueness for the sake of greater descriptive perfection, as in science. The circumstances in which words are used do a great deal to make clear how the emphasis falls among the three sign functions, but there is always room for misunderstanding. Many a breach of promise suit arises out of the fact that his motivational "I love you" was interpreted by her as an expressive "I love you" with reference to marriage, home, and children! The entanglement and the disentanglement of the expressive, descriptive, and motivational functions of language constitute much of the comedy and tragedy of human relations.

Part of the problem in the use of words is the fact that words both denote and connote; that is, words not only represent things, but they also convey what these things have come to suggest to people. The word "dog" denotes a domesticated canine, but in addition the word has acquired a host of connotations — low, cowardly, snarling, uncouth, ill-tempered. Often new words are invented with the same denotation as established words to convey new connotations or to avoid the customary connotations, for example, cur, mutt, and *canis familiaris.* The above suggestions that are clustered around the meaning of "dog" might be called the public connotations of the word, since they are the fringe of meaning for most people. In addition there are private connotations. A man who has recently been bitten by a dog has a very different reaction to "dog" than has a child who has just been given a puppy. Since everyone's experience is different from everyone else's, the words used by the sender always have somewhat different meanings for the receiver. Words not only help give definite form to problems so that one can keep track of them, but words sometimes also create problems of their own.

3. *Classification and definition*

Consider an infant's limited grasp of the world. With no words to label things, no experience which relates things, no conception of cause and effect, he must find life a "blooming, buzzing confusion." When he has troubles, he is unable to identify them for lack of ideas that would connect things together. But not for long. Very early the infant remembers and classifies; he begins to make sense of the infinite sensations which crowd each other.

Classifying and defining give order to experiences and ideas. The result of classifying is not knowledge, but neither can one know without classifying. When one classifies, he divides a subject into groups depending upon his interests and purposes. Human beings, for example, can be classified into men and women, rich and poor, bourgeois and proletariat, lost and redeemed. The Chinese language has terms for over one hundred family relationships for which there are no terms in English. Since classifications depend upon the use the classifier has in mind, schemes of classification come and go. None has ultimate finality. The classification is always directed by some problem, but it must also be guided by the characteristics of the material to be classified.

Not only do we have classes of individuals, but we also have classes of classes. John and June are classified as sophomores; sophomores are classified with freshmen, juniors, and seniors as college students; college students belong to the class of people; and so we could move on and on to increasingly general classes. In biological classification the ladder of generality is most elaborate: variety, species, genus, family, order, class, phylum, kingdom. If this seems to make biology extremely complex, think how much more complex our knowledge of the world would be in the absence of general names. Indeed scientific knowledge would be impossible were there no class names. Each leaf on each tree would have to be considered separately! A new object is not so new when we relate it to a class of familiar objects. Classifications are a way of relating the unfamiliar to the familiar, the old to the new. The question "What is that?" must be answered by assigning the unknown object to a familiar class. This is the first step in identifying any problem.

Logicians have devised rules for good classifications. One is that the classes to which an object is assigned must be appropriate; for example, human beings cannot be classified according to the size and shape of their horns, since they have none. Secondly, the principle by which things are divided into classes must be the same at every level of classification within a system. Consider the foolishness of trying to classify men into these four classes: redheads, those with an I.Q. over 125, club-footed, and unmarried. Thirdly, the classes used should include all individuals who are to be classified; for example, to classify men according to the color of hair would exclude the completely bald from the class of human beings. Fourthly, the classification should exclude all individuals who ought not to fit into the class. There is a story that the students in Aristotle's school in ancient Athens once ridiculed Plato's classification of man as a featherless biped by sending a plucked chicken to Plato's Academy.

Definition, like classification, consists essentially in exchanging the unfamiliar for the familiar. Ideally the defining words can be used in place of the defined words, although this is an ideal which is only approximated because of the varying connotative meanings of words. The necessity for definition of concepts comes about in a curiously circular process. Because of the vagueness of the words we use in our ordinary conversation, we must create other words, which in turn must be defined in the words of ordinary conversation. Sometimes in order to make our ideas clear we must use unfamiliar words; at other times clarity requires that we convert these back into the small coin of ordinary communication.

To define is to outline the limits of what is included in the referent of a word. As words are used, their original meanings expand. If we look at any page of a dictionary, we shall notice that many words have a variety of meanings. According to *Webster's New International Dictionary*, the noun "work" has twenty different meanings, the intransitive verb "work" has sixteen meanings, and the transitive verb "work" has eighteen meanings. As words become older they must carry heavier duties; hence great care must be exercised that a word is being used in the sense we intend. "Words strain, crack, and sometimes break, under the strain," says T. S. Eliot.

There are three kinds of definition: (1) reported, (2) stipulated, and (3) descriptive. A reported definition is a statement of what people usually mean when they use a word or phrase. This is the kind of definition found in a dictionary. This sort of careful statement of the meaning of a symbol is correct or incorrect according to whether or not it truly reports what people have meant by the symbol being defined. The person doing the defining is not creating the meaning of the word; he is reporting it. The symbol being defined has meaning as a result of agreement between symbol users, but this agreement existed before the definition was stated. In most cases the agreement upon a meaning is a matter of custom, and it usually grows unconsciously. If a symbol is used to represent something new, in its first use its meaning is usually evident from the circumstances in which it is used. By repetition, this meaning becomes fixed firmly enough to evoke the same response even though circumstances may no longer make the meaning obvious. A reported definition is an attempt to make clear just what is agreed upon in those customs of symbol usage that grow so consciously. Since customs in the use of symbols change continually, the task of giving reported definitions is never done.

Stipulated definitions declare what will be meant by a word in the future. Of course, no one can guarantee how other people will use a symbol; so a stipulated definition is a declaration of intention by those who draw up the definition. Giving such a definition amounts to saying, "When we use this symbol, it is to be understood to mean so-and-so." When writers find it necessary to invent special technical terms, the meaning of the new terms is stipulated. Also, if common terms have become so vague by varied use that our ideas cannot be made sufficiently clear by them, it is common practice to stipulate a restricted meaning for use in a given book or article. This was the purpose of some of the definitions given in this book, for example, the definition given of a problem situation. A stipulated definition is not subject to error. A stipulated definition may be awkward, but it cannot be wrong, because the symbol's meaning is established by the given definition. In stipulating a definition a person is reporting his future use, and his responsibility is to state his meaning clearly, and then to use the word in the way he says he will. In *Through the Looking-Glass* Humpty-Dumpty chose to use "glory" to mean "a nice knock-down argument." As Humpty-Dumpty pointed out, this use of the word was justifiable since a word "means just what I choose it to mean — neither more nor less." But Alice was also justified in saying that Humpty-Dumpty should not blame his hearers for not understanding him, for he had failed to tell them in advance what the word was to mean. If a person uses words to represent unconventional meanings, he must first make their meanings clear with a stipulated definition or he will probably not be understood.

A descriptive definition outlines the limits of the referent of a word in a different sense from a reported or stipulated definition. In all definitions some distinguishing characteristic must be noted that sets members of the referent group apart from other things. Most groups have a number of distinguishing characteristics, not just one. Human beings may be distinguished from all other things by the fact that they have a sense of humor, or by the peculiar shape of their teeth, or by their use of tools, or by the fact that they can assume responsibility for their own evolution. There may be important characteristics that distinguish human beings from all other things that have never been noticed. As we learn more about any group we discover more characteristics which distinguish its members from the members of other groups. In reported and stipulated definitions one distinguishing characteristic is as good as another if it will effectively separate the things referred to from all others. A descriptive definition, however, is an attempt to describe the most important of the characteristics by which the referent of a given symbol differs from other things, whether or not these are the characteristics by which the group is customarily distinguished.

Let us examine the definition of "planet" as an example of the development of a descriptive definition. At one time the correct reported definition of a planet was "a wandering star." The ancients noted seven objects in the sky that did not remain in the same spatial relationships to the thousands of fixed lights of the night sky. These seven were the sun, the moon, Venus, Jupiter, Mars, Mercury, and Saturn. A descriptive definition of "planet" would describe what it is about these wandering stars that makes them different. To be sure, they wander, but if wandering is only a manifestation of some much more fundamental difference, a descriptive definition would delimit the group of planets by describing this underlying distinction. In the course of many centuries of investigation it was found that most of the objects conventionally referred to as planets behave as they do because they revolve around the sun. The appearance to us of wandering roughly distinguishes the group of things objectively set apart by the fact that they revolve around the sun. The descriptive definition of "planet" outlines the distinguishing characteristics of this natural group, not the conventional group which, at the beginning, had been the subject of study. The groups were not quite the same. For example, the sun wanders in relation to the stars visible near it at sunset or at sunrise. But this appearance of wandering is caused by quite different objective relations from those that cause Venus, Jupiter, Mars, Mercury, and Saturn to wander. The sun was included in the reported definitions of the ancients, but the referent was retrimmed in making a descriptive definition to exclude the sun, since its case was a different kind. The earth, which we do not see as a wandering star, was not part of the conventional meaning for "planet," but was included in the descriptive definition, for the earth has the same objective relations although we are never in a position to observe them from outside.

There are several methods of making clear the limits of the referent of a word. These methods apply whether one intends to report a definition, to stipulate one, or to delimit a natural group. The meaning may be made clear by directing attention to instances of that to which the word refers, as by pointing. When this is done, a word is said to be ostensively defined. The difficulty with defining ostensively is in isolating attention to the right things. Suppose we wished to show someone what we mean by the word "bicycle" by pointing to a bicycle and saying, "That is what I mean." How is he to know what we are pointing to, unless he already knows something of the meaning of "bicycle"? We are pointing to a patch of color. Is it the color we mean? We are pointing to some metal. Is "bicycle" a name for that kind of metal? We are pointing eastwards. Is it a direction to which we refer when using this word? Or is it a thing in that direction which we can pick out and do something with, and, if so, which thing? In practice, ostensive definitions depend on a series of pointings under different circumstances. We learned what is meant by "water" by hearing this word applied to many situations. Perhaps the first case was in taking a bath, another case was while drinking, and another was when rain was falling. What was meant by "water" was something present in all these situations. Irrelevant characteristics of these situations were dropped out of attention by their absence in later cases of pointing. We probably learned the English words for many common objects by ostensive definitions. Although efficient in conveying the broad outlines of a meaning, ostensive definition does not readily make clear the finer details of what is included and what excluded.

Most words may also be defined operationally. For example, a spectrum is what one will see if a prism of flint glass is put in the sun so that the sun's light can shine through against a wall or sheet of paper beyond. An operational definition, such as this one, tells us how to find or produce what is referred to by the word to be defined. It does not tell us what is there when we do find it. It is like a map which tells where to find a certain city, but does not tell what the city will be like. Since operational definitions guide indirectly to instances, they too are sometimes vague, but they are peculiarly well adapted to defining words which tend to get out of touch with reality and to defining words that refer to things of which we know very little, as, say, newly discovered objects in physics or chemistry.

A third method of defining is by verbal equivalence. A word may be defined verbally by giving a more familiar word or set of words which mean the same as the word to be defined. Two conditions must be met by any adequate verbal definition: (1) the defined word and the defining words must really be equivalent, and (2) the defining words must be more clearly understood than the defined word. It would not do to report the meaning of "chair" as "an article of furniture upon which to sit." The first condition is not met by this definition, for although all chairs are articles of furniture upon which to sit, not all articles of furniture designed for sitting are chairs. Such a definition includes too much, since stools, benches, and couches are included mistakenly in the referent of "chair." To make of a verbal definition an assertion starting with "all" and then to test this assertion for reversibility as was done above is a good way to find out if the defined word and the defining words are really equivalent. The second condition for an adequate verbal definition would not be met if we were informed that a wife is a female spouse, for we are almost certainly more vague about the meaning of "spouse" than about the meaning of "wife." To explain the more familiar word with one which is less well understood does not make clearer the meaning of the word to be defined, which is the purpose of any definition. Similarly, the defining words are not more clearly understood than the defined word if they depend on an understanding of the word to be defined in order to be understood. Sponges are what sponge-divers dive for. But this circular definition does not make the meaning of "sponges" clearer, since we must already know what is meant by a sponge to understand the words used in the definition. Negative definitions, as, for example, "A chair is an article of furniture in which you cannot sleep comfortably," also usually fail to meet this second condition for a good definition.

Classificatory definitions are the most common form of verbal definitions. In this form the referent of the word to be defined is located in some larger, clearly understood class and then essential characteristics are named which distinguish the referent from other things in this larger group. For example, man is an animal that thinks, or man is an animal that tells lies and writes literature, or man is an animal that makes love at all seasons.

4. *Alternative ways of stating a problem*

To understand a problem clearly we ought to state the problem fully, using clearly defined words and using sound classification to state the relation of the elements to one another. But in addition we may need fresh insights into the problem, and for this nothing is more effective than to state the problem in a variety of ways. A problem becomes clearer as we state it from many different views. One of the greatest scientific geniuses of all time, Charles Darwin, did this in trying to solve the problem on which he spent most of his life. He began *The Origin of Species* with these words: "When on board H.M.S. 'Beagle,' as naturalist, I was much struck with certain facts in the distribution of the organic beings inhabiting South America, and in the geological relations of the present to the past inhabitants of that continent. These facts, as will be seen in the latter chapters of this volume, seemed to throw some light on the origin of species — that mystery of mysteries, as it has been called by one of our greatest philosophers." Darwin's problem was "What is the origin of species?" but if we examine *The Voyage of the Beagle* and the first two chapters of *The Origin of Species* we shall find his problem stated in a variety of ways:

1. How can Mr. Lawson, the Vice-Governor of the Galapagos Archipelago, tell from which island a tortoise comes merely by looking at the tortoise?

2. Why do the tortoises from Charles and Hood Islands have their shells in front thick and turned up like a Spanish saddle, while the tortoises from James Island are rounder, blacker, and have a better taste when cooked?

3. Why are the marine Amblyrhynchus larger at Albemarle Island than on the other islands of the Galapagos Archipelago?

4. Why are the mocking-thrushes from Charles Island of one species, those from Albemarle Island of another species, and those from James and Chatham Islands of a third species?

5. Why are 30 of the total flora of James Island confined to this island, 26 of the total flora of Albemarle Island confined to this island, 16 of the total flora of Chatham Island confined to this island, and 29 of the total flora of Charles Island exist only there?

6. Why are there two varieties of rats on Ascension Island: black rats with fine glossy fur on the grassy summit of Green Hill and brown rats with less glossy and longer hairs near the settlement on the coast?

7. Why do individuals of the same variety of older cultivated plants differ more from each other than do the individuals of any variety in a state of nature?

8. Why is there no case on record of a variable organism ceasing to vary under cultivation?

9. Why are "sporting plants" or bud-variations rare in nature but not rare under culture?

10. Why do domesticated plants and animals revert to the aboriginal stock when they are allowed to run wild?

As Darwin continues to raise such questions it becomes increasingly clear to the reader, as it must have become clearer to Darwin, that these are all variations of the big question: "What is the origin of species?"

Perhaps you may wonder if these questions that Darwin put to himself are not part of the process of collecting information to solve his main problem rather than steps in the clarification of that problem. In other words, aren't we getting ahead of our story? Of course, these various ways of stating the elements of his problem arose out of the relevant information Darwin was collecting. Stating the problem clearly and usefully assists in the collection of relevant information, and the collecting of information assists in stating the problem clearly and usefully. The steps in problem solving are never as sharply defined as might be suggested by our chapter headings. In critical thinking we do not run through the operations in chronological order. Rather we run back and forth through the operations; and even as we are at the final stages of drawing the conclusion, we may have an insight which will force us to go back to the analysis of the problem and restate it in a clearer fashion.

4

Stating the Problem Usefully

In the last chapter we considered the importance of stating the problem clearly. Now we turn to the importance of stating the problem usefully. A man with a problem may have a perfectly clear conception of the nature of the problem, knowing exactly what is needed, and still be unable to deal with it because he cannot formulate it in a way so he can do any-thing about solving it. The statement of the problem indicates the direc-tion in which a solution might be found. To anticipate a bit — we can say that a clear and useful statement functions as a hypothesis before the hypothesis. That is, when a problem has been clearly and usefully stated, we know wherein the difficulty lies and in general what must be done in order to overcome the difficulty and solve the problem. For example, when epidemics swept over medieval Europe, the problem was, at least in one sense, quite clear. Men, women, and children were dying like flies, and the problem was how to keep one's self and one's loved ones from getting the illness. But the problem was not usefully stated when the epidemic was identified as arising from God's wrath against his sinful creatures or as the result of the evil eye or of the influence of devils and demons, for then there was little one could do to solve the problem. Of course, charms, fetishes, incantations, magical potions, and esoteric rites were tried as preventives and cures, but they were not markedly successful in warding off or curing the illness. Lest we hastily conclude that only medieval minds stated their problems in such unuseful ways, we might recall that during World War II one of the most sophisticated religious periodicals in America constantly maintained that the war was the judg-ment of God upon the people of America for national sins. This same periodical also urged that America fight with all her strength to win the war — a strangely inconsistent position, since this seemed to be saying that America ought to act to frustrate God's judgment. Or did the editors believe that fighting the war was divine judgment, whereas losing the war was not divine judgment? How much more useful would have been the statements of these two problems if they had been expressed as: What is there that we eat, drink, or touch which causes this epidemic? What social, economic, and political forces brought on this war?

1. *Relation of the problem to the difficulty*

The first awareness of a problem situation is the feeling of an unanalyzed difficulty, a dumb awareness that something is wrong. Analysis of the difficulty begins so quickly that it is well nigh impossible to isolate the sense of the difficulty from the analysis. We would have to empathize the experiences of a newborn infant or of an animal of one of the lower species, if we wished to understand these first feelings in the total problem solving process. If the problem is to be solved, it must first be identified and stated. Then it can be dealt with; otherwise it remains a restless feeling which persists either until the feeling is past or until we have become so accustomed to the difficulty that it loses its poignancy.

There are certain dangers in the formation of a useful statement of the problem in relation to the difficulty. We shall consider two: (1) the danger of fragmenting the problem, and (2) the danger of becoming sidetracked from the problem. A problem is fragmented when only some of its parts are stated. A problem is sidetracked when a closely related problem and not the real problem appears in the statement, and hence in the conclusion. Few, if any, problems are simple problems. Most problems are multiple, complex, and mixed with other problems. Problem situations do not come in neatly wrapped, hermetically sealed plastic bags; instead, each problem situation is so entangled, both in its internal parts and in its external relations, that an attack on any problem is likely to set off a chain reaction among problems.

A problem is fragmented when it is broken down into its parts and attention is given to only some of the parts. As an example of a fragmented statement of a problem consider the not unusual plight of a college sophomore in the midst of an hour essay examination. He is doing quite well until, upon glancing at his watch, he realizes that he has only ten minutes in which to write the last half of the examination. He loses some time and disturbs his concentration on the exam by quickly running over in his mind a few statements of the difficulty he faces. He formulates his problem in three ways:

1. Will I fail the course if I flunk this exam?
2. Will the professor let me have ten extra minutes?
3. Will I lose my board job if I write ten extra minutes and arrive late for work?

Each of these may be fragments of his total problem, but the student is indeed foolish to use some of his precious time on these fragments. The core of his problem is: "What can I put down in the remaining time which will best answer the remaining questions?" If he spends time on the other three statements of his problem, he will miss the possible solution of the core of his problem.

Sidetracking a problem is closely related to fragmenting a problem. The difference is that when a problem is sidetracked and a secondary problem is solved, we have the illusion that we have solved the problem. Of course, we have solved a problem, but it is a secondary one that has been confused with the basic problem. The secondary problem is a deceptive snare which seduced us into thinking we had faced the basic problem. As an illustration we shall consider a problem situation in which, much to the surprise of many people, sidetracking did not take place.

During the school year 1956–1957 a number of acts of violence occurred in a high school at Clinton, Tennessee. The high school board and the principal, in accord with a decision of the Supreme Court of the United States, allowed Negro students to enroll in this formerly all-white high school. Some members of the community, not wishing Negroes in the school, formed an anti-integration group known as the White Citizen's Council to protest the integration of the school. A Federal Court injunction ordered racial integration in the school, but the Negro students continued to be threatened, and violence broke out against a white minister who attempted to accompany the Negroes to the school. In the summer of 1957 eleven of the segregationists were tried in a Federal District Court on the charges of stirring up community discord in violation of the Federal Court injunction. The case was tried before an all-white jury of ten men and two women. The problem before the jury was to determine whether the eleven accused were or were not guilty of stirring up discord in violation of the injunction, but the highly explosive issue of integration of white and colored people was involved, and it had been believed by many Americans both in the North and in the South that no white Southern jury would bring in a verdict that could be interpreted as supporting integration. In other words, it was commonly believed that a white jury trying a case that related to integration would become sidetracked to a related problem and render a verdict in keeping with their prejudices about the social organization of white and colored rather than stick to the problem involved in the trial.

The jury which heard the Clinton case, however, convicted seven of the racial segregationists of criminal contempt and acquitted four of the co-defendents. When some Southern leaders, who were disappointed with the verdict, argued that the case had been tried before a group of men and women who were not "real true Southerners," the *New York Times* sent a correspondent to interview each of the members of the jury. The correspondent reported that all the members of the jury were natives of east Tennessee, that only two of them had ever lived north of the Mason-Dixon line, that each was born of Southerners, and that all had married Southerners. He also reported that eleven of the group did not believe in "mixing the races" and that the other was "more or less neutral" on integration. The quoted remarks of jury members was further evidence that the jury had refused to be sidetracked from their problem which was "Are the accused guilty of criminal contempt?" to another problem which many had confused with the problem, "Do we favor integration of the schools?" Some of the jury members spoke to the correspondent as follows: "When a man goes to jury, he swears to go by the evidence presented in searching for a decision . . . the trial wasn't concerned with integration itself. . . . We didn't let integration or segregation come into our discussion. We merely decided whether or not Judge Taylor's order was violated. . . . I'm not for mixing the races, neither do I believe in violating the law." The ability of the jury to resist sidetracking was praised by a number of United States senators. A Southern senator said it "completely refutes the charge that Southern people are unworthy of trust and perjure themselves in this type of case." A Northern senator added, "No longer can it be said that a jury in the South arbitrarily refused to convict." To refuse to be sidetracked by emotional involvements is a hallmark of critical thinking.

2. *Relation of the problem to the solution*

A problem well stated is half solved. This has become almost a proverb, but it must be qualified by the words "if there is a solution." It would be a serious error to believe that every problem is solvable — an error which is still made, especially in America. An American corporation is reported to have had this motto on its wall: "The possible we do immediately; the impossible takes a little longer." Vigorous young America has cherished the belief that through perseverance she can attain anything she wants; she can build bridges, dam rivers, conquer disease, feed a growing population, find new sources of power, win wars, and even change the weather. The Korean stalemate was a new experience for America; she fought and did not win. Perhaps it was a maturing experience for the American people, since maturity in men and nations includes the recognition of the problems that cannot be solved. For example, an immature person takes a strangely unrealistic attitude toward the problem of death; it is an event which happens only to others. A philosopher has recently said, "Modern man has forgotten that Nature intends to kill us, and Nature always succeeds." It is a sobering and maturing experience to realize that death happens to all. "How can I avoid death?" is a problem with no solution. A useful statement of a problem must recognize whether or not the problem is one that can be solved. A well-known modern prayer embodies this wisdom: "O Lord, give me strength to change the things that must be changed, patience to endure the things that cannot be changed, and wisdom to know the difference."

Sometimes a problem can be solved in a way quite different from that suggested by the original statement of the problem. When Alexander the Great was confronted with the Gordian knot, a knot with which a Phrygian king had bound his chariot yoke so tightly and intricately that no one could untie it, and a knot about which an oracle predicted that he who could untie it would become the master of the world, Alexander solved the problem in a way different from the solution implied in the statement. He drew his sword and cut the knot with a single stroke. Of course this was not an untying of the knot, but it did separate yoke and tongue as untying would have done. Sometimes a fresh statement of a problem may suggest an unthought-of solution.

Again the problem may be one that cannot be solved now, although it can be solved at a later time. Most parents learn from experience that some behavior problems in their children cannot be solved until the child has grown older. The dangers of expecting a level of behavior beyond that of a child's capabilities are repeatedly pointed out by psychologists. For example, it is frequently affirmed that weaning the child too quickly from breast or bottle may manifest itself in thumb-sucking, nail-biting, insomnia, and other symptoms of insecurity.

As an example of the useful statement of a problem with relation to the solution we shall consider a problem that confronts many professional baseball players. Most baseball players tend to hit to a certain part of the field. A few years ago a big-league player hit well, but usually he hit deeply into left field close to the foul line. Opposing teams therefore shifted their outfielders to the left and most of his fly balls were caught. This player's problem admitted of a number of statements implying a variety of possible solutions, e.g.,

1. How can I hit fly balls into right field?
2. How can I hit a little harder so my flies become home runs?
3. How can I learn to hit more balls on the ground?

The first statement might imply a thorough revision of stance at the plate, timing of swing, size and weight of bat, grip on the bat, etc. The player believed that any change in these matters would cause him to bat poorly. The first statement might suggest that he ought to learn to hit from the left side of the plate. This, however, was rejected since such a drastic change would be very difficult for a player of his age. To become a good switch hitter requires years and years of training, and this player had only a few more years to play in the major leagues. Hence statement number one was eliminated as impossible. The second statement did not seem promising either since the player felt that he was hitting almost as hard as he could; if he were to swing harder, he would disturb his timing and would strike out more often. He and his manager rejected the second statement. The third statement was also rejected because the team had many players who hit usually on the ground, and they wanted a few who could hit high fly balls. All the statements of the problem were therefore rejected either as impractical in that they would require changes the player could not make, or as involving changes that would not be good from the standpoint of the team. The problem was stated therefore in a different way. Instead of asking how the player might be changed, they asked how the field might be changed to fit the player! It was finally decided to fence off a small part of far left field and to declare that any ball going over this fence would be a home run! They had at last stated their problem so it could be solved; they had arrived at a useful statement.

A second consideration in providing a useful statement of a problem has to do with the component parts of a problem. As we have already noted most problems have parts, but these parts are not always obvious. The division into parts and the ordering of the parts is guided by the interests of the person confronted with the problem. He may arrange the parts in a variety of ways; from simple to complex, from easy to hard, from near to remote, from well-known to less well-known, from that which can be handled alone to that which will require a great deal of help from others, from the least urgent to the most urgent, etc. The acid test in the organization of the parts is the removal of the difficulties and the achievement of a solution.

3. *Relation of the problem to other problems*

Problems do not stand alone. They are related to other problems. The statement and solution of other problems give clues for the understanding of a given problem and the statement and solution of that problem give clues for the statement and solution of other problems. Originality in the sciences is highly regarded, yet the geniuses in science are quick to deny that originality accounts for much of their greatness. Newton said that if he had seen farther, it was by standing on the shoulders of giants. Not only does a scientist profit from the studies of related problems in his field, but he also learns from studies in other fields which appear to be unrelated to his own. Wallace and Darwin developed their theories of evolution after reading Malthus on the problems of human population.

Problem solving is an endless process, because the problem solver is also a problem creator. The invention of automobiles solved part of the problem of transportation and at the same time it created problems of roads, bridges, traffic regulation, policemen and police courts, insurance, registration, licenses, etc. As an example of how problems create problems we shall consider in some detail the problems that have developed from the introduction of a few pairs of rabbits into Australia.

Shortly after the revolt of her American colonies England began sending to Australia her undesirable citizens and political prisoners. These settlers, although now banished from their home country, wanted to make the new land much like the old. They brought seed, sheep, and fowls to remind them of England. Recalling the fun they had had in the old English sport of "chasing the hare," they imported a few rabbits. A man named Henty is known to have brought in several pairs in 1834, although probably some were imported into Australia prior to that date. Thus rabbits were introduced to solve a problem: the problem of homesickness for England among the exiles. But in a short time the rabbits became problems themselves. The natural enemies of the rabbit were not found in Australia; consequently, the rabbits reproduced much faster than hunters could kill them. It is estimated that a single pair of rabbits can in five years increase to twenty million rabbits! As the rabbit population of Australia grew, their food became inadequate to sustain them. Rabbits ate every bit of green grass; they killed the shrubs by eating the green bark; they even climbed trees to get at the green leaves. They migrated from east to west following the seasons of the continent. The Australians, realizing that they were faced with serious problems, tried every conceivable method of control. Bounties were placed on the rabbits, and hunters were hired to kill them. Even though a hunter shot as many as four hundred a day, the rabbit plague continued. The daring idea of building a rabbit-proof fence that would divide Australia in two, thus keeping the rabbits in one half of the continent, was conceived and carried out. A fence called "No. 1 Rabbit Proof" was built from the Southern Ocean to the Indian Ocean. It was even extended into the water of the oceans to make certain that the rabbits would not swim around it, and it was sunk four inches in the ground so the rabbits could not burrow under it. The fence was 1138 miles long and 42 inches high. It was made of seventeen gauge wire in an inch and a quarter mesh. When this fence became ineffective, because it had been broken so often by kangaroos and other large animals of Australia, in spite of the fence riders who kept it in repair, a second fence was built. Additional fences were built around farms. In New South Wales alone there were 44,000 miles of rabbit-proof fence in 1929. Gates were placed across roads and railroads which were kept closed except when an automobile or a train was passing through. During droughts rabbits died at the fences until the dead bodies formed ramps over which the starving rabbits crossed to the other half of the continent. At least once a train was stopped by rabbits moving along the tracks seeking food and water. Traps and poisons were used — and new problems were created. After many sheep and cattle were killed by phosphorus-saturated bran, the bran was buried so the rabbits had to burrow to get at it. Thousands of valuable insect-destroying birds were poisoned by the bran. Poison was put in some of the water holes which were fenced to keep out sheep and cattle and let rabbits get to the water. In one year three million rabbits were poisoned at a single water hole. But again new problems were created: many cows were killed in chewing the carcasses of poisoned rabbits to get the salt of their bodies. West Australia one year turned two hundred cats into the rabbit districts to exterminate the pests, only to discover that within a year the cats were living peacefully with the rabbits in their burrows! Foxes were introduced, and the foxes now kill 100,000 sheep annually!

In the early nineties Australia hoped that some bacillus might be found that would rid her of her rabbit plague, but none was found which would not endanger other animal life. Some hope was held that perhaps the rabbits might be turned into an asset by shipping frozen rabbits and skins to Europe. In 1924 the exported meat and skins added three million pounds to Australian income and resulted in the extermination of twenty million rabbits. In 1951 the Australian government tried a new solution to its problem: it spread among the rabbits myxomatosis, a virus disease which has almost killed off the rabbits in England. This seems to have been partially effective, since as a result of increased pasturage wool production in Australia jumped seventy million pounds annually. But it did not end the difficulty. The latest effort to find a solution has been initiated by Australia's Commonwealth Scientific and Industrial Research Organization. In 1955 this organization resorted to a poison known as "1080." This poison, known chemically as sodium fluoroacetate, is of American origin where it is used in rat poison. Great hopes are held for the effectiveness of this poison since it is tasteless and odorless, and rabbits have proved to have the uncanny ability to identify dangerous foods by taste and smell. All these problems were created simply because a few early Australian settlers wanted to solve the problem of their nostalgia. Problems — like rabbits — reproduce their kind!

EXERCISES

Statements of Problems

Directions: Here are brief descriptions of problem situations followed by a number of attempts to state the problem. Some of the statements evade, or postpone, or fragment, or miss the problem. The student should select from among the options the statement which gives the clearest and most useful presentation of the problem. Of course he should be prepared to defend his choice. If some of these do not seem to be "exercises" in the traditional sense, then regard them as examples of what we have been thinking about in Part One.

A. A man has a blowout on the Pennsylvania Turnpike. He puts on the spare tire, but after driving a few more miles this tire also goes down. His problem is:
   1. Why aren't the tires made now as good as those made a few years ago?
   2. How far can one drive a car on a flat tire?
   3. What can be done to stop people from throwing nails and glass on the highways?
   4. Why are patrol cars and emergency cars never around when a fellow needs help?
   5. What is the quickest way of getting to a filling station to get a new tire or to have one of these repaired?
   6. Why don't they put two spares on cars?

B. Two young men while climbing the rock slide of Mt. Colden in the Adirondacks come to a place where they cannot advance and they cannot climb off safely. They are on a ledge about two feet wide. The ranger station is two miles away. They have with them a first aid kit, some sandwiches, a flashlight, a pencil, some paper, and matches. They attempt to state their problem in six different ways.
   1. We must take off our shoes and toss them down the mountain side. Also we must toss away everything we are carrying. Then maybe we can be light enough to crawl over the rocks without slipping.
   2. We must stay where we are and yell for help.
   3. We must stay here. When it gets dark, we must burn everything, even our clothes, to make a light signal.
   4. We must draw straws to see which one of us slides down the rocks. There is a 50-50 chance he will be killed, but when his body is found that will touch off a search for the survivor.
   5. We must make ourselves comfortable for the night. We must flash S.O.S. signals with the flashlight every fifteen minutes during the night. When we are missed back in camp, a searching party will be sent out.
   6. We must start writing messages for help, and throw them into the wind.

C. Hank is working his way through college washing dishes in a restaurant.

The proprietor has spoken very sternly to his help about breaking dishes. One day after going for three months without breaking a dish, Hank slips on a wet spot on the floor and drops a tray of dishes. The proprietor is out of the restaurant at the time. Hank asks six other students who work there what he ought to do. Each answer shows a different conception of Hank's problem.

1. Throw the broken dishes at the boss.
2. Toss the pieces in the garbage, and don't tell the boss.
3. Start looking for another job.
4. Tell the boss about it when he gets back. Tell him you are sorry, and you'll be more careful. And offer to pay for them.
5. Give the janitor a kick in the pants for not wiping up that wet spot on the floor.
6. Tell the boss he ought to get plastic dishes.

D. A factory worker misses his bus one morning. He is due at the factory in thirty minutes. The factory is three miles away. If he arrives late for work, he will probably lose his job. The next bus will come by in one hour. His problem is:

1. How can I get even with that bus driver?
2. What is the best way to secure another job?
3. Is hitch-hiking legal in this state?
4. What is the cheapest means of transportation I can get which will get me to work in thirty minutes?
5. Why didn't I buy that good used car last week?
6. Can I still do the Boy Scout pace?

E. Mr. Zurf has a lovely home on the west side of Shady Street. He reads in the paper that the city council is considering the widening of Shady Street by cutting four feet off the lawns on the west side of the street. Mr. Zurf has four large maple trees within three feet of the street. His problem is:

1. How much is maple wood per cord?
2. When is the next meeting of the city council, and how many of the residents of Shady Street will go with me to the meeting of the council to find some solution to this problem which will be agreeable to all of us?
3. What is the best way to make the council members take that four feet off the east side of the street?
4. Why does the paper print such rumors?
5. Who is the best lawyer to help me bring suit against the city?
6. Why do the members of the city council pick on the poor people who live on our side of the street?

F. Mr. Stone discovers one cold winter morning that during the night the gas furnace has gone out. His problem is:

1. Can I slip out of the house before my wife wakes up?
2. How much does it cost to convert a gas furnace to coal?
3. Why doesn't the gas company stop shooting air through the gas mains?

4. Is the pilot light on, and if it is not, how can it be safely lighted?
5. How many matches will it take to light the pilot, check the gas meter to see if gas is going through the pipes, and look for a leak in the gas pipes?
6. Can I get a good job in Florida?

G. Frank is an usher in a large movie theatre. One evening he discovers that a fire has started in the men's room. His problem is:
1. Where is the fire extinguisher?
2. Where is the nearest fire station?
3. Why are men so careless with cigarettes?
4. Can I run into the front of the theatre and yell "FIRE" before the fire spreads beyond the men's room?
5. How can I inform the people in the building of the fire and get them out of the building without causing a panic?
6. Where is the manager?

H. The mother of a four-year-old girl, Mary, discovers that the child is frightened almost hysterically by the telephone and the doorbell. Her problem is:
1. Should Mary and I go for a long visit to my country cousin's home?
2. Could we get along without a doorbell and a telephone for about six months?
3. How can I help Mary to build up pleasant associations with the telephone and the doorbell?
4. How could I have failed so miserably with my child?
5. Why don't they make telephones and doorbells that don't frighten children?
6. Where can I get some attractive earmuffs for Mary?

I. A large family with a modest income agrees that the car which they have been using for eight years is no longer safe to drive. They have decided to get a new car but are undecided as to make and model. One night at dinner the parents and their four children express themselves as to what they need in the new car.
1. One of those small foreign cars would suit our pocketbook just fine. I hear they run fifty miles on a gallon of gas.
2. The new car must be pink with black trim. That is the classiest color.
3. Our problem is to find a six-passenger car which is not too expensive to maintain and which will give us good service for six or seven years.
4. Well, we must not get a car less expensive than the Smith's. We don't want people to think that we are poorer than the Smiths.
5. Whatever we get, it's got to be a convertible. They are swell for getting sun tans while driving.
6. Just so it has a big trunk compartment. I hate having to pack groceries in the back seat of the car when we go to the supermarket.

J. Mr. Hockson is awakened out of sound sleep by his wife who whispers in his ear that she thinks she hears a burglar downstairs in the living room. His problem is:
1. How soon can I go back to sleep?

2. Why do women keep imagining things?
3. Where's my gun?
4. Why didn't I put that cat out when I went to bed?
5. What sort of noise should I make to frighten away that prowler without getting him so excited that he will take a shot at me?
6. What is the quickest way to call the police?
7. What evidence is there that there is a prowler downstairs?

K. Senator Horn has served two terms in office and will be seeking a third term at the next election less than one year away. He is known among his colleagues and among his constituents as a man of complete honesty. He has just received a letter from a manufacturer offering him $100,000 to vote "Yes" on a bill that is before the Senate. It so happens that he has already decided to vote "Yes" on the bill, although he has not yet made known his thinking to anyone. His problem is:

1. How can I accept that money and escape income tax on it?
2. What will be the best way of making it known to the public that I am accepting the money, but not as a bribe?
3. How much will it take to make my secretary keep his mouth shut about this money?
4. How long can I consider this before I have to make up my mind?
5. What will be the best way of rejecting this money and letting it be known in the Senate and among my constituents that my vote cannot be purchased for any price?
6. Why do people do such things as this?
7. Why didn't I announce last week how I was going to vote?

L. Mr. Franklin takes great pride in his lawn and is consequently distressed by the crabgrass which appears in his yard each year. He consults a number of people about what he should do. Which individual indicates by his advice that he clearly understands Mr. Franklin's problem?

1. Stop fussing. Admire the crabgrass for its hardiness. See how life fills every nook and cranny of space.
2. Plow up your entire lawn. It isn't worth all the time and money you spend on it.
3. Give your whole lawn a liberal sprinkling of salt.
4. Post a sign in the center of your lawn marked "CRABGRASS EXPERIMENT."
5. Spray with a crabgrass poison and then fertilize your lawn heavily after the first frost so the grass will become so thick that the crabgrass will not be able to get started next summer.
6. Take a nice long vacation each year from the middle of July to the first heavy frost. Then you'll never see the crabgrass.

M. Eight-year-old William has moved with his parents to a new community and has enrolled in a new school. At the first recess one of his classmates makes fun of him and finally hits him in the nose, bringing blood. William's problem is:

1. Why did Mother and Dad move to this neighborhood?
2. Where is the office of the school nurse?
3. What is the best way to take blood out of a white shirt?
4. How can I establish myself in this school so I shall be accepted by all my classmates?
5. What will Mother and Dad say about this?
6. How can I get even with this guy?

N. Mr. Dicks has spent ten pleasant years as clerk in a men's store. In his pay envelope he finds the following note: "As you know our business has been falling off for six months due to new competition. We regret therefore that we are forced to discontinue your services beginning next Monday." His problem is:

1. What is the best way to warn all my friends not to trade here?
2. What is the best way to induce all my friends to trade here so I can get my job back?
3. Where's the nearest tavern?
4. Where can I find a job similar to this one that will give me sufficient income to support my family?
5. What is the best way of driving this new competitor out of business?
6. Why doesn't my employer satisfy himself with a smaller margin of profit?
7. Where can my wife and I go for a few weeks until my employer realizes what an essential man I am in his business?
8. Shall I tell my wife?

Classifications

Directions: Make at least one good classification for each of the following:

1. cats
2. things on which to sit
3. vegetables
4. college professors
5. Boy Scouts
6. musical instruments
7. movie stars
8. boys (by a sorority)
9. girls (by a fraternity)
10. paper
11. paintings
12. economic systems
13. socks
14. things to drink
15. medicines
16. football players
17. parents
18. lamps
19. sea craft
20. eyes

Definitions

Directions: Mark the following definitions according to these characteristics:

a. Includes some things that ought to be excluded.
b. Excludes some things that ought to be included.

c. Repeats the word that is to be defined, either directly or indirectly.
d. Negative when it could be affirmative.
e. Obscure or figurative.
f. A good definition.

1. A woman is one of Nature's agreeable blunders.
2. A plastic is a material capable of being molded.
3. A piscatory tribe is one that lives by fishing.
4. Love is a tickling under the heart which you can't scratch.
5. History is a record of all past events.
6. Consistency is the hobgoblin of little minds.
7. A soporific drug is a drug that produces sleep.
8. Cowardice is the lack of courage.
9. A bonfire is a large fire made in the open air for the purpose of roasting wieners.
10. A kiss is an anatomical juxtaposition of two orbicular muscles in a state of contraction.
11. A kiss is a rosy dot over the "i" of loving.
12. A furnace is a mechanism placed in the basement of houses to supply heat.
13. Number is the class of classes.
14. Man is the only animal that can make a fool of himself.
15. A husband is a man whose wife is living.
16. A husband is a married man.
17. A swastika is a symbol or ornament in the form of a Greek cross with the ends of the arms bent at right angles all in the same direction, usually clockwise, and each prolonged to the height of the parallel arm of the cross.
18. A swastika was the symbol of German Nazism.
19. A college student is a young man or woman who is going to a school more advanced than high school.
20. A college student is a person who is studying at an educational institution that is not an elementary or a secondary institution.
21. Knowledge means to know something.
22. A novel is a thing like *The Tale of Two Cities.*
23. Home is where the heart is.
24. A cow is a bovine ilk, the one end moo, the other end milk.
25. A brick is a piece of building material made of red clay baked in a kiln.
26. A Puritan is a person who pours righteous indignation into the wrong things.
27. Virtue consists of states of character in virtue of which we stand well or badly with reference to the passions.
28. Time is a temporal slab of eternity.
29. A circle is a figure whose radii are equal.
30. A moving picture is a picture that moves.

31. Patriotism is the last refuge of a scoundrel.
32. A cuckoo-pint is a common European arum with lanceolate erect spathe and short purple spadix.
33. A cause is an antecedent event.
34. Evolution is a change from a nohowish, untalkaboutable, all-alikeness to a somehowish and in general talkaboutable notall-alikeness by continuous somethingelsifications and sticktogetherations.
35. Truth is not a diet.

Uses of Words

Directions: Words are used for three purposes: Expression, description, and motivation, although seldom, if ever, are words used for only one of the purposes. Indicate which of the following statements are largely expressive, largely descriptive, and largely motivational.

A. From a broadcast of a football game —
1. Haskins has the ball and moves to the four-yard line before he is stopped.
2. What a play! What a plunge! Just like a steam roller! Haskins has infinite power.
3. It is a grand afternoon. Why don't you and the Mrs. jump in the car and rush out here to see the game? You'll regret it if you don't.
4. Against a gray October sky the four horsemen ride again.
5. Never have I seen such a game. It has been thrills from start to finish.
6. Haskins has the ball again. He's a good back. Wish all you listeners were here. My wife wouldn't come because she had to do a big washing. Woman's work is never done, so she says. Well — Haskins made it.
7. Let me tell you, Haskins is the best player of them all. You are going to hear a lot more about that boy.

B. From a history book —
1. A fragment of the barons held out stubbornly at Kenilworth until December of 1266 when disease and famine compelled them to surrender.
2. Famine! Disease! Death! Have you ever seen a rotting corpse? Then you know why the barons surrendered.
3. Do not forget Kenilworth! This is what happens when the common people unite against their masters. Workers of the world unite and throw off your chains!
4. It was a sad day for England when the barons were forced to surrender at Kenilworth.
5. Never again would the barons be able to ignore the needs of the common people. Let this be a reminder to those who would oppress their fellowmen.
6. The sufferings of innocent peasants at the hands of vicious, bloodthirsty barons was ended at Kenilworth.

C. From a news story on a play production —
1. Seldom has this community witnessed such a display of talent. The scenery was complete in every detail, the costumes were authentic, and the actors were well trained. In all it was an evening one will remember for years.
2. If you did not see the play last night, you missed a treat. Never again should you let such an opportunity pass you by.
3. The thespians who manifested their rare talents last evening gave this community fresh insight into the theatre as a reflection of man's weal and woe.
4. The audience clapped for ten minutes.
5. Wave upon wave of thunderous applause brought forth innumerable curtain calls after this most magnificent production.
6. When you go downtown tomorrow buy a ticket for the next play. It will be even better.

D. From a record of discussions on the floor of a legislative body of a mythical state — (Many errors in thinking are found in these excerpts. Try to identify the errors.)
1. There is evidence to show that there is a devilish, fiendish conspiracy back of this. The maniacs who propose this new method should be clamped in jail before they harm peaceful, honest, tax-paying, law-abiding citizens.
2. Last year one of my secretaries came from Adelpolis. She was good. This year I got two more from Adelpolis. They also are excellent. If you want a fine secretary, you cannot go wrong by getting one from Adelpolis.
3. You all know the great contributions of Darwin and of Newton to our understanding of the physical and biological worlds. Such men of learning can certainly say something of significance to us about how taxes should be raised. Allow me to quote from them on these issues.
4. We know, my friends, that all wars are evil, and we also know that sins are evil. It follows therefore that wars are not only evil, they are sins.
5. My worthy opponent from the illustrious state of Missolina, the land of the sky blue waters, has in his diatribe besmirched the honor of every young mother who like a madonna holds her babe to her breast.
6. Can we trust the four nations who have signed the pact? Gentlemen, are you not aware that these nations have of their own will signed the pact? Now, since we trust these nations by putting our signatures to the pact, let us proceed to bring in a new era of good will.
7. Would you turn your own mother out into the cold? Would you refuse to defend your sister against one who would do her harm? Would you allow another to strike a blow upon your loving and faithful wife? Would you stand by and watch tragedy overtake your daughter? The answer is NO. You would come to their defense. Now, gentlemen, the great nation of Iwanda has been to us like a mother, a sister — yea, even like a wife and a daughter. Can we refuse to come to her aid? The answer again is No! No!! No!!!
8. The bid of the U.L.B. Company was the best bid, everything considered.

This is obvious since the U.L.B. Company won the contract. Some have pointed out that there may have been some shady dealing in the awarding of the contract, since my brother owns half interest in the U.L.B. Company. Gentlemen, you forget that the contract was awarded in this case, as in all cases, to the *best* bid.

9. I cannot give my consent to this appointment. Mr. Smooth ten years ago did not return a dollar to a department store in this city when an error was made in his account. A man who is willing to accept money dishonestly, who refuses to meet his financial obligations, is unfit for a position such as this one. Holy Writ tells us that all men are either saints or sinners. Mr. Smooth is certainly no saint. Therefore he is a sinner, and is not to be trusted in this or any other responsible position.

10. Ten years I served on this committee; fifteen years I worked faithfully in these halls; twenty years I have held public office; thirty years I have studied and interpreted the laws of this land. Now my opinion is that we must vote "Yes."

11. A new tax at this time will be strong medicine, I know. But as my dear old mother used to say, "Strong medicine is good for the soul." Now according to the best medical definition of the word "medicine," a medicine may serve any of three purposes: purgation, stimulation, or sedation. The body of our state needs stimulation. Let us hope this tax will be the proper medicine.

12. I accept the truth of this theory of capital punishment. And I shall tell you why. It is because there are fifty arguments for it, and only twenty-one against it.

13. There may be some people who can share the views of my opponent, but I am obliged to think like common folk. God loves the common people; that's why he made so many of them. And the common opinion is not the opinion presented by my opponent.

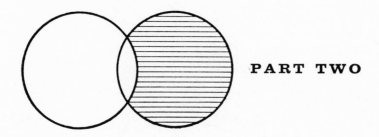 PART TWO

The Formation
of Hypotheses

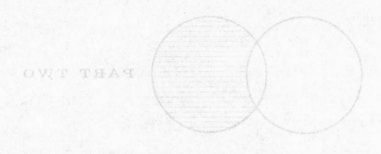

The Formation
of Hypotheses

Collecting Information

In Part One we considered the analysis of the problem. We saw that if a problem has been well analyzed, we know what is the difficulty, and we know the area of experience where we might find a solution. If the problem is poorly analyzed, we have only a vague conception of the difficulty and hence little reason for preferring one course of action to another. If problems were merely puzzles proposed to our minds as a pleasant way to pass the time, it would not matter much whether problems were carefully analyzed before a solution is reached. Questions, riddles, and puzzles of the How-smart-are-you? type which appear in newspapers, magazines, radio, and television are evidently very popular, even though one may reasonably doubt that knowing the names of all the world's welterweight boxing champions or the location of the Cauca River is a fair test of intelligence. Brain-teasers are good fun. But in our Atomic Age there are problems which affect man's basic values and man's continued existence on this planet. These are the problems to which we must bring our best critical thinking. Today's culture and civilization is the result of solutions to yesterday's problems. Tomorrow's culture and civilization will be determined by how well we solve today's problems. Only as we become better critical thinkers will we improve the world, and improve ourselves for significant living in the world.

In Part Two we shall examine the formation of suggestions and hypotheses which point to a solution of the problem. This formation process ordinarily follows the analysis of the problem, although, as we have already noted and as we shall note again, the analysis of the problem and the formation of hypotheses — as well as the other "steps" in critical thinking — must not be assumed to be distinct either chronologically or logically.

One of the dangers in treating critical thinking systematically, as we must treat it if we are to make sense of it in a volume like this, is the danger of creating the illusion that critical thinking follows an irreversible step-by-step order. While studying the parts and sub-parts of critical thinking, we must continually remind ourselves that critical thinking is an organic unit which cannot be fully understood by dissection. With this caveat we continue dissecting! In Part Two we shall examine the formation of hypotheses under three headings: (1) collecting information, (2) making information manageable, and (3) producing hypotheses to be tested.

1. *Identification of relevant material*

The information at hand will rarely be just the information needed for the solution of the problem. There may be a dearth of information or there may be such a wealth of information that we do not know which is pertinent and which is not pertinent to the solution of the problem. In general it is preferable to have abundant information, even if most of it appears to be irrelevant, than to have a meagre amount of relevant information. In other words, in solving problems it is wise not to be hasty in rejecting that which may seem to be quite remote from the problem. Watson was always discarding the clues which Sherlock Holmes used to solve a murder case. Particularly when dealing with a problem that is both novel and difficult, wisdom dictates that we cast around for any insights which might help in the solution.

The first stage in the forming of hypotheses is an almost uncritical gathering of information. We say "almost" because there is operating at this early stage a "proto-hypothesis" by which information is selected or rejected. The procedure of psychoanalysts is interesting in this connection. A psychoanalyst may spend many weeks collecting information, most of which is irrelevant. He listens and takes notes as the patient talks. Psychoanalysts seem to laymen to be exasperatingly slow in their treatment, but they have learned to avoid hasty conclusions in dealing with the ills of the human personality. The dislike of a playmate in the first year of school fifty years ago may be the clue a psychoanalyst needs to determine why a business executive cannot work harmoniously with his associates. Information does not come conveniently labeled RELEVANT or IRRELEVANT. Sometimes great imagination is required to distinguish the relevant from the irrelevant. For example, how difficult it was — and is — for man to realize that phases of the moon affect the tides of the ocean, and spots on the sun affect the weather on the earth, but the positions and states of the heavenly bodies have no effect on the fortunes of men and nations.

We may have relevant material right in our hands and not use it because we have not stated the problem in such a way that the material is relevant. For example, the ancient Egyptians and Babylonians collected observations of lunar and planetary movements for centuries, but they did not develop a science of astronomy. Simplicius, a Greek philosopher, recorded a rumor that there were astronomical records in Egypt extending back 630,000 years and in Babylon back 1,440,000 years! More reliable is the report of James H. Breasted that Egyptian records of observations of Sirius (the Dog Star) extend back to 4241 B.C. The ancient priests of Egypt, who made and recorded these observations, knew that the length of the year was about 365 days, and they believed that Venus and Mercury revolved round the sun, but their information was largely used for practical purposes such as the orientation of pyramids and temples to the sun or stars. They were also able to predict with accuracy the yearly inundation of the Nile valley. The Babylonians were able on the basis of their extensive observations to predict lunar and planetary movements in the sky. They had arrived at a period of time known as the *saros*, a period of 6585 days, and they discovered that a solar eclipse occurred at every saros interval. But with such data in their possession, the Babylonians turned to astrology rather than to astronomy. It remained for the Greeks to take these records and develop a science. In the words of Peter Doig, the editor of the *Journal of the British Astronomical Association*, ". . . although the Egyptians and Mesopotamians had gone further than the ancient Greeks in mathematics and in astronomical observation, their studies had an almost entirely utilitarian object. The Ionians and later Greeks took up these matters in a more purely intellectual manner and built the foundations for a science of Astronomy."[1] In later times the Babylonian records of eclipses were put to scientific uses. Ptolemy used them to improve his tables for prediction of the movements of the sun and the moon; and in recent years they have been useful in the discovery of a slight lengthening of the earth's period of rotation. The information collected by the Egyptians and the Babylonians was relevant for the development of astronomy, but the ancient observers did not recognize this relevancy because they related the data to the problems of agriculture, architecture, and fortune-telling rather than to the development of a rational science of the heavenly bodies.

[1] Peter Doig, *A Concise History of Astronomy* (London: Chapman and Hall, Ltd., 1950), p. 25.

Sometimes a problem may be clearly and usefully stated, yet we are unable to develop a hypothesis which leads to a solution because the relevant data cannot be separated from the irrelevant data. This is often the complication faced by detectives. Clever criminals sometimes deliberately create misleading evidence. J. Edgar Hoover, Director of the Federal Bureau of Investigation of the United States Department of Justice, in his book, *Persons in Hiding*, gives many examples of the difficulty in distinguishing relevant and irrelevant evidence. One of his stories is that of a criminal known as Machine-gun Kelly, who was terrorizing the Midwest in the early thirties of this century. Kelly was dominated by his beautiful and ruthless wife, Kathryn. One of their most notorious crimes, and the one for which they received life sentences, was the kidnapping of Charles F. Urschel, a millionaire who was taken from his home in Oklahoma City in July, 1933, and held for $200,000 ransom. Mr. Urschel was blindfolded and taken to the ranch of Kathryn's mother. Two days after the kidnapping Kathryn visited a detective in Forth Worth, Texas. The visit was obviously to give evidence to the detective that Kathryn Kelly was not involved in the Urschel kidnapping. Her presence with a detective should itself be evidence that she was not the kidnapper, and in addition Kathryn told the detective that she had just driven from St. Louis to Fort Worth. But the detective made three observations: (1) Kathryn did not appear as tired as a person would be after driving that distance; (2) there was an Oklahoma City newspaper on the front seat of her car; (3) there was red mud on the wheels — like the red soil of Oklahoma. The detective, deciding that Kathryn's presence in Fort Worth and the story of her trip were irrelevant evidence whereas his three observations were relevant, reported this information to the F.B.I. But by the time special agents reached Kathryn's Fort Worth home, she was gone.

When Mr. Urschel was safely returned to his home, against the argument of Kathryn that he be killed, he gave the F.B.I. a great deal of information. As Mr. Hoover says, "Mr. Urschel's photographic mind had pictured almost every move, action and surrounding of the days in which he had been held for ransom." The most helpful information was his memory of a conversation of his kidnappers that a passenger plane which usually passed over the hideout house on Sunday morning had been forced to detour because of a rainstorm. This seemingly insignificant item led to the location of the place where Mr. Urschel had been held and to the arrest of Kathyrn's mother and stepfather. Kathryn now devised ingenious methods to throw the F.B.I. off the trail. She wore a red wig, she made her husband dye his hair and wear octagonal glasses; she disposed of her luxurious sixteen-cylinder car and drove a small pick-up truck; and she persuaded a hitchhiking couple to allow their twelve-year-old daughter to travel with the Kellys. This last move resulted in their capture, for the F.B.I. learned they were using the girl as a decoy, and when the girl sent a telegram for her parents to meet her, she was met by the F.B.I. who learned from her the new hideout of the Kellys. An early morning raid took them by surprise and they were captured without resistance. The F.B.I. had correctly distinguished relevant and irrelevant evidence.

2. *What has been done by others*

In the collecting of information we cannot afford to ignore what has been done by others. Even in routine matters we continually make use of information gathered by others. For example, most people wash their hands before eating partly because they were so trained in childhood, and partly because of the discoveries of bacteria and their relation to diseases by the French scientist, Pasteur. Even if it were possible to solve problems without reliance upon what others have done, the brevity of life and the multiplicity of problems would make such behavior foolish. On the other hand, if men stay too close to what others have done they will merely repeat others' conclusions and failures.

The making of knowledge is a cumulative process. Consider the invention of the airplane. Men for centuries admired the flight of birds, but it was not until the late fifteenth century that a thorough study was made of how birds fly. Leonardo da Vinci carefully observed birds, noticing how they used wings and tail to utilize air recoil and resistance. Then he drew plans for wings that man might use, and later, following these plans, made a few of these wings. Da Vinci went about as far as man could go in the absence of suitable power for flight. In the last half of the nineteenth century successful gliders were made by Le Bris of France, Lilienthal of Germany, Chanute of Illinois, and Montgomery of California. Samuel Langley experimented at the turn of the century with a small steam engine to propel his flying machine. Meanwhile the gasoline engine had been invented. Orville and Wilbur Wright, making use of what others had done, made the first flight in a self-propelled machine on December 17, 1903. Learning how to fly was a human process covering four centuries of study and experimentation. The process now continues as man plans for interplanetary travel.

The solution of many, if not most, of the problems to which men direct their attention comes about in similar manner. The solution is a group endeavor. In the solution of complex problems the necessary cooperation is often a cooperation in space as well as in time. Men and nations work together that all might profit from the solution. An International Geophysical Year in which scientists of all nations pool their information about the nature of the physical universe is but a dramatic illustration of cooperation that goes on all the time. Sometimes national interests may seem to require that specific knowledge be confined within a certain nation or within a certain group of nations, but eventually the information becomes disseminated throughout the world. Knowledge cannot be confined within the boundaries of nations, or races, or centuries.

3. *Authorities*

An American philosopher has said that nine-tenths of what we hold to be true comes to us from the testimony of others. The exact percentage is impossible to ascertain, but surely nine-tenths is a conservative estimate. We know that Columbus discovered America in 1492, that light travels 186,000 miles per second, that the word "deity" is not correctly spelled "diety." We know all of these on the basis of authority. A history textbook, a physics textbook, and the dictionary are the sources of these items of information. Parents were our first authorities, and for many years mother and father were for us sources of infallible information. As children we accepted their word as completely reliable on all topics. Later the opinions of older playmates, of teachers, and of religious leaders were probably also accepted authoritatively. Newspapers, magazines, books, radio, and television were added as authorities. (A twelve-year-old boy recently argued that the tablets on which God wrote the Ten Commandments still existed because he saw them in a motion picture!) Long before reaching high school the average child has discovered that some authorities are not entirely dependable and that authorities sometimes contradict each other. Some young people while going through the storm and stress period of the early teens rebel against all authorities; they will believe nothing told them by others — so they say. But as they grow older they realize that there is much that cannot be known except by authority, and that much which would be known by personal experience is better accepted authoritatively. A bottle marked POISON could be tested to see if it is poison, but it is wiser to accept the label at face value. With the proper equipment a student might be able to measure the speed of light, but it is a great economy of time to accept the measurements of competent physicists. The events which antedate one's birth can be known only by appeal to the authority of older people, or to written history, or to the archaeological remains. Even one's own birth must be established by authority! Many people have had the curious experience of searching for a birth certificate, a doctor's record, or a family Bible to establish the fact of their own birth.

In the previous paragraph we used the word "authority" as an undefined word. Now we ought to ask, "What is an authority?" and "How do authorities come to be?" A simple definition of an authority is that it is one whose opinion has been found to be trustworthy. Albert Einstein is an authority in physics, George Kennan an authority in international relations, and Robert Moses in city planning; but if Einstein writes on international relations, or Kennan on city planning, or Moses on physics, they do not write as authorities. An authority is one who has studied a topic until he knows it so well that his opinion carries weight, both when he speaks about a matter to which he has given years of research and also when he speaks about matters which are closely related to his research. That is, while Einstein did not study primarily in spectroscopy, his opinions in this field would be far more authoritative than those of Kennan or Moses. Incidentally, specialization is becoming so necessary in the sciences that within a field like physics there are specialists whose studies are so pin-pointed that they experience difficulty in communicating with other physicists who have specialized in other aspects of physics.

Some people have almost a mental block about the matter of authorities because it connotes for them what might be called authoritarianism. Authoritarianism is the blind use of authorities. Most people have heard of the use to which Aristotle was put in the Middle Ages. He was quoted as the infallible source of all information about the physical universe. Debates were settled by looking in the writings of "The Philosopher" for the answer. If Aristotle did not happen to give the information, the pious scholar would say, "We must wait for God to reveal the answer."

Authorities may be used in two ways: dogmatically or critically. When an authority is used dogmatically, the user is saying in effect, "Here is what my authority says. It must be so because he says so." (*Ipse dixit* was the scholastic phrase.) When an authority is used critically, the user is saying in effect, "Here is what my authority says. His statement is reached by using the following methods and the following reasoning. I invite you to try his methods and his reasoning to see if you come to the same conclusion." There is a legend that before the destruction of the Alexandrian museum the Kalif Omar said, "If the books in the museum agree with the *Koran* they are useless and need not be preserved; if they disagree with it they are pernicious. Let the books therefore be destroyed." The Kalif was using the *Koran* as a dogmatic authority. In the fourteenth, fifteenth, and sixteenth centuries Aristotle was used equally dogmatically; for example, in the middle of the fourteenth century the Inceptor in Arts at the University of Paris was asked to swear that he would teach nothing inconsistent with Aristotle, and as late as 1624 the Parliament of Paris passed a decree threatening with death those who held or taught anything contrary to Aristotle. National Socialism was used authoritatively in Nazi Germany just prior to World War II. Goebbels, the Minister of Propaganda, said in 1934, "Since we National Socialists are convinced that we are right, we cannot tolerate anybody else who contends he is right."

The chief difficulty in the dogmatic use of authorities is that the conclusions and the methods by which the conclusions are reached are separated. In case someone doubts the truth of the authoritatively supported statement, he has no information as to how he might discover the truth for himself. Authorities that are used dogmatically were not necessarily dogmatists in their own researches. Aristotle, for example, reached his conclusions about plants and animals by observing them. He wrote down what he saw and appealed to his readers to look and decide if they saw what he saw. He did not claim to be the dogmatic authority the scholastics claimed he was, and he did not treat his scientific and philosophical predecessors as he was treated by the scholastics. An authority ought to be regarded as he regarded his predecessors. Pascal made this point clearly when he wrote, "What can be more unjust than to treat our ancients with greater consideration than they showed towards their predecessors, and to have for them this incredible respect which they deserve from us only because they entertained no such regard for those who had the same advantage (of antiquity) over them?"

The psychological state which usually accompanies the dogmatic use of authorities is tenacity. Tenacity is compounded of two operations: the repetition of an idea and the refusal to entertain alternative ideas. While we may feel like saying, "I thank God I am not as other men in this regard," a closer look might reveal a number of ideas which we hold by tenacity, that is, ideas we entertain as true or right simply because we have never bothered to question them, such as, heaven is above the earth, men are stronger than women, chopsticks are crude tools for the dining table, mothers always love their children, coffee wards off sleep, and potatoes make people fat. The wisdom of proverbs and folk tales is wisdom acquired through repetition. Coué would improve the world by having every man and woman recite several times each morning upon rising, "Day by day in every way I'm getting better and better." Hitler said any idea oft repeated becomes an accepted idea. Aldous Huxley in *Brave*

New World describes how "Elementary Class Consciousness" was drilled into children through hypnopaedia (sleep teaching). The Beta children slept in a nursery where all night they heard over and over again the words "I'm so glad I'm a Beta . . . Gammas are stupid . . . and Epsilons are still worse." It is a great comfort to possess a few beliefs which one does not doubt. Lincoln Steffens once was asked by a business executive not to remind him of his past miscalculations, for, as the executive said, he could not act if he were at the same time to question his own judgments. One of the best-known examples of the tenacious holding to authority is that of the seventeenth-century professors in Florence who refused to look through Galileo's telescope. Even today there are people who follow the method of tenacity: Christians who refuse to read the *Koran*, Communists who will not examine democracy, and capitalists who close their minds to socialism. For all who refuse to examine new ideas out of a desire to hold to established ways of thought and action, W. K. Clifford recommended "the still small voice that murmurs 'fiddlesticks.' "

Galileo claimed there were moons around Jupiter, but Francesco Sizzi argued that there can be only seven planets in the sky because there are but seven openings in the head, but seven metals, and but seven days of the week. He continued with marvelous enthymematic reasoning: "these satellites of Jupiter are invisible to the naked eye, and therefore can exercise no influence on the earth, and therefore would be useless, and therefore do not exist." As a final flourish he added, "Now, if we increase the number of the planets, this whole and beautiful system falls to the ground." Sizzi's argument by analogy and his appeal to the beauty of the medieval system are amusing to us, but we should recognize that this Scholastic was giving reasons for his position. He was not simply using an authority dogmatically, as Martin Luther did when he opposed Copernicus in this fashion: "This fool wishes to reverse the entire science of astronomy. But Sacred Scripture tells us that Joshua commanded the sun to stand still, and not the earth." When a man quotes an authority and then gives reasons and evidence for the truth of the opinion of the authority, he is not using his authority dogmatically; he is asking that the view be accepted because it is rational and because it has supporting data.

4. *One's own experiences*

Information derived from one's own experiences is more convincing than information that may be collected from the experiences of other people. Personal experiences are more than our experiences — they are ourselves. The Scottish philosopher, David Hume, put it this way: ". . . when I enter more intimately into what I call *myself*, I always stumble on some particular perception or other, of heat or cold, light or shade, love or hatred, pain or pleasure. I never can catch *myself* at any time without a perception, and never can observe any thing but the perception." No doubt you have noticed how difficult it is to give up that which you have learned by personal experience. Such experiences have a vividness which reported experiences cannot have. For example, if you live in New York City, you probably have walked many times in Central Park. You know its mall, its skating rink, its lakes, and its Metropolitan Museum of Fine Arts. You know Central Park. Let us assume you have never been to Chicago, although you have read a great deal about Chicago and you have talked to many who have been there. You know from the experiences of others and from the authorities you have consulted that Chicago has a downtown park called Grant Park. You may even know that the park has a band shell, a Chicago Museum, a Shedd Aquarium, and an Adler Planetarium, but your knowledge of Grant Park is not as certain as your knowledge of Central Park. You would argue more emotionally for the exactness of your knowledge of Central Park than you would for the exactness of your knowledge of Grant Park. After all, you have seen Central Park. Surely one can trust one's senses.

That is exactly our problem: Can one trust his senses? If you recall the last magic show you attended, you know that you cannot always trust your senses. You knew that the magician did not actually draw the rabbit out of the hat because he showed that the hat was empty only a second before the rabbit appeared. And if you really had believed your eyes when he seemed to be sawing the lady in half, you probably would have fainted. But you do not need to go back that far in memory to get to a situation in which eyes were defective as collectors of information. Just recall your last motion picture. Movies are really "stillies." The motion is but an illusion created by presenting a series of still shots in rapid succession. If the projector were slowed down so that you saw one picture each second instead of twenty-four, then you would realize that movies do not move — and the usual one and one-half hour show would last thirty-six hours. As a matter of fact, you do not have to recall a sense deception. You can have one right now. Just look up from this book at two objects which are about the same size, one which is close to you and the other which is some distance away. The farther one looks smaller. Perspective is such a universal experience that we do not think of it as an illusion. We are so accustomed to seeing things in perspective that we make allowances for it. We know that the rails which seem to meet a half mile down the railroad track do not meet. An amazing instance of correction of visual images is demonstrated by a simple piece of apparatus, found in most psychological laboratories, called the Ames demonstration. It is a trapezoid window sash which slowly revolves on a vertical axis. At one phase of its revolution the wider end of the window is farther away from the eyes and the narrower end is closer to the eyes, but this is so foreign to the human visual expectations that the eyes make a correction and will not see the window revolve; instead, it seems to swing back and forth with the wider end always closer to the observer.

Even when our senses are not playing tricks on us they give us only limited views of the world in which we live. Visible light is only a narrow band in the electromagnetic spectrum which ranges all the way from the low-frequency forms of radiation such as radio waves to the high-frequency forms such as X-rays and gamma rays. All these waves from the standpoint of physics are the same kind of things. Theoretically the human eye might have been sensitized to X-rays; in that case the human world would be an uncolored world. A chest X-ray is as much a photograph of a person as is the photograph taken by means of a box camera. Individual men and women differ widely in their ability to perceive even the narrow band of visible light; the wearing of glasses is obvious evidence of this divergence. Some birds such as the hawk and the eagle are able to see distinctly at much greater distances than man can, and the common housefly has a composite eye which gives it a much broader range than has the human eye. Many lower animals have keener awareness of sounds and odors than has man, but man has been able to overcome the dullness of his senses by scientific instruments which amplify his sensations a thousandfold. Many of these instruments give him only indirect sensations, or, as Eddington has said, they reduce reality to pointer readings.

Observations are always affected by perspectives and contexts. Things are always sensed from some point of view and are interpreted in a frame of reference. Sensation is never pure sensation, that is, sensation is never an unadulterated imprint of the external world upon the sense organs of man. The physical conditions determine the nature of the sensed object. That is why a careful shopper will insist on examining a new suit in daylight as well as in artificial light before he buys it. The emotional state of the observer is also important. A ten-year-old boy walking past a cemetery on a moonlight night is in no emotional state for the making of accurate observations. Fear, anger, exultation, and other strong emotions affect the ability to hear and see accurately. Observations are also affected by the different assumptions with which one comes to the object. Martin Luther once threw an ink well at the devil. Today the satanic apparition would probably be identified as a sudden gust of wind which billowed the curtains. New England Puritans saw witchcraft where we today would see only senility or mental illness. But we must not conclude that Luther and the Puritans had assumptions which clouded their observations, whereas we see things as they actually are. Rather we have substituted another set of assumptions. Observations are sensations plus interpretations.

The limiting conditions of all observations produce three sorts of errors: (1) errors of non-observation, (2) errors of mal-observation, and (3) errors of memory. The first sort of error may be either one in which a person sees something when nothing is there, or an error in which the person fails to see what is there. Lady Macbeth's awareness of the blood of Duncan on her hands was a case of seeing what was not there. A husband who fails to see the new styling of his wife's hair commits the other error of non-observation. All of us are guilty of failing to observe what is often right in front of our noses. Daily we pass objects which we do not consciously notice. Several years ago when "Information Please" was a popular radio program, the board of experts were asked one evening to hold a card under their chins; then they were asked to state the color of the tie they were wearing. The experts failed, and a copy of the *Encyclopaedia Britannica* was sent to the person who submitted the question. Errors of mal-observation are those errors in which one observes something but does not identify it correctly. A dark object in the meadow is seen as a cow until we get close enough to realize it is a bush. Often a mal-observation is the result of reason acting adversely on sensations. Medieval artists for centuries painted young children with the body proportions of adults. Early Egyptian painters put both eyes on the same side of the nose when they drew a human profile. The third class of errors, the errors of memory, are too well known to need elaboration. Memories are not only selective, they are also constructive. We remember what we want to remember, and we alter it so it fits our purposes. Some of our memories get better in the recounting!

Our own experiences, in spite of all their limitations, constitute a paramount source of the information we need as we move on to the formation of hypotheses and ultimately to the solution of problems. After having collected the information we next attempt to make the information manageable.

6

Making Information Manageable

1. *Importance of relationships*

Problems are not solved merely by collecting relevant information. A man with extensive knowledge is not necessarily a critical thinker; as a matter of fact, a man with a *World Almanac* type of mind — a veritable walking glossary of facts — is likely to be a boring conversationalist, a pedantic student, and a bumbling problem solver. The critical thinker discovers and creates relations between items of information. Information becomes manageable when it is related to other information.

A professor of geology in a small Midwestern college collected rocks within the geographical limits of his state for more than fifty years. These rocks were kept on the shelves of a large classroom. His classes in geology were the most popular on the campus because he shared with his students the circumstances under which each rock was collected. Many of his friends and colleagues advised him to write the story of the collection, and he assured them that he would when he retired from teaching. He commonly justified his lack of publications by quoting from the Old Testament book of Job: "O that my enemy would write a book!" The year before he reached retirement age the professor died of a heart attack. The college was left the large collection of unlabeled rocks. The new professor of geology spent many months in identifying the rocks, but the important information of where, when, and how the rocks were found was lost forever. Merely to identify rocks establishes too few relationships, whereas to discover more relations — particularly of the type this geologist held in memory — changes a rock collection into a source of scientific hypotheses. After the professor's death this collection served largely as a display of the many varieties of rock found in the state, but as long as the professor lived and remembered the circumstances under which the rocks were collected, the collection served to raise stimulating questions: "Why did I find this specimen twenty feet underground at least one thousand miles south of the usual outcropping of such rock? What circumstances might have caused this rock to appear on the surface fifty miles west of our campus when we ordinarily find such rock well below the surface? How far did this pioneer have to travel to quarry this rock which formed the foundations of his house and barn?"

Information that is not classified, ordered, and related with respect to other information is almost useless in the solving of problems. An unclassified file of fingerprints of the citizens of the United States would be of small aid to the Federal Bureau of Investigation in tracing a criminal. In the absence of a classification system, the task of identifying the fingerprint left by a bank robber with one of the millions of fingerprints on file would be a case of looking for a needle in a haystack. Again, to make another analogy, the attempt to use unrelated information in problem solving would be like playing football without rules. A football game in which the object of the game was merely to transport the ball from one end of the field to the other might deteriorate into a situation in which one team brought out bulldozers in order to break through the opponents' defense. In the past, even wars were governed by rules: the rights of non-combatants, the respect for a flag of truce, the agreement to allow the Red Cross to tend to the wounded, and the attempts to control the use of poison gas. Many of the former humanitarian restraints on warfare are meaningless as man enters the Atomic Age. Now with horror he envisions the possibility of a genocidal conflict. Efforts to control atomic weapons are tragically important, since in atomic conflict "victory" will likely come to the participant that soonest violates the rules.

Completely unstructured information is difficult to conceive. Certainly it would be non-verbalized, or perhaps more accurately, non-communicated, since to communicate implies to order. Perhaps the Hebrew myth of the building of the tower of Babel is an illustration. According to this story the men of the land of Shinar set themselves to the building of a tower whose top would reach the sky. When the gods saw what was being accomplished, they came down and confused the people's languages. The building came to an end when communication ceased. While the myth was probably fashioned to account for the multiplicity of languages of man, it serves our purposes better as a clue to the implications of unstructured information. To communicate is to organize information. To say "This is an apple" or "That is red," and to communicate to another in one's speaking, is to bring some order into information, since the words "apple" and "red" are names of classes — the class of apple things and the class of red things. Philosophers have occasionally tried to state what might be the nature of unrelated information. Kant, for example, used the term "sense manifold" to designate that which when related spatially and temporally would be a human sensation; but since space and time are the necessary forms of all man's sensing, he found himself unable to say anything about the nature of the sense manifold. What we have in mind is not merely random information; rather it is an experience or a thought that does not fit anything we have previously experienced or thought. Science fiction stories appeal to some people because of the novelty of the events depicted, but a science fiction story with absolutely no similarity to events of ordinary life would be but a riddle. Perhaps the nearest any person comes to experiencing unstructured information would be within an outlandish dream. The admonition to pinch oneself to see if the experience is a reality or a dream might be stated philosophically in this way: attempt to establish a normal relationship within the "abnormal" to determine the reality of the events. There is a curious statement in one of the dialogues of Plato in which he attempts to speak meaningfully of space abstracted from spatial things. After confessing that space in this sense is "apprehended without the help of sense, by a kind of spurious reason, and is hardly real," he confesses, "Of these and other things of the same kind, relating to the true and waking reality of nature, we have only this dream-like sense, and we are unable to cast off sleep and determine the truth about them."[1]

Let us beware that we do not turn with repugnance from the never-never world of unstructured information and swing in pendulum fashion to completely organized information. This is the fallacy of grade school science textbooks which attempt to convince the school boys and girls that the whole world economy was involved in the preparation of their breakfast, or that no one sneezes without affecting the Great Wall of China! Philosophers who have argued that everything is related to everything else may be stating — or overstating — a fact about our world, but the notion of relations in such a view of the world must for such philosophers be carefully defined, or the idea confuses rather than clarifies the human grasp of the world.

[1] *Timaeus*, 52.

The desire to establish relations between items of information can become a passion which leads a person to assume relations where none exist. Among uncivilized men — and even among those whom we may call semi-civilized — the wish to know the future results in a wide variety of fortune-telling: astrology, numerology, palmistry, phrenology, spiritualism, counting of tea leaves in the bottom of a cup, noting the grouping of long and short lines in the shells of turtles, studying the flight of birds, examining bubbles of oil in water, etc. The intent of all forms of fortune-telling is to relate present events with future events. One ingenious method of relating events which was practiced for centuries by the Delphic Oracle was to request the pilgrim, after he poured out his problem before the priestess, to stuff his ears with wax and to go at once into the marketplace. When he reached the marketplace, he was to remove the wax. The first words he overheard were the answer to his problem. Although most of us would regard such ordering of events as mere happenstance, we would soon discover that a person who is convinced of merit in one mode of fortune-telling is a very stubborn person. A friend once wasted the better part of an evening trying to talk a firm believer in astrology out of his belief. The only measure of success he had came when he shifted ground from refutation to ridicule. He argued that an examination of the entrails of sheep was far more reliable as a means of learning about the future than a study of the position of the stars at the moment of one's birth. The believer in astrology would not accept this; he felt that stars were better than entrails for such purposes, although he finally confessed that there was no inherent reason for the validity of one method of fortune-telling over another method. His final defense was that he had found the stars too reliable to be rejected!

Many of man's superstitions are cases of bad relating of information. Superstitions about black cats, the number thirteen, seeing the moon over the left shoulder, and walking under ladders are relationships which have been established on insufficient evidence — at least so the non-superstitious contend. Most American brides laugh at the notion of "something old and something new, something borrowed and something blue" — yet, just to be safe! — these same brides carry out the four prescriptions in their own wedding. Some forms of insanity are extreme forms of bad relating; for example, a woman may develop a habit of touching a certain part of the door panel each time she goes through doors in order to avoid bad luck, until this becomes such an obsession that she spends many of her waking moments re-establishing favorable relationships with doors.

It would be untrue to assume that the establishing of bad relations among items of information is found only among the superstitious and the insane. All of us are sometimes guilty of seeking relationships which only subsist in our hopes and imaginations. In our anxiety to make knowledge manageable we may press far beyond the evidence for connectives. A humorous incident of this sort occurred several years ago in the zoology department of one of the best graduate schools in the United States. A young professor in the department was studying the functioning of the thymus gland in mammals. Believing that the thymus had something to do with the development of fetuses, he put his belief to the test by stimulating the thymus glands of one group of pregnant white mice and not stimulating the thymus glands of another group. The results were astonishing. The young of the first group were born with their eyes open and were much more developed in every respect than were those of the second group. The professor reported his discovery in a paper before a national scientific organization. However, when other zoologists tried the same experiments in their laboratories, they did not get the same results. After considerable puzzlement the young professor found a variable which he had not taken into account. His student assistant, a young girl secretly in love with her professor, had come to the laboratory each morning before the professor arrived, and had carefully substituted mice several days old for the newborn! She thought she was contributing to his happiness by arranging matters so that his hypothesis was confirmed.

The critical thinker is cautious lest he become involved in a case of bad relating; he is also open to new possibilities of relating. The attitudes of caution and adventure must somehow be combined in the same person. The human ability known to psychiatrists as ambivalence is the despair of logicians. The statements "I love you" and "I hate you" are assumed by logicians to be mutually excluding — if one is true, the other is false — yet, as Freud pointed out, and as most people know by self-examination, the two emotions may be held simultaneously by one person toward another person. Man can love-hate in spite of the logical exclusiveness of the concepts. The critical thinker must perform a similar act of ambivalence: he must rigorously hold to his own theories and at the same time remain open to new counter theories.

2. *Discovering and creating relationships*

In this discussion of the process of relating information that has been collected for the solution of a problem the reader may have observed that some relations seem to be *found* and others seem to be *made*, or more precisely, some aspects of relations are found and some aspects are made.

For example, the pilgrim to the Delphic Oracle *discovered* the relationship of before-after between the words spoken to him by the oracle and the words he heard when he removed the wax from his ears when he reached the marketplace, and the pilgrim *created* the relationship of question-answer between the words of the oracle and the words in the marketplace. The words he heard in the marketplace were of themselves chronologically posterior to the words of the priest; they were not of themselves the answer to his problem — that was a created relationship. Of course, the Delphic priest, were he here, would inform us that due to our ignorance of the way in which Apollo works, we unbelievers conclude that the temporal relationship is real and the oracular relationship is unreal, but if we knew the hidden ways of the god, we would then understand that the words overheard in the marketplace are temporally related and oracularly related in manners which are realistic and objective.

David Hume regarded the distinction between two types of relations as basic to his philosophy. He wrote early in his volume *A Treatise of Human Nature*, "The word relation is commonly used in two senses considerably different from each other. Either for that quality, by which two ideas are connected together in the imagination, and the one naturally introduces the other . . . or for that particular circumstance, in which, even upon the arbitrary union of two ideas in the fancy, we may think proper to compare them."[2] Later in the same work Hume makes the same distinction in slightly different language: "These relations may be divided into two classes; into such as depend entirely on the ideas, which we compare together, and such as may be changed without any change in the ideas."[3] The former, which Hume itemizes as the relations of resemblance, contrariety, degrees of quality, and degrees of quantity, yield knowledge of an absolute sort. An example would be the knowledge of the equality of the sum of the interior angles of a triangle and two right angles. This knowledge is not derived from, nor confirmed by, the physical measurement of triangles. The latter, which Hume itemizes as identity, situations in space and time, and causality, yield knowledge that is at best only probably true. This distinction between relations depending upon ideas only and relations which he calls "matter of fact" is the basis of Hume's distinction between rational knowledge and empirical knowledge. Hume's thinking rests upon notions of the nature of the external world which we need not go into here. What does interest us is that Hume felt the necessity, as do we, to distinguish relations derived from an examination of ideas and those derived from an examination of facts.

[2] Part I, Section V.
[3] Part III, Section I.

Returning to our distinction between created and discovered relationships, there is no intention to imply that one type is preferred to another. All that is intended is that the critical thinker must be perfectly clear about which sort he is dealing with. If they are discovered relationships, he must be certain that the relationships are actually there. Did the shot precede the scream? Was the gun used in the robbery the same gun that the sporting goods store sold on June 3? Was the witness standing not more than fifty feet away from the door of the grocery? And if they are created relationships, he must apply a wide variety of tests: Could the juxtaposition of these notes arouse the emotion appropriate to memories of unrequited love? Does this vaccine have the potentiality of reducing the pain of cancer? Does colored advertising increase the sale of this product? Which translation of this French word most nearly represents in English the subtleties of this term? Is this theory of atomic energy consistent with what we already know about the nature of the atom? Should animals be classified in terms of their food habits, or their means of locomotion, or the state of their young at birth? Man must continually check his created relationships with refined observations and experiments. For example, rabbits are classified in the Mosaic Law among the cud-chewing animals! Created relationships in the absence of discovered relationships could result in an imaginary world far removed from realities. To retreat occasionally to worlds of fantasy may be a pleasant relief from the stern realities of life, but such worlds are not places for permanent residence. On the other hand, he who eschews altogether the created relationships dooms himself to a world of dullness, stagnation, and uncreativity. He would never be one who

> "Finds tongues in trees, books in the running brooks,
> Sermons in stones, and good in everything."

3. *Systematizing the information*

Information takes on different meanings according to the classification into which it is put. Within a matter of minutes a person may be a bus rider, a shopper, a pedestrian, a victim, and a patient. The variety of classifications of people is seemingly endless: sex, race, age, color, religion, nationality, height, weight, shape of head, color of hair, physiological type, personality type, intelligence quotient, education, wealth, fingerprints, lodge memberships, political affiliation, etc. In some situations one classification may be extremely important and another classification may be entirely irrelevant. Some objects are classified quite differently by different peoples; for example, a sycamore tree may be for the botanist, *Platanus occidentalis*; for the poet, white fingers reaching into dark blue sky; for the pioneer, a nuisance, fit only for fuel; for the landscape artist, a backdrop for shrubs; for the lumberman, mere pulpwood; for the historian of religions, the symbol of Osiris; for the homeowner, a messy tree, the sort to plant secretly in the yard of one's enemy; for the nurseryman, the tree of song and poetry, a beautiful tree and one that should be more widely planted. Not only men and trees, but also events, acquire different meaning and significance according to the relationships they are given: the Declaration of Independence so warmly presented in Lincoln's Gettysburg Address — "Four score and seven years ago our fathers brought forth upon this continent a new nation, conceived in liberty and dedicated to the proposition that all men are created equal." — is vastly different when described in the scholarly, critical — and British — manner of the *Cambridge Modern History*: "On July 4, 1776, Congress passed the resolution which made the colonies independent communities, issuing at the same time the well-known Declaration of Independence. If we regard the Declaration as the assertion of an abstract political theory, criticism and condemnation are easy. It sets out with a general proposition so vague as to be practically useless. The doctrine of the equality of men, unless it be qualified and conditioned by reference to special circumstances, is either a barren truism or a delusion."

Sometimes men forget that a wide variety of relations can be established between events. A curious example of such an erroneous relating of events is found in the history of the Sikh religion. In the late seventeenth century the leader of Sikhism, a man named Govind Singh, believed that the peaceful Sikhs should be emboldened to become a military society. He called together a large group of the followers of the religion and announced to them that the goddess Kali demanded human blood before better times could come to the Sikhs. Kali, he said, required five human sacrifices. Was any man willing to be killed to appease the goddess? Five men volunteered. Govind Singh led one of the men into a tent; a swish and a thud were heard, and Singh emerged wiping blood from his long sword. The crowd was silent with horror, as one by one the remaining four men went into the tent for execution. But after the fifth swish and thud, Singh and the five men emerged from the tent dragging with them the carcasses of five beheaded goats! While the people were still under the emotional excitement of the wrong relationships they had established in their interpretation of the events, Singh called for a new dedication like the dedication of these five men who had been willing to die to appease Kali.

Information that has been collected may be related in many different ways. The obvious types of relationships are the serial, the quantitative, the chronological, the spatial, the logical, the causal, and the categorial. The *serial* relationship is perhaps the simplest type. Other appropriate names for this type of relationship are the indexical and the alphabetical. It consists of assigning numbers or letters to discrete units. In this form of relating the numbers 1, 2, 3, etc., or the letters *a, b, c,* etc., mean only that 2 is after 1 and before 3, or that *b* is after *a* and before *c.* There is no other unit of the kind between 1 and 2, or between 2 and 3; and there is nothing of the kind between 1 and 3 other than 2. Things that are serially ordered do not form a continuum. Sometimes serially related things may be described as if they were not discrete units, but this is to be regarded as a verbal necessity and not as a violation of the discrete nature of the units. For example, a certain American university once reported that the average family of its graduates had one and three-quarters children. Many humorous remarks were made about the three-quarters children of alumni. Again the serial ordering of information may denote a second ordering, or it may not. For example, numbers assigned to students in a large classroom could designate their relative height, weight, cumulative point hour ratio, or even the order in which they entered the room on the first day. A completely random serial ordering of the students is not as easy to achieve as one might at first suppose.

The *quantitative* relationship and the serial relationship may both be called numerical relationships, but there is a significant difference between them. The ordering 1, 2, 3, may be either a serial ordering or a quantitative ordering. A serial ordering is a sort of naming. There is no implication that by adding 1 and 1 the result will be 2. For example, when a group of soldiers count off, Tom becomes 1, Dick becomes 2, Harry becomes 3, etc., but this does not mean that Tom plus Dick equals Harry. Yet in the quantitative ordering the cumulative relationship of the units is an essential characteristic; one dollar plus two dollars certainly does equal three dollars. Whereas in serial ordering 2 merely comes after 1 and before 3, in quantitative ordering 2 comes after 1 and before 3, and in addition 2 is 1 plus 1, as well as 3 minus 1. If the difference between serial ordering and quantitative ordering becomes confusing, a simple rule of thumb is to use *a, b, c,* for serial ordering, and to use 1, 2, 3, for quantitative ordering.

The *chronological* relationship is a species of the serial relationship. This relationship brings in the notion of a temporal before and a temporal after. There is no need to become involved in the metaphysics of time with such problems as its absoluteness or relativity, or its independence of or dependence upon perceiving agents. We here confine ourselves to the experiences of before and after. As to what time is, we can by-pass the issue with the clever observation of Augustine: "What, then, is time? If no one ask of me, I know; if I wish to explain to him who asks, I know not." Temporal ordering is important in man's life, yet it is not an ordering that can be applied to all man's life and thought. Items of information in mathematics and logic are not chronologically ordered. "*When* does 2 plus 2 equal 4?" or "*When* does 'A implies B' mean that it is not true that there can be an affirmation of A and a negation of B?" are foolish questions. They imply a temporal ordering of the non-temporal. Man has been described as the time-binding animal — the animal that remembers the past and anticipates the future; man might also be described as the time-eliminating animal — the animal who is able to entertain objects of thought which are non-temporal. If for God a thousand years are as a day and a day as a thousand years, then, in the words of a modern astronomer, God is indeed the great mathematician — the being for whom all knowledge is non-temporally ordered.

The *spatial* relationship is closely related to the temporal relationship. Einstein, as every high school boy knows, contended that space and time are four dimensions of events. Man locates where an event is when, and when an event is where. The newspaper report of an airplane collision in the air would need to include altitude, latitude, longitude, and time. A principal difference between space and time is the excluding characteristic of space and the non-excluding characteristic of time. Two things cannot be in exactly the same space; but two acts can occur in exactly the same time. Among the subclasses of spatial ordering can be listed the ordering of spatial things according to color, or shape, or size, or position.

The *logical* relationship is a species of ordering of items of information such that from one, or from several, a conclusion may be drawn. The units of this form of ordering are statements, that is, sentences which have meaning. To have meaning, however, is not the same as to make sense. Logic textbooks are full of illustrations such as: If all mugwumps are bombats, and if all bombats are fuzzy-gigs, then all mugwumps are fuzzy-gigs. As a matter of fact, writers of logic textbooks are partial to this sort of argument, for it forces the student to make a distinction between the truth of sentences and the validity of arguments. Logical meaning has to do with the internal structure of arguments; it need not refer to any space-time reality. Logical relationships are the relationships of ideas to ideas, not the relationships of ideas to realities, nor the relationships of realities to realities. When we are dealing with logical relationships, we are concerned with what we mean when we say such and such, not with whether when we refer to such and such we are denoting anything that is real in the space-time world.

The *causal* relationship is one of the most important relationships in the scientific enterprise. Much of scientific research is a quest for answers to "What brought this about?" or "What will this bring about?" There are two opposing views of causality in modern philosophical thinking: the necessary connection view and the regularity view. According to the former theory the causal relationship is rooted in the nature of the world. Bread nourishes and strychnine poisons, because it is the "nature" of one to nourish, and it is the "nature" of the other to poison. Even if no person had ever eaten bread or consumed strychnine, it would be theoretically possible to relate bread to nourishment and strychnine to death. This view can be called the rationalistic view, since the cause and the effect are determined by appeal to reason alone. According to the regularity view the causal relationship is rooted in human expectations based on previous experiences. This could also be called the expectancy view. After one has observed that the eating of bread is followed by physical well-being and that the consuming of strychnine is followed by death, one tends to associate nourishment with bread and poisoning with strychnine. Supporters of the regularity theory contend that observations condition us to expect nourishment from the one and death from the other. But the supporters of the necessary connection theory accuse the supporters of the regularity theory of failing to distinguish between cases in which one event happens to follow another event, e.g., thunder after lightning, and cases in which one event is "really" the cause of another event, e.g., nourishment after eating bread.

Finally there is what might be called the *categorial* relating of information. By "categorial relating" we refer to the selection of basic terms used by both the common man and by the scientist to talk about a subject matter. Some languages specialize in certain kinds of categories. The English language and the Chinese language have interesting differences in this respect. One difference is that English tends to reify that which Chinese tends to keep as a process.[4] For example, in English the fist is a thing, whereas in Chinese a fist is something one can do with the hand — the fisting of the hand! A second difference is that the English language makes sharp distinctions between right and wrong, form and matter, yes and no. But in Chinese terms like Yin and Yang, which suggest to the speaker of English such dichotomies as negative and positive, wet and dry,

[4] See Alan W. Watts, *The Way of Zen* (New York: The New American Library of World Literature, 1959), p. 19.

female and male, mean for the Chinese a harmonious opposition. Yin and Yang are concordant in the Tao. Even the word "No" (*wu*) in Chinese does not mean total negation; it means absence from the immediate scene. Originally *wu* meant "forty men disappear into the woods"![5] By categorial relationships we mean more than the selection of the language one uses to express information; we mean also the selection of the basic terms used to deal with a subject matter. For example, if we read an essay in economics which utilizes such basic terms as proletariat, bourgeoisie, exploitation, revolution, surplus value, and exchange value, we would suspect that the author was a Communist. A second essay in which the basic terms are employee, employer, profit, loss, supply, demand, stock, bonds, dividends, competition, and free enterprise would probably be the work of a Capitalist. Another example can be selected from metaphysics. Some metaphysicians think of the world as composed of fixed quantities; they use terms like substance, property, accident, being, essence, matter, form, and structure. Other metaphysicians think of the world as being in constant change; they use such terms as event, duration, flux, process, creativity, relatedness, occasions, novelty, and becoming. One of the classical philosophies of India, the Nyāya-Vaiśeṣika, lists the following as the categories for relating information about the world: substance, quality, action, universal, particular, relation, and non-existence. The last category has four sub-categories: (1) mutual negation, e.g., the non-existence of red color in a blue ball; (2) absolute non-existence, e.g., the non-existence of color in air; (3) destruction, e.g., the non-existence of a piece of wood after it is burned; and (4) previous non-existence, e.g., the non-existence of a pot in the clay before it is fashioned into a pot. A Western metaphysician might be able to utilize these four forms of non-existence in expressing his own view of reality, but he would probably discover that the use of such basic terms would tend to shape his view of reality. The selection of the categories for the relating of items of information to each other is a very important aspect of critical thinking.

After the critical thinker has placed his information in the relationships appropriate to his subject matter, he moves on to the formation of hypotheses.

[5] Frederic Spiegelberg, *Living Religions of the World* (Englewood Cliffs, N.J.: Prentice-Hall, Inc., 1956), p. 302.

7

Producing Hypotheses

Early in these considerations of what is involved in problem solving, hypotheses were described as possible answers. The word "hypothesis" is derived from two Greek words meaning "to place under." It is that which when placed under the information gives a rational explanation for a state of affairs. We have noted already that there is what might be called a proto-hypothesis at work in the collecting and organizing of information. Information is collected and made manageable according to guiding ideas as to what information is relevant and what organization assists in the solution of the problem. But, whereas the proto-hypothesis is assumed and often implicit, the hypothesis is consciously and deliberately formed to relate the information directly to the conclusion of the problem. Perhaps the hypothesis might be called a "proto-conclusion" in the sense that it is a possible conclusion which, if it survives what we shall call examining and testing, becomes the conclusion. When distinctions are made among hypotheses, theories, and laws, these distinctions designate degrees of generality, scope, and certainty. Hence, Darwin's hypothesis of evolution and Einstein's hypothesis of relativity are called "theories," whereas Kepler's hypothesis of planetary motion and Galileo's hypothesis of falling bodies are called "laws." Since all the important generalizations of the sciences are hypothetical, it is unfortunate that the word "hypothesis" is not used throughout. When a scientist becomes convinced that the evidence for a hypothesis is overwhelming, he may eschew words like "theory" or "law" and call the hypothesis a "fact," that is, a true statement. For example, Wells, Huxley, and Wells give the title "The Incontrovertible Fact of Evolution" to Book III of their volume, *The Science of Life*. In other contexts the hypothesis may be so basic to a body of knowledge that many items are deduced from it. In such cases the hypothesis functions as an axiom.

Hypotheses may serve a variety of overlapping functions. They may be efforts to reach a conclusion to a problem. The problem may be a practical problem such as how to get from Times Square to Columbia University in thirty minutes; or it may be a theoretical problem such as how to make sense of the doctrine of the Trinity. Sometimes hypotheses are designed to clarify a puzzling situation. There is need to give significance to an object or an experience which would otherwise be relatively meaningless. When one is awakened by a sound in a darkened room a hypothesis is needed to answer "What was that?" Sometimes the object or event is identified, but one wishes more specific identification. We may know that the object in the tree outside our window is a bird, but we desire to know what sort of bird it is. Again hypotheses may function as answers to the problem of what to do. Hypotheses are sometimes directed toward courses of action. A party of mountain climbers a few years ago found a girl lying unconscious on the trail where her horse had thrown her. The nearest automobile was three miles away by mountain trail. Many hypotheses for action were presented before the party agreed that one hiker should go down the trail to get a stretcher while the other hikers should stay with the girl. Sometimes the function of hypotheses is to make predictions possible. A high school boy might impress his friends by tossing a stone down an abandoned well, clock the fall as two seconds, and then announce that the well is about 64 feet deep. He would be making a practical use of the hypothesis $S = 1/2 \, gt^2$. These are the chief functions of hypotheses: (1) to reach a conclusion to a problem; (2) to clarify a puzzling situation; (3) to imply a course of action; (4) to make predictions possible.

The discerning reader may have noticed that in the last paragraph when speaking of hypotheses the plural displaced the singular. This was intentional. We are to be aware at the beginning of this chapter of the importance of producing many hypothetical conclusions to a problem. It is a case of not putting all one's eggs in one basket. In addition it is a reflection of the fact that most problems have many facets, and rarely would the critical thinker happen directly on a single hypothesis which will account for all sides of the problem. Often the causes of the problem are multiple. A homeowner who wants to know why a large tree is losing its leaves ought to consider a number of hypotheses: lack of moisture, insect attack, disease, poor soil, etc. There is always the possibility that none of his hypotheses is the correct one, as in the case of the man who discovered too late that the boys who mowed his lawn had killed many of his trees by repeatedly hitting the trunks with the lawnmower.

1. *No rules for the production of hypotheses*

If any step in problem solving is more important than the other steps, that step is the production of hypotheses. So it is not strange that men have sought an infallible technique for the forming of hypotheses. Surely there must be some formula, some yoga, or some charism which will lead to the creation of significant hypotheses! This is the area peculiar to genius. But alas! the geniuses have not been helpful in explaining how they work at this stage of critical thinking. A nineteenth-century American mathematical wizard, when asked how he could compute so rapidly replied, "God put it into my head, and I can't put it into yours." "I frame no hypotheses," said Newton. This oft-quoted remark of Newton's should never be quoted except in context: "I have not been able to discover the cause of those properties of gravity from phenomena, and I frame no hypotheses; for whatever is not deduced from the phenomena is to be called an hypothesis; and hypotheses, whether metaphysical or physical, whether of occult qualities or mechanical, have no place in experimental philosophy." So Newton was not really denying that he framed hypotheses; instead he was saying that all scientific research — including the formation of hypotheses — must be restricted to the world of our shareable and testable experiences. On another occasion when questioned as to the origin of his hypotheses, or "bold guesses" as he preferred to call them, he replied, "I keep the subject of my inquiry constantly before me, and wait till the first dawning opens gradually, by little and little, into a full and clear light." But many men have kept a problem constantly before them, yet for them there was no "dawning" that gradually opened into "full and clear light." Persistent attention to a problem sometimes only results in a headache! To put oneself in the same situation as another is no guarantee that one will undergo the same experience. An Indian professor stated that he once meditated all night at the very spot where the father of Rabindranath Tagore had spent an all-night vigil resulting in a mystical experience which altered his entire life. When asked what he got out of his attempt to duplicate Tagore's experience, the professor replied, "I was eaten by mosquitoes!"

There are no rules for the forming of hypotheses; neither are there trade secrets which when discovered will in Pygmalion fashion turn the humdrum intellect into a critical thinker bordering on the level of genius. Yet there are some broad suggestions which may be applied to hypothesis formation.

One of these suggestions is that hypotheses appear only in the context of a problem, and the more clearly a problem is defined the more likely will hypotheses appear. Contrariwise, the less clearly the problem is defined, the less likely will hypotheses appear. In the early days of archaeology, the science — if it was a science at that time — was simply a search for what was hidden. Archaeology was a sophisticated game of hide-and-seek with hider and seeker separated by many centuries. The ancients buried things; the moderns dug them up! The object of the search was to collect as many ancient objects as possible. Today archaeologists define their problem much more comprehensively. They seek pots, shards, bones, arrowheads, etc., as did their archaeological predecessors, but now they set for themselves problems regarding the times in which the artifacts were made and used. They do not disturb a fragment of a clay pot until they have photographed it, sketched it, located it with reference to other natural and man-made objects. Anyone who has ever watched an archaeologist squatting in a dusty hole wiping dust from a bit of pottery with a small camel's hair brush does not need to be reminded that archaeology is far more than digging up ancient remains. The caution does not end with this. Because of the awareness of the limitations of our present knowledge of ancient civilizations and also because of the steady growth in information about historical and geological periods, a current practice is to leave unexcavated a considerable portion of each tell so that archaeologists of another generation will have virgin digs.

The second fact to be noted about the formation of hypotheses is that they do not appear in the absence of information. The problem solver does not invent a hypothesis and then enrich it with supporting observations. Kepler wrote in a letter to a friend, "You believe that I start with imagining some pleasant hypothesis and please myself in embellishing it, examining it only later by observations. In this you are very much mistaken. The truth is that after having built up an hypothesis on the ground of observations and given it proper foundations, I feel a peculiar desire to investigate whether I might discover some natural, satisfying combination between the two." The man best informed about a subject matter is the man most likely to form hypotheses. Familiarity with the subject matter is a necessary cause, although not a sufficient cause for the formation of hypotheses. Machinists like the Wright brothers invent the airplane, and musicians like Handel and Bach compose oratorios. Machinists do not compose oratorios, and musicians do not invent airplanes. This is so obvious that to state it seems a bit silly. Yet it must be said, for many people seem strangely surprised by what other men have produced, forgetting that in most cases the end product is the result of years of concentrating on a certain problem and collecting much information relevant to that problem. Ordinarily masterpieces in any field do not appear unpredictably.

On the other hand, many persons well informed in a field do not bring forth startling discoveries. W. D. Bancroft, in an interesting series of lectures on "The Methods of Research,"[1] classifies scientists into "accumulators" and "guessers." The accumulators are those who collect specific observational and experimental data. Collection seems to be completely satisfying to them. The guessers (he says a guess is a judgment made from inadequate evidence) attempt to create explanations to account for what the accumulators find. This classification seems puzzling, if not misleading, because accumulators surely do not collect data in the absence of a problem they wish to solve, and guessers certainly do not guess in the absence of facts. Bancroft's classification is suggestive, but not very precise.

As people move from the open-eyed years of childhood into maturity they become increasingly accustomed to sensing and knowing what they wish to sense and to know. They pay attention to only limited portions of their surroundings. To illustrate this point a certain university professor once asked a large class of senior students to name the color of the shutters on the library not more than fifty yards from the classroom window (without looking at the library, of course!). After he had been told that the shutters were white, or green, or brown, he asked the students to look out the window. The library had no shutters! These students had regarded the library as a place to go for a book, a place to meet a friend, a building on the campus, and not as an aesthetic object. If these students had known their professor better, they could have turned the tables on him by asking him what he ate for lunch. That would have stumped him, since for him food is stuff to sustain the body; he gives no special attention to it. His wife has long ceased to ask him what he wants to eat at the next meal, and is almost reconciled to the fact that he does not know what he is eating during a meal! There are some people who have retained the attitude of childlike wonder toward some parts of their experience. They are probably the better problem solvers because they are keenly aware of problems and facts. A genius is he who can return to childhood at will. In him problems and information cross-fertilize.

A third point to note about the formation of hypotheses is that they are formed at the end of study, not at the inception. Because hypotheses often have appeared in leisure moments — while taking a bath, or dozing before a fire, or daydreaming under an apple tree — some have supposed that a striking hypothesis is the gift of the gods, that men may be grateful for their appearance, but do little about their coming. These sudden in-

[1] *The Rice Institute Pamphlets*, 15, 1928, pp. 167–286.

sights or flashes of genius, however, usually follow long periods of study, even if they are not the direct result of study. David Hume said, "Reason alone can never give rise to any original idea." If hypotheses are emergents, they emerge usually from a well-stocked and trained mind; they are not the autochthonous products of an intellectual vacuum.

The last suggestion to be made about the general nature of hypothesis formation is that the process is highly subjective. The selection of hypotheses depends upon the objective facts and also upon the hopes, values, and desires of the problem solver. A hypothesis is a very personal affair. It is the thinker's brain child. Men do not ordinarily nor easily turn against their own children. Scientists are not robots; they feel the same emotions as the non-scientists. They know probably better than the average man how difficult it is to see that which repudiates one's expectations. The Ames demonstration, to which we have previously referred, neatly shows how difficult it is to see that which violates what is known about perspective. When watching the apparatus in action we *know* that the larger end of the revolving isosceles trapezoid is at one stage nearer to us than is the smaller end, but our eyes refuse to see it that way! A scientist who believed that birds fly at much faster speeds than is commonly supposed actually clocked birds flying at 240 miles an hour! There is an old and pregnant saying among scientists that no one believes a hypothesis except its originator, and that everyone believes an experiment except the experimenter. That is, each scientist is at the same time anxious to establish his hypothesis and aware of the possibility of error in his experiments. A careful reading of books on the scientific method will often result in the discovery of two statements which when put together are most puzzling: "The vast majority of hypotheses prove to be wrong." and "Scientists cling to their hypotheses long after they are disproven." Someone has said that scientists clinging to disproved hypotheses resemble hens sitting on boiled eggs! Copernicus seems to have been an exception to the rule; he wrote to Pope Paul III, "I am not so much in love with my conclusions as not to weigh what others will think about them."

Sometimes the subjectivity of hypotheses is frankly admitted. For example, F. Sierksma of the University of Leiden, in a recent study of sacred cairns, pointed out that there are two general hypotheses as to the motivation for constructing cairns — the pastoral hypothesis, i.e., cairns are built by travelers as good luck charms of the road, and the agricultural hypothesis, i.e., cairns are built as magical means to secure fertility of fields and animals; he then presents his own hypothesis and admits his bias: "Here the present writer only begs to differ, because he simply prefers pastoralists to agriculturalists. Aware of the fact that the pastoralists have their negative as well as their positive aspects, he prefers their ability to develop a personality that is characterized by individualism, freedom, honor, pride, realism (without prudery but not without poetry)."[2] Sierksma admits in the next paragraph that his is a subjective opinion, yet he sticks to it. The fact that Sierksma likes the personality of primitive pastoral peoples better than the personality of primitive agricultural peoples does not seem to be reason sufficient for preferring a pastoral hypothesis regarding the constructing of cairns to an agricultural hypothesis. At least his prejudice nicely illustrates the subjectivity which enters into all framing of hypotheses.

There is a passage in the writing of Ernst Mach, the Austrian physicist, which also illustrates the difficulty scientists experience in rejecting a hypothesis they have formed. Mach, writing in the fifth edition of his book, *The Analysis of Sensations*, in 1906, quotes from a paper of his written in 1863 in which he defended the view that the electric processes in the nerves explain the difference of quality in sensations, and then adds, "Even to-day I have not succeeded in getting rid of this idea, and I cannot refrain from bringing forward evidence that confirms it in essentially the same form, as for instance by referring to the presence of an identical current in different electrolytes."[3] Yet early in this same book when arguing that there is no real permanency of the ego, Mach takes a quite different position regarding his earlier scholarly endeavors: "Many an article that I myself penned twenty years ago impresses me now as something quite foreign to myself."[4] Mach was more interested in preserving his hypotheses than in preserving himself!

Even though most hypotheses prove to be wrong, some prove to be right — and occasionally this is due to the tenacity of their originators. Faraday's hypothesis on electricity came at last to be accepted, partly because he persisted in holding to it. His stubbornness in holding to this hypothesis must however be counterbalanced with other words of Faraday: "The world little knows how many of the thoughts and theories which have passed through the mind of a scientific investigator have been crushed in silence and secrecy by his own severe criticism and adverse examinations."

[2] "Sacred Cairns in Pastoral Cultures," *History of Religions*, Vol. 2, No. 2, Winter 1963, p. 240.

[3] *The Analysis of Sensations*, translated from the first German edition by C. M. Williams. Revised and supplemented from the fifth German edition by Sidney Waterlow (Chicago and London: The Open Court Publishing Company, 1914), p. 371.

[4] *Ibid.*, p. 4.

2. Role of analogy

The process of producing hypotheses may be divided into two parts: the planned and the unplanned. The identification and clarification of the problem and the collection and organization of information are elements of the planned part. They lead directly to the formation of hypotheses. After the problem has been clarified and the information has been organized, the critical thinker turns to the specific attempt to create hypotheses which may lead to a conclusion to the problem. We have already noted that there is much that is personal and subjective in the forming of hypotheses. Analogies play an important role in this early stage of creation of hypotheses. An analogy is a noting of likeness or resemblance between two things. Analogous reasoning consists in arguing that because things agree in one or more respects they also agree in other respects. Some hypotheses are analogies; they grow out of an imagined application of principles of one subject matter to those of another subject matter. Other hypotheses originate as the discovery of previously unnoticed connections. Scientists have pointed out that between the defining of the problem and the collecting of information on the one hand and the actual forming of the hypothesis on the other, there is a twilight zone of daydreaming — a fermentation of ideas — in which analogies sometimes play important roles. It is not completely unplanned behavior; rather it is the making of comparisons with the minimum of critical examination. Kekulé, who formulated the idea of the benzene ring, claimed that the idea first came to him as he daydreamed before a fireplace of wiggling snakes that had seized their own tails.

A distinction must be made between analogies used as tools of explanation and analogies used as aids to hypothesis formation. The first usage is the metaphorical; it is the enrichment and clarification of an exposition. For example, in Buddhistic scriptures words are described as fingers that point to the moon, or as rafts used to cross a stream. How foolish, continues the Buddhist, to look at the finger and never see the moon to which the finger points, or to become so attached to the raft that, after crossing the stream on the raft, a traveler puts it on his back and trudges through the forest with this load. By using these analogies the Buddhist writers help us to understand that words are but pointers to realities and techniques of accomplishments; they are not real or valuable in themselves. Some modern semanticists say there are two uses of language: the communicative and the pragmatic. Analogies as explanations illustrate the first use. As a second example of the explanatory force of analogies, consider the following from Bertrand Russell. Lord Russell does not like a type of philosophy now current among professional philosophers; this is a philosophy called Language Analysis or Linguistic Philosophy. Russell believes, exactly as do the Buddhists, that language should be treated as a means of communicating about a real world rather than as an end in itself to be studied for its own sake. He accuses linguistic philosophers of becoming finger-conscious, and thus forgetting the moon to which the finger points. But Russell uses a different analogy: "When I was a boy, I had a clock with a pendulum which could be lifted off. I found that the clock went very much faster without the pendulum. If the main purpose of a clock is to go, the clock was the better for losing its pendulum. True, it could no longer tell the time, but that did not matter if one could teach oneself to be indifferent to the passage of time. The linguistic philosophy, which cares only about language, and not about the world, is like the boy who preferred the clock without the pendulum because, although it no longer told the time, it went more easily than before and at a more exhilarating pace."[5] Russell's biting metaphor has other implications, e.g., linguistic philosophy is a useless activity like a runaway clock which does not tell time but merely runs at a terrific pace. One of the problems of the use of analogies for explanation is that there is no rule as to how far the comparison should be extended. Should we infer from Russell's analogy that just as a runaway clock soon comes to an abrupt halt, so linguistic philosophy will soon run its course and cease to exist?

The uses of analogies as explanatory devices and as aids in the formation of hypotheses cannot be sharply distinguished, since one of the functions of hypotheses is to explain. For example, when Thomas Hobbes compares the state to an organism — "by art is created that great Leviathan called a Commonwealth, or State, in Latin *Civitas*, which is but an artificial man" — he is both clarifying the nature of the state and also formulating a theory of the state which is rich with implications for man's life within society. Hobbes is forming a hypothesis which is partly analogical, and he is also using a metaphor to explain his hypothesis. A better example of the use of analogy in hypothesis formation is that of Darwin's use of an idea from Malthus. Darwin informs us that he had been working for fifteen months to find a theory to account for the formation of new species of plants and animals. In October, 1838, he read for amusement an essay on population by Malthus in which the author argued that man reproduces in geometric progression whereas his food supply can increase only in arithmetic progression. In other words, food supply curbs the increase of human populations. Darwin took this idea, which Malthus

---

[5] Ernest Gellner, *Words and Things* (London: Victor Gollancz, 1959), p. 15.

had applied only to man, and developed his own theory of evolution. Darwin explained the event in this fashion: "I happened to read for amusement, Malthus on Population, and being well prepared to appreciate the struggle for existence which everywhere goes on, from long-continued observations of the habits of animals and plants, it at once struck me that under these circumstances favorable variations would tend to be preserved, and unfavorable ones destroyed. The result of this would be the formation of new species."

This, we have said, is planned thinking in hypothesis formation. The critical thinker faced with a problem which he wishes to solve will probably begin by thinking of similar problems, similar situations, and similar processes to find a clue. Darwin found his clue in Malthus' studies of human population; Hobbes found his in the nature of the human body; Kekulé found his in the image of a snake biting its own tail! The structure underlying this type of thinking is: If A is like B in respect to X, then probably A is like B in respect to Y. An analogy may be that which triggers a line of thought ending in a hypothesis; it may be the best way to explain the meaning of a hypothesis; but usually the critical thinker would prefer not to have the hypothesis itself stated in the form of an analogy. To do this would lay the hypothesis open to misunderstandings inherent in any analogy, that is, its extension beyond the confines of the problem which generated the quest for a hypothesis.

3. *Role of intuition and chance*

We noted above that there is a planned aspect and an unplanned aspect in the process of hypothesis creation. Now we are to consider the intriguing unplanned aspect of the process. This may be divided into the subjective and the objective. The subjective is an intuition, a lucky guess, a hunch, or a "eureka" as one scientist has suggested; the objective is chance, luck, accident, or "tyche."

According to Washington Platt and Ross A. Baker in their interesting article, "The Relation of the Scientific 'Hunch' to Research,"[6] nine-tenths of the time in any research laboratory is taken up with work of a mechanical nature. In the remaining one-tenth there may appear the leap of the imagination over the gaps in the evidence and the mental elaboration of the leap. This is the intuition, the insight, the hunch, or whatever name by which it may be called, which comes seemingly without planning, and

[6] *Journal of Chemical Education*, Vol. 8, October 1931, pp. 1969–2002.

which leads to the hypothesis. Darwin said he could remember the very spot in the road, while in his carriage, the insight came to him that culminated in the theory of evolution. Platt and Baker offer two definitions of the hunch: "a unifying or clarifying idea which springs into consciousness suddenly as a solution to a problem" and "a judgment the bases or premises of which are unknown or not clear to the individual having the hunch." In some Oriental philosophies the hunch experience is called "seeing with the third eye." The experience is well known to poets and artists; it is not foreign to scientists. Platt and Baker prepared a questionnaire asking scientists about their hunches. They sent their questionnaire to 1450 scientists selected from the list in *American Men of Science.* They received 232 replies. The first question in the questionnaire was "Have you ever received assistance from the scientific revelation or hunch in the solution of an important problem?" To this question 33 per cent replied "Frequently," 50 per cent "Occasionally," and 17 per cent "Never." We can surmise that scientists, having been trained to think objectively, found difficulty in answering a questionnaire which demanded an introspective analysis. Most scientists probably find difficulty in stating exactly what are the sources of their pregnant ideas. Helmholtz was an exception in that he was most explicit in locating his hunches: he said that his best ideas did not come to him while in the laboratory but "when comfortably ascending woody hills in sunny weather." Platt and Baker conclude on the basis of the replies to their questionnaire that hunches are common among scientists, and that they cannot be directly willed. A few of the scientists reported they had experimented with food, tobacco, and alcohol as stimulants for the production of intuitions. This use of stimuli is strikingly similar to efforts of medieval Christian mystics to foster a mystical experience during the "dark night of the soul." Platt and Baker conclude that the following conditions can be specified for the successful incubation of hunches:

1. The scientist must have great interest in the problem and have a strong desire for its solution.
2. There should be an absence of other problems which would tend to crowd out the first problem.
3. The mind must have available a large store of pertinent information.
4. The information should be stored in the mind in a systematic fashion and should be well digested.
5. There must be a sense of well-being and a sense of freedom from interruptions.
6. There must be an absence of definite obstacles to the proper functioning of the mind.

7. The scientist must engage in certain types of positive stimuli to mental activity such as reading or conversation.

The question whether there is actual chance in the world has been debated by philosophers as separated in time and as diverse in points of view as Aristotle, John Calvin, and C. S. Peirce. We do not wish to become involved here in metaphysical and theological questions about chance such as are connected with doctrines of determinism, free will, fate, predestination, and Divine omnipotence. Rather we are interested in recognizing that unplanned events sometimes stimulate the formation of hypotheses which prove to be satisfactory solutions to problems. An unplanned meeting with another person, or simply being by chance in a certain place at a certain time, may change the whole course of one's life. Lincoln happened to be in New Orleans at the time of a slave auction; Augustine accidentally overheard a child singing a song which turned his religion from Manichaeism to Christianity; Luther's life was changed when his friend was killed by lightning. But we are here concerned with the fact that chance events are sometimes ingredients in the shaping of hypotheses. W. I. B. Beveridge lists twenty-nine examples of scientific discoveries in which chance played a part.[7] Beveridge's account of Ehrlich's discovery of the acid-fast method of staining tubercle bacilli is an interesting example. Ehrlich left some preparations on a stove which someone later lighted. He discovered that the heat of the stove was just what was needed to make the tubercle bacilli take the stain.

One might be tempted to conclude from Beveridge's examples that every scientific laboratory ought to have a bungling assistant to make the mistakes which will lead to the discoveries. But Beveridge does not tell of the accidents which led to nothing! He does list a few working principles for capitalizing on the chance events, which we may summarize by saying simply that the good problem solver is sufficiently awake to his problem to make use of any lucky event which may be later formulated into a hypothesis. We should not overemphasize the hunch in hypothesis formation. There is invariably a long period of gestation of ideas before a hypothesis is born. Norwood Russell Hanson cautions us as follows: "Yet the original suggestion of a hypothesis type is often a reasonable affair. It is not as dependent on intuition, hunches, and other imponderables as historians and philosophers suppose when they make it the province of genius but not of logic. . . . To form the first specific idea of an elliptical planetary orbit, or of constant acceleration, or of universal

---

[7] *The Art of Scientific Investigation* (New York: Random House, Vintage Books, n. d.). First published in 1950. Pp. 37–45, 215–225.

gravitational attraction does indeed require genius — nothing less than a Kepler, a Galileo, or a Newton. But this does not entail that reflections leading to these ideas are nonrational."[8]

4. Considerations of what others have done

Non-scientists suppose that scientists spend most of their time confronting themselves with the experimental facts in the laboratory or in the field. As a matter of fact, most scientists — even the so-called experimental scientists — spend much more time in the library than in the laboratory. Almost any scientist will agree that his biggest job is keeping up with the literature in his field. "Keeping up" is a jest among scientists. In 1952 there were more than 50,000 scientific periodicals. The scientist must select what he is to read, which scientific conventions he will attend, and which lectures he will attend when he goes to a convention. Scientists wish to know what others have done and what others are doing in their field. There is enough work to go around. There is too much work to be done to waste time repeating what others have done. The international cooperation of scientists is sometimes misunderstood by politicians to indicate a lack of national devotion; it is hard for some people to understand how devotion to truth might transcend devotion to one's country. Following World War II one of America's greatest atomic physicists was charged with being a security risk; yet when a leading German space scientist came to America, he was welcomed as one who was changing national allegiance. The manner in which scientists are able to transcend barriers of nation, race, color, and religion is an example of what might be possible for all men when the quest for knowledge supersedes some of the other quests of mankind.

Scientists build upon each other. Darwin claimed to be a schoolboy to Aristotle; and Darwin, as we have already noted, created his theory after having studied Malthus, a political economist. Some of man's most foolish acts have been those in which he has ignored the work of his predecessors. Henry Ford is supposed to have remarked on one occasion, "All history is bunk." But Ford did not ignore the work that had been done in combustion engines when he designed his automobile. The ridicule of history — Napoleon said history is but fable agreed upon, and Voltaire said it is a pack of tricks played on the dead — when examined

---

[8] "Is There a Logic of Scientific Discovery?" in *Current Issues in the Philosophy of Science*, ed. Herbert Feigl and Grover Maxwell (New York: Holt, Rinehart and Winston, 1960), p. 30.

turns out to be a ridicule of the work of historians; it is not the ridicule of the past. Memory that spans generations distinguishes man among the animals. He who ignores the past as he attempts to solve a problem seems less than human. Because man remembers his past, he need not work by trial and error. "There is nothing new under the sun" is often quoted in bitterness; it should be quoted in optimism. Because we do not face entirely new problems, we can seek clues for their solution in the long experience of man.

EXERCISES

Selection of Information

Directions: The following are statements of problems and items of information which are supposed to be relevant to the solution of the problems. Mark the items of information according to these options:

1. Probably relevant to the solution of the problem.
2. Probably irrelevant to the solution of the problem.

Then star the one item most relevant to the solution of the problem, that is, the item of information you would wish to examine first.

A. The Dean of a college suspects two students in a certain dormitory of having engaged in a disastrous prank last weekend. He is trying to complete his evidence before acting on the case. He has the following bits of evidence.

1. These two boys have been in trouble ever since they came to college.
2. They were both out of town last weekend — according to their landlady.
3. They are both the sons of alumni.
4. The dorm director heard them boast several weeks ago that they were going to pull this prank sometime.
5. Both faithfully promised last spring that they would behave themselves if allowed to room together.
6. One of them has been dating the daughter of the Dean.
7. Their parents are divorced.
8. Their nicknames are Bum and Jerk.

B. The Chief of Police in a college town wonders why there are far more traffic accidents in September than in any other month of the year. He jots down on his writing pad the following facts.

1. The college opens in September.
2. Labor Day is in September.
3. There are more left-handed drivers than right-handed in this town.
4. September has less rainfall than any other month.
5. September is the month in which rookie policemen are added to the force.
6. The public school opens in September.
7. Liquor sales are highest in the month of September.
8. There are more Bargain Days among the stores in this month than there are in any other month.
9. Women drivers stop wearing big hats in September.

C. A defeated candidate for public office sits down the night after the election and tries to determine why he lost the election. He notes the following items.

1. The public opinion poll predicted he would lose.
2. His name was slightly misspelled on the ballot.

99

3. There was a thunderstorm during the afternoon of the election.
4. He drives a foreign car.
5. Over half of the voters were of his party.
6. He did not make a statement to the League of Women Voters.
7. He has wavy hair.
8. He promised that if elected he would raise property taxes.

D. Sam Black cannot find his pipe. He is sure that it is in the house. He knows that he smoked it four days ago.
1. His ten-year-old daughter had a birthday party yesterday with ten girl friends. The party was in his home.
2. His wife has threatened to throw out the pipe.
3. His son has been begging to be allowed to try the pipe.
4. His den smells of pipe smoke.
5. A week ago a friend of his who is a practical joker was in his home for the evening.
6. The garbage men picked up the garbage yesterday.
7. He thinks his wife has a guilty look.
8. He has not yet looked in his office.

E. James Moulton, the head of a small department store, discovers that money has been disappearing for one month from the cash box. Eight of his employees have keys to this box. He asks the elevator boy to report any conversation he overhears which might help identify the thief. The elevator boy reports the following snatches of information from the eight employees.
1. "Well, everyone slips some time, you know."
2. "The boss is sure sore. I don't blame him, but he had this coming to him. He's too stingy."
3. "My psychoanalyst has been advising me to give in to some of my baser urges. Today I gave in to one."
4. "For some reason I have been in a nervous sweat for several days. It seems to have started when Moneybags started this rumor about losing some cash."
5. "I am shocked about this discovery, and I for one intend to do everything in my power to bring the guilty one to justice."
6. "Oh, I don't know. There are acts much worse than borrowing a little from the cash box. Suspecting honest people is one."
7. "My kid has got to have some dental work at once. Do you know where I could lay my hands on about $40.00 before next payday?"
8. "Sure I took the money! Ha! Ha! Why, I've been pocketing every $2.00 bill that I've seen for years. Why, I have more than doubled my salary in this store in this way. Ha! Ha!"

F. Two hikers come to an unfordable river. If they can cross the river, they can return to camp by a short cut, but if they have to retrace their steps they will not be back at camp before dark.

1. The day happens to be the first day of daylight saving time.
2. Both of them can swim.
3. One of them catches pneumonia easily, especially when he becomes chilled.
4. The temperature is 70 degrees F.
5. One hiker has developed a sore foot.
6. A telephone construction company has left 500 yards of rubber corded wire on the bank.
7. One hiker has a compass.
8. It looks like rain.

Organizing Information

Directions: Here is an editorial. The statements have been numbered in the order in which they appeared in the editorial.

1. Trucks are pushing the motorists off the highways now.
2. So you can imagine what it would be like in the event of larger trucks.
3. I have been in various states and cities and I have actually seen trucks racing one another.
4. I have been driving the average speed of 50 miles per hour on numerous highways, when trucks have passed me as though I were standing still.
5. Why, a fellow takes his life in his hands whenever he goes out on the highway!
6. Larger trucks on the highway mean more accidents,
7. more damage to roads,
8. and more taxes to keep up the roads.
9. So if you want a place on the highway, you better write a letter to your state representative and ask him to do something about the trucks on our highways.

   a. Which statement is the main conclusion?
   b. Statement 1 is a reason for 2 3 4 5 none of these.
   c. Statement 2 is a reason for 1 3 6 9 none of these.
   d. Statement 3 is a reason for 1 4 7 8 none of these.
   e. Statement 4 is a reason for 6 3 1 8 none of these.
   f. Statement 5 is a reason for 6 7 8 9 none of these.
   g. Statement 6 is a reason for 7 8 9 2 none of these.
   h. Statement 7 is a reason for 9 1 8 4 none of these.
   i. Statement 8 is a reason for 2 3 4 9 none of these
   j. Statement 9 is a reason for 1 2 3 4 none of these.

Organizing Reasons

Directions: List the statements for the following as in the exercise above on trucks on the highway, and indicate which statements are reasons for which.

1. You are well aware that your work with us has for some time been unsatisfactory. Output in your department has dropped 40 per cent in the last four months. There have been two wildcat strikes in your department in the last three months. A group of your men have complained about your inability to control the department. Therefore, you will be dropped from the payroll at the end of this week.
2. The solar system is most evidently not a product of chance. The common direction of orbital motion for every one of the 1300 known planets is alone sufficient to settle this; and the small eccentricities and inclinations of the larger planets add proof upon proof.

Evaluation of Evidence

Directions: Each of the "conclusions" is to be evaluated on the basis of the data given according to the following options:

1. There is evidence *sufficient* to establish this conclusion.
2. There is *relevant* evidence for this conclusion.
3. There is *no relevant* evidence for this conclusion.
4. There is evidence which *refutes* this conclusion.

(N.B. The "correct" answer is the strongest possible answer, i.e., sufficient evidence is, of course, relevant evidence, but if the evidence is sufficient, it will be considered a wrong answer to mark it as "relevant.")

1. In a Midwestern city one week there are 54 car accidents in which the driver is left-handed and 18 car accidents in which the driver is right-handed.

Conclusions:

1. Right-handed drivers are less cautious than left-handed drivers.
2. There are both left- and right-handed people among drivers of cars.
3. Left-handed people do not drive cars.
4. All right-handed people should be trained to use their left hands so there will be fewer car accidents.

2. Henry Brown, an inveterate handy man, has been painting his house in the evenings after his day at the office. Each evening after painting he has cleaned his paintbrushes with turpentine, wiped out the turpentine, and then washed the brushes with soap and water. But his brushes are hard each evening when he starts to paint. He knows that he is not getting his brushes clean enough. Upon the suggestion of the local paint store manager for one week he has followed the same procedure for the cleaning of brushes except that he has substituted denatured alcohol for the turpentine. He discovers that after this type of cleaning his brushes are soft and pliable when he starts to paint on the next evening.

Conclusions:

1. Denatured alcohol makes paintbrushes last longer.
2. Soap and water help clean paintbrushes.

3. Denatured alcohol makes paintbrushes less pliable.
4. Turpentine is hard on the hands.
5. Denatured alcohol makes paintbrushes more pliable than does turpentine.
6. Denatured alcohol makes some paintbrushes, when used with some kinds of paint, more pliable than does turpentine.

Invention of Hypotheses

Directions: What would be some of the likely results if the following changes were to take place?

1. An English scholar once said that if some great Power would agree to adjust him so he would always think what is true and do what is right, on condition that he be turned into a sort of clock, he would without hesitation accept the offer. If men were turned into "clocks" like this, what difference would be made in their lives?
2. The Dean of Women in a certain college secures the proper support to enforce this rule: "No woman attending this college shall use lipstick. Anyone violating this rule shall be dropped from the student body."
3. Coffee is discovered to be the direct cause of heart trouble.
4. Because of a diminishing fuel supply, the Congress of the United States passes a law making it an act punishable by ten years in prison for any public building other than a hospital to be heated above 65 degrees.
5. The American telephone companies announce that they have for rental for $5.00 per month an attachment which makes it possible for one to see as well as hear the person with whom he is communicating by telephone. There is no evidence when one is talking over the telephone whether one is being seen by the other party.
6. To save cloth, a War Production Board passes a law that men's trousers must have no cuff, and that the end of the trousers must be at least eight inches off the floor.
7. A city school board announces that because of a river close to the school which fluctuates rapidly with heavy rains, on any day on which one inch of rain has fallen between sunrise and twelve o'clock noon, school will be dismissed in the afternoon.
8. Utopia University decides that man is now moving out of the Written Age and into the Oral Age with more and more communication by voice and less and less by the printed page. Therefore, the university abolishes all work in written composition.
9. A homeowner has at last done what he has threatened to do; he has covered his entire lawn with asphalt, and has painted it green.
10. Water contracts when it freezes.

Analogies

Directions: Indicate whether the following explanations are

1. Analogical
2. Genetic
3. Purposive

1. Light is particles of energy moving in a sustaining body called ether.
2. Light is radiant energy which, by its action upon the organs of vision, enables them to perform their function of sight.
3. Rain is moisture which drops from the clouds in order that crops may grow.
4. Rain is caused when clouds have acquired more moisture than they can hold.
5. A book is composed of paper, ink, thread, and glue.
6. A book is the product of hours of labor.
7. A book is the effort of an author to convey ideas to his readers.
8. A book is a one-way conversation — you can't talk back to the author.
9. Paint is the carpenter's friend; it can hide a multitude of errors.
10. Paint is usually pigments suspended in a liquid.
11. An automobile is a means of transportation.
12. An automobile is the result of hours of labor on the drafting board plus the work of hundreds of workmen in several factories.
13. Man may be explained as the resultant of a long period of evolutionary development.
14. Man exists in order to glorify his Creator.
15. Man is a machine into which food is poured and in which thought is produced.

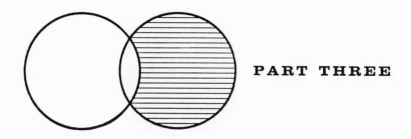

PART THREE

The Examination
of Hypotheses

8

Recognizing Assumptions

A tempting way to begin this chapter is to say, "Now that we have the problem clearly and usefully stated, the information collected and made manageable, and the hypothesis formulated, we can push on to the next step — the examination and testing of the hypothesis." But such a beginning would be misleading. Critical thinking does not move neatly through clearly distinguishable and separable steps, even though our study thus far may have suggested this notion. The critical thinker seldom, if ever, moves smoothly from problem identification to information organization, to hypothesis formation, to hypothesis examination, to hypothesis testing, to a conclusion. He is more likely to flit back and forth through what we have called the five parts of problem solving. A problem solver, unlike Lot's wife, may at any time look back. Information collecting and hypothesis forming, for example, take place constantly throughout the whole process. Perhaps there is more of this sort of activity during the early stages of the process, but at any time new information may be added, new hypotheses may be formed, and the problem may be redefined.

1. Deduction and induction

So, without committing ourselves to a rigorous chronological ordering of the parts of the total process, we can proceed with the examination of the hypothesis. A hypothesis is — or can be — formulated in words. Then the problem solver sets himself to the study which we have chosen to call examining and testing. By examination we mean the formal analysis of the stated hypothesis. By testing we refer to the empirical aspects of the analysis, that is, observing and experimenting. The examination of hypotheses is a part of formal logic or deduction. The testing of hypotheses is a part of induction.

Deduction is that form of reasoning in which an effort is made to determine what statements necessarily imply; or, to state the same idea conversely, it is that form of reasoning in which the conclusion follows necessarily from the given statements. The statements in deductive reasoning are called premises. When the relation between premises and conclusion is such that the conclusion is forced by the premises, the relationship is said to be valid. Logicians speak of both the validity of the argument and the validity of the conclusion. The premises are never said to be valid; they are either true or false. A valid conclusion is one that is logically certain. Logical certitude in a deductive argument has no degrees.

The validity of the conclusion follows from the form of the argument, not from the truth of the premises. Hence this type of reasoning is called formal. When we know that a conclusion is valid, we know nothing about its truth; all we know is that there is a statement — or there are statements — from which this conclusion is derived by necessary implication. In valid deductive arguments the premises may be true and the conclusion true, the premises may be false and the conclusion false, the premises may be false and the conclusion true, but there cannot be a valid deductive argument in which the premises are true and the conclusion false.

Induction is that form of reasoning in which the argument proceeds from observations and/or experiments to general conclusions of varying degrees of probability. The probable truth of inductive conclusions can always be increased by more evidence, but they never can attain the logical certitude of deductive conclusions. The starting points of induction are empirical evidences. In other words, inductive conclusions are never valid in the same sense as are deductive conclusions. Whereas the truth of the premises within deduction is irrelevant to the deductive correctness (i.e., validity) of the argument, the truth of the evidence within induction is crucial to the inductive correctness of the conclusion. Deduction yields logical certainty; induction yields logical probability. Deduction attempts to draw out what is necessarily contained within the premises; induction attempts to formulate a generalization which goes beyond the evidence, but to which the given evidence points.[1]

[1] See Douglas Johnson, "Mysterious Craters of the Carolina Coast," *American Scientist*, Vol. 32, No. 1, 1944, pp. 1–22, for an excellent example of how deduction and induction interplay in the research into the causes of a geological phenomenon in South Carolina.

The examination of a hypothesis may work either backwards or forwards, that is, we may examine what the hypothesis assumes, or we may examine what the hypothesis implies. For example, a mother says to her young son as he starts to school in the morning, "John, take your umbrella, or your clothes will be thoroughly wet by the time you reach school." Her words assume that it is now raining, or that it will be raining before John can reach the school building. Her words imply that if John takes his umbrella he will not get wet. There are other assumptions and other implications involved. She assumes in her statement that John will put up his umbrella upon taking it, that John will actually get all the way to school, that this is a school day, that John has not already left the house, etc. She implies in her statement that it is impossible that John take the umbrella and get wet, and that if John does not take the umbrella, he may or may not get wet. While an examination of assumptions and implications of hypotheses is clearly a deductive study, an examination of all assumptions and implications would include psychological and sociological elements also. For example, John and his mother may understand each other so well that by the tone of her voice John understands that he had better obey his mother regarding the umbrella or she will report his misbehavior to his father who will settle matters with him that evening before dinner!

2. *Thinking in context*

All acting and all thinking take place in context. Sometimes this fact is stated by saying that the same act or the same idea has different meaning in different frames of reference. This statement cannot stand up under examination, for it assumes that there is a sense in which one can speak of the same act or the same idea in different contexts. But that is just the point at issue. An act or an idea is what it is partly because of its context. In the opening scene of "Romeo and Juliet" Sampson and Gregory, servants to the Capulets, discuss how they will act upon meeting Abram and Balthasar, servants to the Montagues. "I will bite my thumb at them; which is a disgrace to them, if they bear it," boasts Sampson. When he is accosted by Abram, "Do you bite your thumb at us, sir?" Sampson, discovering in an aside with Gregory that the law will not be on their side if he answers "Yes," replies, "No, sir, I do not bite my thumb at you, sir; but I bite my thumb, sir." Sampson denies that he bites his thumb in the context of biting it against the Montagues, but does not state in what context he bites his thumb. There are hundreds of contexts:

the act could be a sign of tension, or a signal by a baseball manager to his batter, or an expression of masochism, or a prearranged signal between a husband and wife that it is time to leave the party, etc. Sampson seems to claim that he bites his thumb in no context.

Ideas, words, images, and signs of all sorts belong in contexts. The same words will have different meanings depending upon who says them, under what conditions, to whom, with what intonations, and with what accompanying actions. The words "This I found on the floor" have vastly different meaning in the two following situations: (1) spoken by a janitor of an office building at a friendly card game to his fellow employees in jest as he holds in his hand a playing card; (2) spoken angrily by the United States Representative to the United Nations at a regular meeting of the General Assembly to the leaders of an enemy nation as he holds in his hand a small microphone.

Francis Bacon in the early years of the seventeenth century concluded that the reigning scientific attitudes and methodologies perpetuated errors rather than discovered truths. He offered a new procedure for the scientific and philosophical investigation of the natural world. He called his book *The New Organon* to make obvious in the title what was patent in the work itself: he offered a methodology to displace the total logical works of Aristotle commonly called by Aristotelian scholars *The Organon*. Bacon wrote like a lawyer arguing a case, rather than like a scientist solving a problem; or, as was said of him, he wrote philosophy "like a Lord Chancellor." Well he might! He was Lord Chancellor! Although he received many high appointments under James I — Solicitor-General, Attorney-General, Privy-Councillor, Lord Keeper, and, finally, Lord Chancellor — his great aim in life was to prepare the way for a total renovation of the sciences. He longed to be the John the Baptist of the scientific revolution. When he lost his high position, after being charged with bribery and corruption in the exercise of his office, he returned to scientific writing and experimenting. He died as the result of exposure while testing the preservation of meat by packing it in snow.

Bacon sought a method of discovery in the sciences which, as he said, "leaves but little to the acuteness and strength of wits, but places all wits and understandings nearly on a level." He would put in place of the scholastic "Anticipations of Nature" a "just and methodical process" which he called the "Interpretation of Nature." By this he meant that man was to come to Nature without preconceived notions of what he would find, and through patient observation and experimentation learn of Nature. He believed that the methods of the reigning sciences of his day were largely systematic devices for ordering information already established. He proposed that there be methods for "new works," and even for "new sciences." While Bacon held that "Our only hope therefore lies in a true induction," he was much more explicit in defining what was wrong with the old than in clarifying the new. His most notable contribution to the new scientific method was his clever analysis of the "Idols of the Mind," the "false notions which are now in possession of the human understanding, and have taken deep root therein." These, warned Bacon, "must be renounced and put away with a fixed and solemn determination." In other places in *The New Organon* Bacon fears that the Idols "will again in the very instauration of the sciences meet and trouble us." And well might he fear! But Bacon's Idols are not what he thought them to be. His desire that the understanding be thoroughly freed and cleansed, that man enter the "kingdom of man" with the purity and simpleness implied in the Biblical warning that except men become as little children they cannot enter the Kingdom of Heaven, was a foolish and impossible desire. Bacon's Idols of the Mind should not be understood as "false notions" which must be eliminated before man can know his world; rather they are an imaginative listing of the contexts within which man thinks. They cannot be eliminated; they are the conditions of knowing. We should become aware of them; we should guard ourselves against being taken in by them. Considered in this light, a study of the Idols can be extremely valuable to the critical thinker.

According to Bacon man thinks in four contexts: (1) within the framework of his humanity, (2) within the limitations of his individuality, (3) in words, and (4) in systems.

The first context reminds us that man thinks as a human being. He is not a lower animal, and he is not a divine creature. All men share the limitations of human nature. According to Bacon these are: the supposition that there is more order and regularity in the world than is apparent to man; a tendency to interpret evidence as supporting rather than weakening received opinions; a tendency to associate things that happen to strike the mind simultaneously; the supposition that the entire world is purposeful, because man finds himself to be a purposing agent; a tendency to believe what one wants to believe; a universal dullness and incompetency of the senses; a proneness to give reality to abstractions. The list is incomplete. More examples of general human cognitive frailties could be added. These contexts of man's thinking ought not to discourage him from the effort to know his world; they ought to warn him that in the words of Protagoras there is a sense in which man is necessarily the measure of all things *for man*. Bacon thought that the Idols were to the sciences as "the refutation of sophisms is to common logic." This is not the case. Errors may creep into man's thinking through the "Idols of the Tribe," but these are the ways of human thought. No man can escape his humanity. He needs however to remind himself that as a finite creature he knows his world finitely. Let God have the infinite point of view! Man's quest for certainty must be a quest for the certainty that is humanly possible.

The second context of human thought reminds us that each person thinks in the context of his own peculiarities — his childhood training, individual psyche, and his particular experiences. Of the many idiosyncrasies Bacon might have selected, he mentions four: (1) some persons become attached to a favorite subject and see everything in terms of that subject; (2) some see differences, while others see only resemblances; (3) some look for novelty, others for antiquity; (4) some analyze, others systematize. Public speakers are constantly bothered by people who hear them only in the context of their own prejudices and obsessions. A superpatriot finds Communism in a lecture on art; a pacifist hears his ideas defended in a talk on architecture; a Moslem may take offense where there was no reference to his faith. There is a story of a Frenchman who remarked while standing on the roof of Notre Dame that the roof tops of Paris reminded him of a woman's curves, and then added in explanation, "Everything reminds me of feminine curves!"

The third context of human thought is the fact that man thinks in words. In order not to become involved in a well-known pyschological quarrel, perhaps we should say that man *expresses* his knowledge in words. Bacon thought these Idols were the most troublesome of all. "The high and formal discussions of learned men end oftentimes in disputes about words and names," he said. Bacon mentions only two of the many problems in the use of words: using words for things that do not exist, and using words confusedly and ill-definedly. Bacon would not have us go as far as Bergson, who defined metaphysics as the science that attempts to dispense with words altogether. Zen Buddhism also makes this effort. Zen philosophers, for example, contrast the experience of talking about water to the experience of immediate contact with water. Of course there is a difference. But does having a glass of cold water suddenly thrown into one's face help one know water? Knowledge is a secondary kind of experience; experiencing water thrown in the face is not knowing at all. Bergson and others have attempted to distinguish between "knowledge of" and "knowledge about." Water tossed in the face is "knowledge of"; water as H_2O is "knowledge about." "Knowledge of" is direct experience, not knowledge. When we know, we stand off from the object of knowledge, and refer to it in words. The use of words is a limitation — often a very confusing limitation — but "knowing without words" is not knowing at all. There is much truth in the old saw, "If you can't say it, you don't know it."

The last context of human thought Bacon called the "Idols of the Theater." He used the word "theater" because he regarded the systems of philosophy as stage-plays. The three he singled out are rationalism, empiricism, and the "superstitious school." The ones he selected are not important for us here. Each individual over the course of his years of thought tends to favor one intellectual approach to the world in which he lives. The sociologist comes to view his problems sociologically; the psychologist, psychologically; the physician, medically. A woman approaches her world from the feminine point of view; a man approaches his from the masculine point of view. Each should be aware of his own bias, as one of a certain sex, a certain vocation, a certain school of thought. But how can one renounce and "put away with a fixed and solemn determination" the contexts of thinking? Man thinks always in contexts. To be aware of this fact is not to transcend it, although the awareness is essential in critical thinking.

3. *Locating assumptions*

We said above that one looks backward to locate assumptions. The assumptions are the intellectual background of a line of thought. They are basic, yet they may not be stated. Part of the charm of assumptions is frequently their hidden quality. "Have you stopped beating your wife?" or "Does your home town have another horse yet?" are far more arresting than "You beat your wife" or "Your home town is a one-horse town." But hidden assumptions are not always charming; they can be devastating to critical thinking. To be clear in an argument one should always identify the assumptions. The relation of assumptions to argument is analogous to the relation of prejudice to human relations; they may be especially vicious when they play their roles without being noticed, but when brought into the open, they can be controlled.

Sometimes philosophers have claimed that they can form a system without assumptions. Carl Jung said Zen Buddhism is a philosophy without assumptions, and S. Alexander affirmed, "The method of naturalism is to study our prepossessions without prepossession. It is in fact to preserve in dealing with human values the same neutrality as natural science preserves in dealing with its subject-matter."[2] Neither Jung nor

[2] "Naturalism and Value," *The Personalist*, October 1928, p. 244.

Alexander is correct. No philosophy is without assumptions, or, as we said in the previous sections, all thinking is in context. Does not Alexander see that the selection of his method rests on a prepossession for that method? If the followers of Zen and naturalism do not recognize their own assumptions, they fail as philosophers, for one of the chief functions of philosophy is to make the implicit explicit. Scientists and philosophers who think they can act in their fields without assumptions mistake the notion of assumptions. Assumptions are the points from which one starts. One cannot go anywhere without starting somewhere. Assumptions are the primitive ideas — the unsupported ideas which are the support of other ideas. A system without assumptions would be circular. To try to create such a system would be as foolish as the attempt of the citizens of the mythical Chinese community who tried to support themselves by doing each other's laundry, or as Oliver Herford's playful "Alphabet for Celebrities" which contains the following lines:

> Q is for Queen, so noble and free;
> For further particulars look under V.
> ....
> V is Victoria noble and true;
> For further particulars look under Q.

The Declaration of Independence is an excellent example of the proper use of assumptions. This document was prepared as it says out of "a decent respect to the opinions of mankind." One-eighth of the document is an actual declaration of independence from the British Crown; seven-eighths of it is a justification for the declaration. The argument leading to the declaration begins with an identification of the assumptions: "We hold these truths to be self-evident, that all men are created equal, that they are endowed by their Creator with certain unalienable Rights, that among these are Life, Liberty and the pursuit of Happiness." Jefferson did not argue in defense of these "truths." They were his assumptions. He knew that in every system there must be some unsupported supporting ideas, and he chose to rest his case — and the case of the colonies — before the moral judgment of the world upon the self-evident character of universal human equality and the unalienable human rights of life, liberty, and pursuit of happiness.

There are three kinds of assumptions: axioms, postulates, and suppressed or hidden premises. An axiom is a statement to which people in general agree, a universally accepted truth. A postulate is a statement for which general agreement is requested in the absence of proof. Not all logicians or mathematicians distinguish axioms and postulates. The difference be-

tween axioms and postulates as used here lies in the attitude of the pro-
poser of the statement to those whom he wishes to convince. When presenting an axiom, he says in effect, "This statement is one which I am
sure that you will agree to as soon as you understand it." When presenting
a postulate, he says in effect, "This statement is one which I want you to
accept for the purposes of the argument." Axioms are self-evident in
themselves; postulates become self-evident by agreement. The third kind
of assumption — the suppressed or hidden premise — appears in what is
known as enthymemes of the first and second orders, that is, syllogisms
with either the major or the minor premise missing.[3] The assumption is
the missing link of the argument which the reader or hearer is expected
to supply. For example, in the argument "You can't do that! Don't
you know you're under twenty-one?" the missing premise is "All people
under twenty-one cannot do that." In "My daddy is very brave, because
policemen are very brave" the assumption is "My daddy is a policeman."

Euclid's *Elements* and Lewis Carroll's *Alice's Adventures in Wonderland*
when placed in juxtaposition beautifully illustrate two diverse ways of
presenting assumptions. In Euclid all the assumptions are stated. The
Elements begins with the definitions of twenty-nine terms to be used in
the work. (Definitions may be regarded as a type of assumption.) Following the definitions are three postulates, each beginning with the significant words "Let it be granted. . . ." The first Euclidean postulate is
"Let it be granted that a straight line may be drawn from any one point
to any other point." Euclid does not ask that we agree that this is actually
the state of affairs in this world, or in any world; he merely asks us to
grant this idea as a primitive idea in the system he is formulating. Next
he gives twelve axioms. These are not preceded by "Let it be granted. . . ."
They are statements Euclid believes his readers will accept because the
truth of each statement is convincing: "Things which are equal to the
same thing are equal to one another." "If equals be added to equals the
wholes are equal." "The whole is greater than its part." There is still
another sort of assumption which can be noted when one looks at Euclid.
He defines "point," "line," "straight line," etc., but in the definitions
other words are used which are not listed among the definitions. These
are the defining words. Some of the defining words are words which
need no definition. Words such as "a," "which," and "no" do not need
to be defined before they are used in a defining sentence. But on the
other hand there are undefined-defining words such as "parts," "magni-
tude," "length," and "breadth." The word "part," for example, appears

---

[3] See Chapter 11.

in Definition 1 and Axiom 9. Is there general agreement as to the meaning of "part"?

Following the Definitions, Postulates, and Axioms in Euclid are the Propositions, that is, the problems and theorems solved and established by use of the definitions, axioms, postulates, and the earlier solved problems and established theorems. The whole system is of such a consistent order that, if a postulate or an axiom were lost, a careful student should be able by an examination of the proofs to formulate it.

Alice's Adventures in Wonderland is quite a different system! In Wonderland the assumptions are not given, and the assumptions appropriate to the usual world do not fit. It is a world in which rabbits wear watches in their waistcoats, all animals talk, cakes and drink make one shrink or stretch, a cat can vanish leaving only a grin, etc. Alice found that her mind did not work in normal patterns: "Let me see: four times five is twelve, and four times six is thirteen, and four times seven is — oh dear, I shall never get to twenty at that rate! However, the Multiplication-Table doesn't signify! let's try Geography. London is the capital of Paris, and Paris is the capital of Rome, and Rome — no, that's all wrong, I'm certain. . . . I'll try and say 'How doth the little' — and she crossed her hands on her lap as if she were saying lessons, and began it, but her voice sounded hoarse and strange, and the words did not come the same as they used to do." The delight we find in reading Alice's adventures is that the assumptions of the reader — whether old or young — usually prove to be incorrect. For example, at the Mad Hatter's tea party the March Hare said to Alice, "Take some more tea." "I've had nothing yet," Alice replied in an offended manner: "so I ca'n't take *more*." A child can appreciate this unexpected reply, but the Hatter's retort is based on another assumption regarding the word "more," one whose subtleties only the mathematician can fully appreciate; "You mean you ca'n't take *less*," said the Hatter, "it's very easy to take *more* than nothing." In Euclid's system, we said, we could supply a missing assumption; but in Alice's world we cannot. Truly, the words do not come the same as they used to do!

Let us not forget where we are in our analysis. We are now looking at the role of assumptions in critical thinking. Assumptions appear at every point in the total process of problem solving, but it is especially important that they be identified at the part of the process we have called the examination of the hypothesis. To become sensitive about assumptions while forming hypotheses might put unneeded restraint on the delicate creativity which is integral to hypothesis formation. Now, however, it would be tragic not to become aware of the assumptions, for if they are not located in the examination of the hypothesis they are likely to pass through the observing and testing stage without evaluation. Furthermore, the assumptions must be inspected in order to set up reliable tests.

We must not underestimate the difficulty in locating assumptions. Our comparison of assumptions and prejudices may be used again. Assumptions, like prejudices, often operate unconsciously. A recent volume makes a careful study of the race prejudice in Protestant Sunday School materials designed to combat race prejudice! A well-known news commentator on a recent half-hour television program on the caste system of India began and ended the program with the observation that on no subject is there so much hypocrisy as in discussions of caste and race problems. During the program he showed Indians arguing that the caste system of India is a better solution than is the segregation system of the United States, that the caste system shows the Americans how their racial problems can be settled, that the caste system is not a struggle between races, and that no important white person joined in the Freedom Rides in the United States. All of these arguments show the blindness of the Indians, said the commentator. One portion of the film pictured an American girl arguing with Indians that the Negro-white relationship in the United States is not as bad as the Indian caste system, because Negro women are hired to tend white children; Negroes are not untouchables. Other portions showed Indians who were not allowed to draw water from village wells, and Brahmins refusing to eat with an outcaste person. The commentator did not mention that there are separate drinking fountains for Negro and white in some parts of America, nor that blood has been shed in efforts to desegregate schools, swimming pools, and lunch counters. He ended the half-hour program with an attack on the hypocrisy of Indians, but failed to mention the hypocrisy of Americans. It is always easier to see the other person's prejudices — and assumptions — than to recognize one's own.

4. The challenging of assumptions

The reaction to new ideas seems to pass through three stages. First the idea is opposed as being radically new; then it is opposed as being unimportant; and finally it is accepted and identified as an old idea refurbished. In fact, most new ideas are refurbished old ones. How really few new ideas there are in a generation! William James deserted experimental psychology because he found the technicians so unfruitful of new ideas: "The results that come from all this laboratory work seem to me to grow more and more disappointing and trivial. What is most needed is new ideas. For every man who has one of them one may find a hundred who are willing to drudge patiently at some unimportant experiment."[4] One way to create a new idea is to challenge an assumption of an established hypothesis. Many of the great discoveries in astronomy were challenges to assumptions: Does the sun stand still? Is the earth the center of the universe? Are fixed stars really fixed?

The most dramatic result of the challenging of a hypothesis in our century is that of Einstein. He challenged a common-sense assumption that one can speak meaningfully of two events occurring at the same time. He formulated the contrary hypothesis that two events may appear to occur at the same time from one point of view and not appear to occur at the same time from another point of view. Hence, he held that the common assumption that events may take place at the same time from all points of view is nonsense.

Sometimes the assumption that is being challenged is so basic to a way of thinking that the challenge itself cannot be understood. Aristotle, for example, was the first in the Western world to formulate the three Laws of Thought: the Law of Identity, the Law of Contradiction, and the Law of Excluded Middle. There are two ways of stating these laws, one for statements and the other for things.

1. The Law of Identity
   For statements: If any statement is true, it is true.
   For things: If anything is A, it is A.
2. The Law of Contradiction
   For statements: No statement can be both true and false.
   For things: Nothing can be both A and not-A.
3. The Law of Excluded Middle
   For statements: Any statement must be either true or false.
   For things: Anything must be either A or not-A.

Aristotle contended that he who would try to deny these Laws of Thought "will not be able either to speak or to say anything intelligible; for he says at the same time both 'yes' and 'no.' "[5] The Buddhist logicians have denied these laws for centuries, but Western minds have until very recent years not been able to make any sense of the Buddhists. Only since the writings of process philosophers like Bergson and Whitehead have Western minds been receptive to Buddhist logic. Once one steps outside the substance philosophy associated with Aristotle, one can begin to catch glimpses

---

[4] Letter to Theodore Flournoy, Dec. 7, 1896. R. B. Perry, *The Thought and Character of William James*, briefer version (Cambridge: Harvard University Press, 1948), p. 198.
[5] *Metaphysics*, 1008 b 10.

of the profundity of the Buddhists who claim that there are no identical real "things" — a "thing" is not the same at different moments or in different places. Every variation in time and place makes a "thing" another "thing." This is a challenge to a metaphysical assumption which when absorbed into Western thought may be as revolutionary as was the challenge of Einstein. But — lest we forget — process philosophies also contain hidden assumptions! Becoming aware of one's assumptions is both difficult and rare.

9

Developing the Implications

of Hypotheses

After hypotheses have been formed as possible answers to a problem, they must be examined and tested before one of the hypotheses is selected as *the* answer to the problem. The hypotheses are studied to determine which one, if any, will solve the problem. To say that we are looking for a true hypothesis would be misleading, since truth may be too rigid a requirement for the hypothesis finally selected. Many untrue hypotheses have functioned usefully: a geocentric world, a flat earth, the fixity of the species, absolute space, and physiological humors are false hypotheses that have served important roles. Hypotheses, though false, are usually better than a non-rational response to the world. De Morgan, an English logician, once said, "Wrong hypotheses, rightly worked, have produced more useful results than unguided observation." Yet a selection must be made among hypotheses, and that selection will have to be made on the basis of certain criteria.

1. *Criteria of a good hypothesis*

In logic textbooks a generation or two ago it was common to list the requirements of a good hypothesis. For example, Hibben in a volume written in 1896 gives as the first requirement: "A hypothesis should be plausible; that is, it should be no fanciful, or merely conjectural, explanation of the phenomena in question."[1] As an example of an unplausible

---

[1] John Grier Hibben, *Logic: Deductive and Inductive* (New York: Charles Scribner's Sons, 1896), p. 301.

hypothesis he refers to Darwin's account of the inhabitants of the Maldiva atolls who believe that corals have roots, and therefore, if rooted out, are permanently destroyed. This untrue hypothesis worked well, since by taking out the "roots" of the coral in their harbors the natives kept their harbors clean. The other requirements of a good hypothesis according to Hibben are: "must be capable of proof or disproof"; "must be adequate"; "should involve no contradiction"; and "should be as simple as possible." Other logicians list "should be consistent with known facts," "should be fruitful" (i.e., predictive), and "should accomplish the purpose for which it is intended."

One of the above criteria requires elaboration. This is the notion of simplicity. The importance of this requirement is well stated by Philipp Frank: "The goal of science in the twentieth century has been to build up a simple system of principles from which the facts observed by twentieth-century physicists could be mathematically derived. It was no longer required that these principles or some of their immediate consequences should be in agreement with our daily experience, or, in other words, with 'common sense.' What was required was a high-grade logical simplicity and agreement with the refined experiments of twentieth-century physicists."[2] Newton would have said that hypotheses should be simple because "Nature is pleased with simplicity, and affects not the pomp of superfluous causes." But today we hold that it is the mind of man, and not nature, that seeks simplicity. The symbiosis of the Smyrna fig and the Blastophage wasp is as complex as a Rube Goldberg cartoon. "Simple" does not mean easy to understand. Einstein's Unified Field Theory is simple, but not easy to understand. "Simple" means contains few elements. Scientists seek to predict the most and to assume the least. If we ask why a hypothesis which contains few assumptions and few items of explanation is better than a hypothesis which contains many, the answer may be the former is more aesthetic! Schrödinger once said that he preferred his theory of relativity to Einstein's because his was more beautiful! In particular, modern scientists do not wish preternatural or supernatural elements in their hypotheses. James Hutton, an eighteenth-century geologist, set for himself this working rule: "No powers are to be employed that are not natural to the globe, no action to be admitted except those of which we know the principle." The rejection of the non-natural does not mean that the scientist utilizes in his hypotheses only those aspects of the world he observes in his daily life. He may employ fictions. Fictions are statements or entities introduced in order that observed facts may be deduced

[2] *Philosophy of Science* (Englewood Cliffs, N.J.: Prentice Hall, 1957), p. 134.

from them. Francis Bacon accused Copernicus of introducing fictions for the purpose of making his calculations turn out well. Some of the fictions that have been employed are Ptolemy's epicycles, Copernicus' movement of the earth, Newton's absolute space, Bergson's vital energy, ether, inertia, genes, atoms, and the corpuscular nature of light.

2. *Implication versus trial and error*

Deduction is a human alternative to animal trial and error. Man elaborates mentally the consequences of hypotheses. He does not need to act upon every idea in order to determine its implications. To put the matter simply, man uses his head to save hands and feet. Legislative bodies are charged with the responsibility of considering the implications of laws before they enact them. Man is able to perform mental experiments as well as physical experiments. A research chemist recently observed that chemistry is becoming so mathematical that a chemist can do most of his research with no more laboratory equipment than pencil and paper. A laboratory scientist sometimes does not see the significance of his own experiment until a pencil-and-paper scientist points it out to him. A remarkable instance of this has taken place in the twentieth century in the work of Albert Einstein. Prior to the latter part of the seventeenth century, astronomers and physicists assumed that light required no time for its propagation. Since a beam of light travels each second a distance eight times greater than the circumference of the earth at the equator, we can easily understand why physicists had concluded that light travels instantaneously. But in 1676, the Danish astronomer Roemer determined the velocity of light by studying the eclipses of the moons of Jupiter. He found that the eclipses were observed earlier when Jupiter and the earth were near to each other, and later when Jupiter and the earth were farther apart. These differences he explained by the hypothesis that light requires time for its propagation. Later, as the result of the studies of Huyghens, Faraday, Foucault, and Maxwell, physicists concluded that light consists of waves of a subtle elastic medium, called ether. Ether waves were compared with water waves and sound waves. They were assumed to follow the laws of Newtonian mechanics, that is, every body perseveres in its state of rest, or of uniform motion in a straight line, unless it is compelled to change that state by forces impressed thereon; the alteration of motion is proportional to the motive force impressed; and to every action there is always opposed an equal reaction. Ether was considered to be a stable continuum in which all bodies reside. It was the stuff of space. Every interstice of space was thought to be filled either with matter or with ether. The earth in its revolutions on its axis and in its orbital movement around the sun was thought to be moving through the ether. It was assumed that the speed of light would vary as the beam of light went with, against, or across the ether stream caused by the movement of the earth, just as greater expenditure of energy is required to row a boat upstream or across stream than downstream. In 1881 Michelson performed an ingenious experiment with an apparatus which he called an interferometer to test the supposed retarding influence of the ether on the speed of light. The experiment consisted in splitting a beam of light and sending the halves at right angles to each other. Mirrors placed at equal distances from the source of the splitting of the beam returned the light to an optical apparatus which could record the difference of time required for the two journeys to a minute fraction of a second. But in all his experiments he found that the velocities of the two beams of light were precisely the same. Michelson had no explanation for this unexpected uniformity.

The Dutch physicist Lorentz offered the explanation that the distance between the optical instrument and a mirror was shortened by the same movement through the ether which slowed the velocity of light. The time consumed by the light rays which traveled at right angles to each other was the same, but the distance traveled varied. This explanation made the whole situation much worse; for now the existence of ether was affirmed, and at the same time the possibility of discovering its existence was denied.

At this point Einstein made the courageous hypothesis that if reliable experiments do not reveal any difference in the velocities of light traveling at right angles to each other, there is no such entity as ether. The constancy of the speed of light which the Michelson experiment shows, said Einstein, is not due to the relation of light to an absolute space filled uniformly with ether, but to its constant relation to an observer. In other words, the observer, not the ether is the point of reference in which the velocity of light is the same in all directions. Light moves at the same rate of speed as measured by an observer regardless of the direction or the velocity of the moving frame of reference, or the direction or the velocity of the source of the light. This means that even though measurements of the velocity of light from the stars are made on a moving planet, and even though the sources of the light are moving, light always has the same velocity.

In defense of his hypothesis of the uniform velocity of light with reference to a material body arbitrarily chosen, Einstein presented his doctrine of the relativity of simultaneity, which is the core of the Special

Theory of Relativity. In the Michelson experiment one kind of simultaneity is embodied: the simultaneous return of the two beams of light. The simultaneity which Einstein denotes in this doctrine is that of two events separated by a great distance. Rays of light from two stars may strike an optic nerve at the same time, but when did these rays of light leave their sources? To determine this the astronomer takes the known distances of the stars from the earth and divides this number by the known speed of light. But how did the astronomer measure the speed of light? This experiment requires two "clocks" at remote distances from each other which are running simultaneously. But alas! simultaneity can be measured only by appeal to the uniformity of the velocity of light, which was the problem at issue! A better illustration of arguing in a circle would be hard to find! To measure simultaneity of events the scientist must have the speed of light, and to measure the speed of light he must have simultaneous events. Einstein concluded that simultaneity of distant events cannot be verified; but since he did not doubt that simultaneity of distant events is possible, that is, is not a meaningless concept, he said simultaneity can only be defined. Simultaneity can only be affirmed from a specific point of view; there is no absolute frame of reference with respect to which events are simultaneous. Einstein's theoretical example is that of a straight railroad track over which a long train is moving at almost the speed of light. Lightning strikes the railroad track before and behind the train. A man located on the embankment halfway between the two points at which the lightning struck says that the lightning struck the track simultaneously at two points. A man on top the moving train was directly opposite the man on the embankment when the lightning struck, but from his point of view the lightning strikes were not simultaneous; indeed, from his point of view lightning struck only once. Therefore, when speaking of events which happen "at the same time" one must add the frame of reference in which the events occurred simultaneously. There is no universal "now."

While our purpose in this discussion of Einstein's analysis of the implication of Michelson's experiment is not to demonstrate that "guessers" are better scientists than "accumulators," we might note that it was Michelson who predicted in the early 1890's that the future of physics would be found in the refinements of the measurements of discoveries already made and not in new discoveries!

3. *The three conditionals*

Michelson's interferometer experiment was based upon this line of thought: if the ether stream affects the velocity of light, that effect will vary according to whether light proceeds with or across the stream. With this hypothesis in mind Michelson designed his apparatus to measure the relative speeds of two beams of light sent at right angles to each other. Michelson's thought after the experiment was this: "If ether affects the velocity of light, then a difference of speed will be indicated by shadow-bands. But there are no shadow-bands. I do not know what conclusion to draw!" Einstein said, "Draw the only possible conclusion: ether does not affect the velocity of light." Then Einstein went beyond this conclusion and presented a radically new hypothesis to account for the negative results: ether does not affect the velocity of light, because there is no ether!

The line of thought evidenced by Einstein is a very common and a very important one used in solving problems of the sort we face every day in our lives, as well as the sort of problems involved in crucial experiments in the sciences. A housewife reasons, "If I add more butter to the dough, the cookies will be crisper." Her husband reasons, "If I spray my roses with rotenone, then I shall get rid of the Japanese beetles." Their ten-year-old son reasons, "If I pack my bicycle coaster brake with vaseline, then I can go faster." Their high school daughter reasons, "If I use purple eye shadow, then John will notice me." These sentences are known as conditionals. We shall hereafter call them statements. The word "sentence" has grammatical connotations which do not concern us here. The word "statement" denotes the meaning aspect of the grammatical sentence. "The rose is red" and "La rose est rouge" are two sentences, but only one statement is expressed in the two sentences. Conditional statements are those with the structure "If . . . . , then . . . ." There are other ways of expressing the same structure:

> "Whenever . . . . , then . . . . . ."
> "When . . . . , then . . . . . ."
> ". . . . . implies . . . ."

By structure or logical structure we denote the if-then nature of these statements as distinguished from whatever content may be indicated by the dotted lines. To make it obvious that the logical structure of statements is distinct from the contents of statements logicians commonly use nonsense words, or untruths, or just letters in place of words in sample statements. Thus:

> If zumgates are frimates, then mumgites are hodites.
> If it rains, then my garden will remain dry.
> If *p*, then *q*.

Conditional statements are divided into two parts: the antecedent and the consequent. The antecedent follows the word "If"; the consequent follows the word "then." The antecedent states the conditions; the consequent identifies a resultant state of affairs. It is quite difficult to state the relationships between antecedent and consequent broadly enough not to prejudice the relation in favor of one of the variety of conditionals. The word "resultant," for example, is misleading because it suggests cause-effect and then-now. These are true only for some kinds of conditionals. Therefore, we must identify the types of conditional statements.

Some conditionals are *causal*. The antecedent expresses the cause, and the consequent expresses the effect.

> If litmus paper is put into acid, then the litmus paper turns red.
> When metal is heated, then it expands.

Other conditionals are *definitional*. The consequent follows as an explication of the nature of the antecedent.

> If anything is circular, then it is round.
> If Smith is a Protestant, then Smith is a Christian.

Some conditionals are *decisional* in nature. In such a conditional the consequent represents a state of affairs which the speaker resolves to bring about if the antecedent becomes or is a reality.

> If our team does not win, then I shall grow a beard.
> If his father is not six feet tall, then I'll eat my hat.

Some decisionals are actually disguised ways of making an unqualified or categorical statement. The statement "If his father is not six feet tall, then I'll eat my hat" is a strong way of expressing "His father is six feet tall." The speaker wishes to show how certain he is that he is correct in his statement by swearing he will eat his hat if he is wrong.

There is a fourth kind of conditional which we may call the *logical*. In this type the statement is a complete logical argument. The antecedent is the logical antecedent; and the consequent is the logical consequent. The word "then" in such a conditional has the force of "therefore."

> If Ali is a Moslem, and Moslems eat no pork, then Ali eats no pork.
> If a helix is identical with a spiral, then a spiral is identical with a helix.

The logical character of these conditionals can be made clearer by identifying the premises and conclusion in each compound sentence.

Premise: If Ali is a Moslem
Premise: If Moslems eat no pork
Conclusion: Therefore, Ali eats no pork.

Premise: If a helix is identical with a spiral
Conclusion: Then, a spiral is identical with a helix.

Regardless of the kind, all conditionals act alike logically. They have the same structure. They function the same way in arguments. In an argument using conditionals there are four possibilities:

1. The antecedent may be affirmed.
2. The antecedent may be denied.
3. The consequent may be affirmed.
4. The consequent may be denied.

We shall simplify by using the traditional horseshoe sign ($\supset$) for the structure of a conditional statement; we shall use p, q, r, etc., for the component elements of the conditional statement, and the stress mark ($'$) for the denial. The expression $p \supset q$ means that if the state of affairs designated by the simple, unconditional statement represented by p is in fact the case, then the state of affairs designated by the simple, unconditional statement represented by q is also in fact the case. Of course, we are not expected to read the formula in the full form! We shall read $p \supset q$ as "If p, then q" or "p implies q," or "Whenever p, then q." The expression p' is to be read as "not p" or "p is denied." There is one more symbol we shall use: the horizontal line will be used to indicate the separation between logical antecedents and logical conclusion, and will be read "therefore," "hence," "so," or "then." So the argument

$$\frac{\begin{array}{c} p \supset q \\ q' \end{array}}{p'}$$

will be read "If p then q, and q is denied, then p is denied," or "p implies q, and not q, therefore not p."

There are four possible types of conditional arguments:

1.	2.	3.	4.
$\dfrac{p \supset q}{p}$	$\dfrac{p \supset q}{p'}$	$\dfrac{p \supset q}{q}$	$\dfrac{p \supset q}{q'}$

These four are known as:

1. Affirmation of the antecedent
2. Denial of the antecedent

3. Affirmation of the consequent
4. Denial of the consequent

Affirmation of the antecedent and denial of the consequent are valid forms; denial of the antecedent and affirmation of the consequent are invalid forms.

When the antecedent is affirmed, the consequent is logically affirmed also.

$$p \supset q$$
$$\underline{p}$$
$$q$$

If friction implies heat, then when there is a case of friction, there is a case of heat. The possibility of getting heat in other ways is left open. The statement simply affirms that one of the ways to get heat is by friction. Friction is sufficient. Sufficient condition means that this is enough, this will do. In the line of reasoning, p implies q, and there is a p, the q must follow. The conclusion is forced. The first premise states "*If* there is friction, then there is heat." The second premise says "There *is* friction" and the conclusion asserts "Then there *is* heat." $p \supset q$ sets up a condition. $\frac{p}{q}$ adds that the condition is met and the consequent follows.

When we deny the antecedent, we deny that the conditions are present which when present would result in the consequent indicated in the first premise.

If there is friction, then there is heat.
There is no friction
$$\overline{\qquad ? \qquad}$$

The temptation is to conclude that there is no heat. Yet our knowledge about the production of heat will not allow us to draw that conclusion, regardless of what we may know about logic. We know that there is no "friction machine" in the basement, yet there is heat in the radiators. In other words, when we deny the antecedent in this example, we are saying that *one* of the sufficient conditions of heat is not present. We leave open the possibility of another sufficient condition being present. The fallacious argument, if p then q, but p is false, therefore q is false, is a very tempting one. There are occasions of course when the implicative relationship is mutual, that is, when p implies q, and q implies p. In such cases denying p allows us to deny q. For example,

If anything is circular, then it is round, and if anything is round, then it is circular.

Here is something that is not circular.
Therefore, here is something that is not round.

Equally tempting is the fallacy of affirming the consequent and concluding that the antecedent is affirmed also. No one would be fooled by

If George is a bird, then George has two legs.
George has two legs.
So George is a bird!

But when the argument is like this, the fallacy may not be so patent:

"Whenever Socialistic principles begin to infiltrate an economy, you will find that men begin talking about the need to broaden the tax structure. My worthy opponent in his last speech said he favored broadening the tax structure. Gentlemen, need I draw the obvious conclusion? Do you not see that my opponent has Socialistic leanings?"

Finally, if the consequent is denied, the antecedent is logically denied as well. If we think about what was said previously about how $\frac{p}{q}$ allows us to assert the consequent independently, we can see that the denial of the consequent allows us to deny the antecedent. If whenever p is true q is also true, then p cannot be true when q is false. Einstein's interpretation of the Michelson experiment was of this nature:

If there is ether, then it affects the speed of light.
But Michelson has established by experiment that the speed of light is not changed.
So there is no ether.

To return to the four possible types of conditional arguments, we find that two of the arguments have valid conclusions, and two do not.

1.	2.	3.	4.
$p \supset q$	$p \supset q$	$p \supset q$	$p \supset q$
p	p'	q	q'
q	?	?	p'

In arguments number 2 and 3, that is, the argument in which we deny the antecedent and the argument in which we affirm the consequent, no conclusion can be reached by deductive processes.

The title of this section is "The Three Conditionals." Our examination thus far has been of but one — the sufficient conditional, although we have hinted that there are other kinds. These others can be dealt with in less detail now that we have considered the $p \supset q$ type. Imagine that a doctor advises an operation for three people — but he advises each in a different way.

> To Mr. A he says, "If you have an operation within a year, you will get well."
> To Mr. B he says, "Only if you have an operation within a year, will you get well."
> To Mr. C he says, "If and only if you have an operation within a year, will you get well."

These three we shall call sufficient conditional, necessary conditional, and sufficient-and-necessary conditional. In the sufficient conditional the physician advises that an operation will make the patient well, but he leaves open the possibility that the patient might get well without an operation. In other words, the operation is sufficient, but not necessary. In the necessary conditional the physician advises that the patient must have an operation to get well, but he admits that perhaps an operation will not make him well. At least he knows that the patient will not get well without an operation. Notice that whereas the sufficient conditional is written "If you have an operation, you will get well" or "An operation implies getting well," the necessary conditional is written "Only if you have an operation will you get well" or "Getting well implies an operation." Symbolically the two conditionals look like this (o = operation, gw = get well):

Mr. A (sufficient conditional)	$o \supset gw$ o ⎯⎯ gw	$o \supset gw$ o' ⎯⎯ ?	$o \supset gw$ gw ⎯⎯ ?	$o \supset gw$ gw' ⎯⎯ o'
Mr. B (necessary conditional)	$gw \supset o$ gw ⎯⎯ o	$gw \supset o$ gw' ⎯⎯ ?	$gw \supset o$ o ⎯⎯ ?	$gw \supset o$ o' ⎯⎯ gw'

Although the invalid forms appear in the same positions in the above pattern of symbolic expressions, you must not conclude that the sufficient conditional and the necessary conditional are identical. This would ignore the change that has taken place in the position of the antecedent and the consequent. Although we may express the sufficient conditional linguistically as "If p, then q" and the necessary conditional as "Only if p, then q," when we place them in logical symbols they become respectively "$p \supset q$" and "$q \supset p$." That is, whereas $o \supset gw$ states an operation (antecedent) implies getting well (consequent), $gw \supset o$ states getting well (consequent) implies an operation (antecedent). If a year after the office conference, we met Mr. B on the street looking very fit, we could say, "I see you had your operation." But if we met Mr. A a year after his conference, and he too was in good health, we would have to ask, "Did you or did you not have the operation?"

Mr. C's recommended therapy may have originally seemed more severe, but at least it had the merit of definiteness: "Have an operation, and you'll get well. Have no operation, and you'll not get well." This is called necessary-and-sufficient conditional, or bi-conditional, or mutual implication, or equivalence. It may be written symbolically

$$(p \supset q) \cdot (q \supset p)$$

The dot ($\cdot$) symbolizes "and." The sufficient-and-necessary conditional statement can also be represented by the sign for equivalence ($\equiv$).

Mr. C (sufficient and necessary conditional)

$o \equiv gw$	$o \equiv gw$	$o \equiv gw$	$o \equiv gw$
o	o'	gw	gw'
gw	gw'	o	o'

Many of the errors in human thinking are errors involving conditionals. We are often tempted to draw a conclusion from the denial of an antecedent or from the affirmation of a consequent; we sometimes confuse sufficient conditionals and necessary conditionals. The exercises on conditionals at the end of Part Three should be carefully studied. Another example may be helpful. A football coach gives this ironclad rule to his quarterback: "Whenever you have a fourth down with two or more yards to go, you are to call a kick play." This rules leaves open the possibilities of kicking on first down, or on second down, or on third down. There is even the possibility of kicking on a fourth-down-with-less-than-two-yards-to-go situation. But the rule eliminates the possibility of not kicking on a fourth-down-with-two-or-more-yards-to-go situation. To emphasize what the rule requires and what it allows, the coach puts the following on the blackboard:

$$4 - 2+ \longrightarrow \text{Kick.}$$
$$\text{Not } 4 - 2+ \longrightarrow \text{Use your own judgment.}$$

The quarterback's sweetheart may not know football, but if she knows the coach's rule — and if she knows conditionals — she can impress her friends in the stadium by saying, "If they do not kick, then it is not fourth-and-two-plus; but if they do kick, then we do not know the down and the yardage." If, before another game the coach changes the rule to: "Only if it is fourth-and-two-or-more-yards-to-go, are you to call a kick play," then the girl will be able to say, "If they kick, then it is fourth-and-two-plus; but if they do not kick, then we do not know the down and yardage." Under the first set of conditions the coach specified what was sufficient for a kick play:

> If 4 − 2+, then kick.
> 4 − 2+ ⊃ kick.

Under the second set of conditions the coach specified what was necessary for a kick play:

> Only if 4 − 2+, then kick.
> Kick ⊃ 4 − 2+

4. *Alternative ways of expressing conditionals*

Arguments embodying conditionals arise in the examination of hypotheses when we work out what differences the hypothesis would make when related to premises supplied by other sources such as laws already held or the results of observations and experiments. Einstein saw that Michelson's experiment was an instance in which, if Newton's laws of motion were applied, nothing would be explained; Darwin believed that if he applied Malthus' thesis on how human population is limited by the struggle for existence he found in all plants and animals, then he would be able to account for the modification of species; Mr. Brown opines that his lawn and the lawn of his friend are not sufficiently different but that fertilizer which helped his friend's lawn will help his; Jack believes that it is not possible for Jane to be a Pi Gamma Delta and not fall in love with himself, the president of the Tri-Kappas. There are many ways of expressing the conditionals. The critical thinker as he examines his hypotheses will want to sharpen his thinking by expressing his conditionals as precisely as possible in a variety of ways, and he will not want to miss a conditional when it appears in another logical structure.

There are three basic logical forms of statements: the conditional, the alternative, and the conjunctive. We have examined the conditional. Now we turn to the alternative and the conjunctive, remembering that they do not express any logical relationships other than those which can be expressed by use of the conditionals. The alternative is a compound statement which affirms one or both of the separable statements which make up the whole statement. The separable statements are called "alternates." The sign for the relationship is ∨. It is translated as "or," "either . . . or," "either . . . or . . ., or both," or perhaps best of all by the joint word, so dearly loved by attorneys and writers of insurance policies, "and/or." Examples of the form are:

Either you are clever, or you are virtuous, or you are both.
Either this country elects a President from the other party, or this country
  goes into bankruptcy.
Love me, or leave me.
This policy pays for fire and/or storm.

The arguments using alternatives following the pattern we used for conditionals are:

1.	2.	3.	4.
$p \lor q$	$p \lor q$	$p \lor q$	$p \lor q$
p	p'	q	q'
?	q	?	p

The alternative may be called the "non-exclusive or." Its fullest translation is "either one or the other, maybe both." As an example of an alternative, consider a lawyer who argues that his defendant was either drunk or temporarily insane at the time of the misdeed. If the court agrees that he was drunk, that does not determine anything about his sanity; and if the court decides that he was temporarily insane, that still leaves open the question of his state of drunkenness. But if the court decided that he was not drunk, then he was insane; and if the court decided he was not temporarily insane, then he was drunk.[3]

The conjunctive is a compound statement which affirms both of the separable statements which make up the whole statement. The separable statements are called "conjuncts." The symbol for the relationship is ($\cdot$) which is translated "and." Unlike the grammatical "and," the logical "and" couples only statements; it does not unite adjectives, nouns, phrases, and clauses. Examples are:

Today is July 4th, and this is New York City.
Venus is the morning star, and my fortune is good.

[3] In addition to the "non-exclusive or" there is also the "exclusive-and-exhaustive or." This we call the contradictive; and for it we use the symbol $\land$. Whereas the alternative means "either one or the other, maybe both," the contradictive means "either one or the other, not both." Examples of this form are:

Either you are on time, or you are not on time.
Either he did or he did not vote in the last election.
Heads or tails.

The pattern for the contradictives is:

1.	2.	3.	4.
$p \land q$	$p \land q$	$p \land q$	$p \land q$
p	p'	q	q'
q'	q	p'	p

The conjunctive statement is said to be true only when both the conjuncts are affirmed. Thus, only if today *is* July 4th and this *is* New York City, can "Today is July 4th, and this is New York City" be a true statement. The whole statement is false if either or both of the conjuncts are false. For this reason a very precise reading of the conjunctive would be "Both today is July 4th and this is New York City."[4]

One matter remains: How do conditionals look when written as alternatives and as conjunctives? How do alternatives look as conditionals and conjunctives? And how do conjunctives look as conditionals and alternatives? The answer is implicit in what we have said thus far about the

---

[4] (This footnote and the remainder of the chapter deal with matters that go beyond the essentials of the art of critical thinking. The student who skips from here to the beginning of Chapter 10 may wish to return to these pages after reading the entire book.) When we try to express the conjunctive argument in the pattern we have previously used for the conditional and the alternative, we run into serious trouble. The conjunctive cannot be so expressed. The reason for this is illuminating in our grasp of these three logical forms. We had no difficulty in so expressing the conditional argument and the alternative argument because in these logical forms there was but *one* pattern which the forms would not allow. The conditional will not allow us to affirm the antecedent and deny the consequent. One thing we know about the conditional — its very nature — is that if the antecedent is affirmed the consequent cannot be denied. This is, in fact, a definition of what we mean by the conditional. Similarly the alternative will not allow us to deny both alternates. This is a definition of the alternative. To repeat: the conditional is defined as that form of reasoning in which it is impossible to affirm the antecedent and to deny the consequent, and the alternative is defined as that form of reasoning in which it is impossible to deny both alternates. But the conjunctive cannot be so defined — or so symbolized in our pattern — because it denies so much! According to the conjunctive it is impossible to deny either or both of the conjuncts! But we are not stymied. If we deny the entire compound statement, and create what is called a "disjunctive," then we are able to express the disjunctive argument in our established logical pattern. A disjunctive, let it be noted, is a contradiction of a conjunctive. The following are two examples of disjunctives:

"It is not the case both that today is July 4th and that this is New York City."
"I deny that both Venus is the morning star and that my fortune is good."

A disjunctive may also be described as a third form of "or."

1. Alternative, or "non-exclusive or": "Either one or the other, maybe both."
2. Contradictory, or "exclusive and exhaustive or": "Either one or the other, but not both or neither."
3. Disjunctive, or "exclusive and non-exhaustive or": "Either one or the other, maybe neither."

The disjunctive argument appears as follows in our pattern:

1.	2.	3.	4.
$(p \cdot q)'$	$(p \cdot q)'$	$(p \cdot q)'$	$(p \cdot q)'$
p	p'	q	q'
q'	?	p'	?

The disjunctive may be defined as that form of reasoning in which it is impossible to affirm both disjuncts.

three forms, but by listing them they may be studied until their equivalence is grasped.

A conditional statement will appear as $p' \vee q$, or as $p \vee q'$, or as $[(p' \vee q) \vee (p \vee q')]'$, or as $(p \cdot q')'$.[5]

Conditional: "If it is a case of friction, then it is a case of heat." $(p \supset q)$
Alternatives: 1. "It is either not a case of friction, or it is a case of heat, maybe both." $(p' \vee q)$
2. "It is either a case of friction, or it is not a case of heat, maybe both." $(p \vee q')$
3. "It is impossible that it is either not a case of friction, or it is a case of heat, maybe both, or that it is a case of friction, or it is not a case of heat, maybe both, or that it is both." $[(p' \vee q) \vee (p \vee q')]'$

Conjunctive: "It is impossible that it is a case of friction and not a case of heat." $(p \cdot q')'$

An alternative statement will appear as $p' \supset q$ and as $(p' \cdot q')'$.

Alternative: "Either you are clever, or you are virtuous, maybe you are both." $(p \vee q)$
Conditional: "If you are not clever, then you are virtuous." $(p' \supset q)$
Conjunctive: "It is impossible for you not to be clever and also not to be virtuous." $(p' \cdot q')'$

A conjunctive statement will appear as $(p \supset q')'$ and as $(p' \vee q')'$.

Conjunctive: "Venus is the morning star and my fortune is good." $(p \cdot q)$
Conditional: "It is impossible that if Venus is the morning star, then my fortune is not good." $(p \supset q')'$
Alternative: "It is impossible that either Venus is not the morning star, or my fortune is not good, maybe both." $(p' \vee q')'$

---

[5] In $[(p' \vee q) \vee (p \vee q')]'$ we have a new form: the contradiction of an alternative. It can be called the rejective form. However, like the conjunctive form, it cannot be expressed in our pattern because it denies so much. It may be defined as that form of reasoning in which it is impossible to affirm *either or both* of the rejects. Conjunction is that form of reasoning in which it is impossible to deny *either or both* of the conjuncts. The other forms we have studied deny less, and are much more explicit in what they deny:

Conditional form: It is impossible to affirm the antecedent and deny the consequent.
Alternative form: It is impossible to deny both alternates.
Disjunctive form: It is impossible to affirm both disjuncts.

10

Examining the Implications of Hypotheses: Immediate Inferences

1. *Forms of categorical statements*

Whether the compound statement be a conditional, or an alternative, or a conjunctive, it consists ultimately of simple statements which are not conditionals, nor alternatives, nor conjunctives. The logical form of compound statements is determined by the connectives "if . . . , then," "either . . . or," and "and." The simple statements within the compound are composed of a subject term, a predicate term, and a relationship. The subject and the predicate are related in an unqualified or categorical manner. For that reason the simple statements within conditionals, alternatives, and conjunctives are called categorical statements. There are a number of forms of these categorical statements.

Some categoricals are *predications*. The predicate term is said to be predicated of the subject term; the predicate term is an attribute or quality asserted of the subject term. Thus in "Our street is narrow" narrowness is asserted as a characteristic of our street.

Other categoricals are *class inclusions*. "Dogs are mammals" does not assert a mammal attribute of dogs; instead, this statement asserts that the class of things called dogs is included within the class of things called mammals.

Class membership is a categorical form which is very closely related to class inclusion, and which can cause considerable trouble to the critical thinker. Traditional logic stemming from Aristotle has sometimes made rather absurd arguments by failing to make a distinction between class membership and class inclusion. The rule of thumb is that when the subject term is an individual the relationship between subject and predicate should be regarded as class membership. If one does not do this, one is apt to assign to the individual characteristics which apply only to the class; for example, "Sitting Bull is an American Indian, and American Indians are vanishing, so Sitting Bull is vanishing." Obviously it is the *class* of American Indians that is vanishing, not the individuals who are members of the class. On the other hand, "Fido is a mammal, and mammals have ears, so Fido has ears" is perfectly correct reasoning. The difference is that whereas vanishing is a characteristic of a class, having ears is a characteristic of individuals included in a class.

A fourth class of categoricals is those statements in which the subject term and the predicate term are identical in meaning. Since these statements are usually definitions, the class can be called the *definitional*. Euclid's definition of a circle is an example: "A circle is a plane figure contained by one line, which is called the circumference, and is such that all straight lines drawn from a certain point within the figure to the circumference are equal to one another."

The fifth class of categoricals is those statements in which the subject and predicate terms are related in a manner such that we must examine the factual nature of the relationship to know how to deal with the statement. Because appeal must be made to material facts rather than to the form, these categorical statements are called *relational* statements. Such relations are "older than," "loves," "played tennis with," "was victorious over," "is north of," "is a friend of," etc. The relational categoricals may be classified according to symmetry and transitivity. A symmetrical relation is one that is reversible. That is, if A is related symmetrically to B, then B is related to A as A is related to B. If A played tennis with B, then B also played tennis with A. An asymmetrical relation is one that is not reversible. If A was victorious over B in the tennis match, then B was not victorious over A in the tennis match. Some relations are non-symmetrical. If Mr. Stuart loves Miss Frank, Miss Frank may reciprocate with love, but she may not. Miss Frank will have to decide that for herself — the structure of the relationship will certainly not force her to love Mr. Stuart! A transitive relation is one in which it is possible to argue that if A has a certain relation to B, and if B has the same relation to C, then A has this relation to C. If A is north of B, and if B is north of C, then A is north of C. But if A is mother of B, and B is mother of C, then A cannot be mother of C. The relation "is mother of" is intransitive. The non-transitive relations are those in which the transitivity may or may not hold — it all depends upon the particular situation. If A is a friend of B, and B is a friend of C, A may or may not be a friend of C. We would have to inquire of A, for we could not determine his attitude toward C by an examination of the meaning of the relation "is a friend of."

2. *Inclusion and exclusion*

Although not all categorical statements can be cast in the form of class inclusion, the study of statements of this type can be very rewarding in understanding the hypotheses which are formed to answer problems. According to traditional analysis there are four basic kinds of statements considered in terms of the degree to which the subject class and the predicate class include or exclude each other:

1. Complete inclusion
2. Complete exclusion
3. Partial inclusion
4. Partial exclusion

Although, as we have stated before, we are not interested in contents when we consider logical structures, we shall take as our first examples statements which are true:

1. All dogs are mammals.
2. No dogs are felines.
3. Some dogs are watchdogs.
4. Some dogs are not house pets.

These four statements can be written in another form which brings out more explicitly the inclusive and exclusive character of the four forms:

1. All dogs are included in the class of mammals.
2. All dogs are excluded from the class of felines.
3. Some dogs are included in the class of watchdogs.
4. Some dogs are excluded from the class of house pets.

This second formulation has the advantage of beginning each sentence with either the word "all" or the word "some" thus clearly indicating which statements are composed of classes that completely include or exclude each other and which are composed of classes that partially include or exclude each other. These four statements have been identified as *A*, *E*,

I, and *O* statements. There are many ways to symbolize the four inclusive-exclusive categorical statements. If we use *S* to stand for the subject class, and *P* for the predicate class, < for inclusion, and ≮ for exclusion, we shall then have the following simple formula for the four statements:

$$A = \quad \text{All } S < P$$
$$E = \quad \text{All } S \nless P$$
$$I = \text{Some } S < P$$
$$O = \text{Some } S \nless P$$

The *A*, *E*, *I*, and *O* statements can also be represented by the use of circles. Two interlocked circles stand for the two classes. The circle on the left, to save confusion, always stands for the class denoted by the subject term and the circle on the right stands for the class denoted by the object term. The shaded portions of the circles stand for areas which have no members. That portion of the circle could be erased to remind us that it does not exist. An X in any portion of the diagram indicates the existence of at least one member of the class. The four statements are diagrammed in the following fashion:

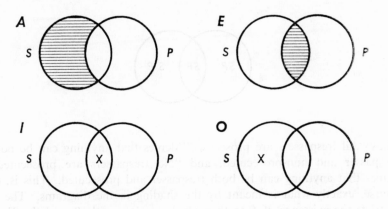

We note that the diagrams of the *A* and *E* statements have shaded portions of the interlocking circles, but no X's; while the *I* and *O* diagrams have X's, but no shading. This indicates an important distinction between the complete and the partial inclusions and exclusions. The *A* and the *E* are universal statements beginning with the word "all"; the *I* and the *O* are particular statements — they use the word "some." The word "all" does not stand for all the members of the class; rather it stands for the class as a whole, whether it does or does not have members: "All dogs — if there are any dogs — are mammals." "No dogs — if there are any dogs — are felines." The universal statements do not denote the existence of members of the class signified by the subject term. The class referred to may be what philosophers call a null class, that is, a class that has no members. When a farmer puts up a sign on his property, "All trespassers are prosecuted," the sign does not inform us that anyone has been or will be prosecuted; rather it tells us that if anyone trespasses, he is prosecuted. The *A* and the *E* statements refer in a negative fashion to individuals. The *A* denies that there is any individual that is both *S* and non-*P*.

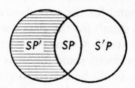

The *E* denies that there is any individual that is both *S* and *P*.

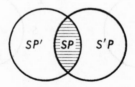

Thus "All trespassers are prosecuted" denies that anything can be both trespasser and non-prosecuted, and "No trespassers are prosecuted" denies that anything can be both trespasser and prosecuted. This is, of course, exactly what is meant by the shading in the diagrams. The *A* restricts the existence of *S* to that which overlaps with *P*, and the *E* restricts the existence of *S* to that which is separate from *P*. While we are here agreeing that the *A* and the *E* shall be treated as non-existential (also called hypothetical or conditional), we must remember that this is what we agree to do when there is no indication from the context as to whether there are members of the class. Sometimes the context of a statement clearly indicates that the class does have members. In such cases the critical thinker will treat the universal statements as existential.

We may now summarize what we have been saying about the universal statements with four diagrams.

1. *A*-conditional: "All *S* is *P*, if there is an *S*." E.g.,

"All trespassers are prosecuted."

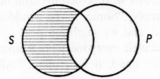

2. *A*-existential: "All *S* is *P*, and there is an *S*." E.g.,

"All dogs are mammals."

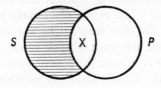

3. *E*-conditional: "No *S* is *P*, if there is an *S*." E.g.,

"No angels are demons."

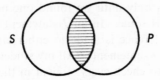

4. *E*-existential: "No *S* is *P*, but there is an *S*." E.g.,

"No dogs are reptiles."

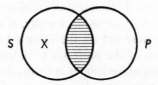

The *I* and *O* statements do refer to individuals within classes. "Some dogs are watchdogs" and "Some dogs are not house pets" denote the existence of individual dogs. In common usage "some" generally means more than one, but in logic it means at least one. One is some. We might

ask, "Well if 'some' means at least one, how *many* can it mean?" The answer is that "some" may mean all. But when it means all, it means all of a class of which there are members. Thus, if at the end of the hunting season, we asked the farmer who posted his land how many trespassers he prosecuted, he might reply, "Some." We would know then that he has prosecuted at least one, and we might suspect — and logic would allow it — that he had prosecuted everyone who trespassed, and there was at least one. On the other hand, if he replied, "All" to our question, he might have meant, "I prosecuted all the trespassers — only there were none."

We shall soon be analyzing arguments in which *A, E, I,* and *O* statements occur. In doing so it will be useful to know something about what is known as the distribution of the subject and predicate terms. A term is said to be distributed when reference is made to all the members (or potential members) of the class denoted by the term, and a term is said to be undistributed when reference is made to only a portion of the class denoted by the term. Let us take the *E* statement, "None of my students last semester were on the Dean's List." If we wished to verify this statement empirically, we would have to look over *all* the names of the students in the professor's class rolls and all the names of the students on the Dean's List. In an *E* statement both terms are distributed. If the professor said, "Some of my students were on the Dean's List," we would need to look over the two lists only until we found one name that was on both lists. One, we recall, is some. In an *I* statement both terms are undistributed, that is, no reference is made to either class as a whole. If the professor had used an *A* statement: "All my students were on the Dean's List," we would need to check every student in the professor's class rolls against the Dean's List. We could not leave out a single name on his list. But we would not need to exhaust the names on the Dean's List. There might be a hundred names left on the Dean's List, but if we had checked all the professor's list of students we could ignore the rest of the names on the Dean's List. In an *A* statement the subject term is distributed and the predicate term is not distributed. Finally, if the professor had said, "Some of my students were not on the Dean's List," we would have to be sure that at least one of the professor's students did not appear anywhere on the Dean's List, obligating us in theory to examine the entire list.

The distribution of terms (or classes) in the four statements then is as follows:

		Subject	Predicate
(A)	All S is P	Distributed	Undistributed
(E)	No S is P	Distributed	Distributed
(I)	Some S is P	Undistributed	Undistributed
(O)	Some S is not P	Undistributed	Distributed

Now that we have examined the distribution of the four statements, we might find it helpful to diagram the four in such a way as to indicate distribution. All solid line circles represent distributed terms; all circles that have any portion of the circumference in dotted lines represent undistributed terms.

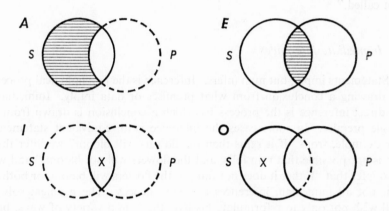

Not all hypotheses will be written in the standardized and stylized forms we have been using in this section. The critical thinker should be able to recognize the logical form when the form is hidden in a linguistic expression. We shall consider a few of the more common variations of the forms.

In those cases in which a statement does not contain the prefix "all" or "some," one will have to examine the context to determine whether the author intended a universal or a particular statement. Thus "Acids turn litmus red" is obviously an *A* statement, but "Allergies are curable" may be an *I*. Individual statements like "Fido is a dog" should be treated as a class membership statement, and thus avoid the troubles of Aristotelian logic in trying to make this into an *A* statement — "All of Fido is a dog"!

"All . . . are not" is an ambiguous form that ought to be avoided. A motorman yelling "All of you cannot get on" may mean either "None of you can get on" or "Some of you cannot get on." On the other hand, "Not all . . ." is a variation for "Some . . . are not . . . ."

Statements beginning "Only . . ." or "None but . . ." or "None except . . ." or ". . . alone . . ." as in "Only water expands when frozen" should have the order of the terms changed in order to fit the standard pattern: "All that expands when frozen is water."

"All except . . ." and "All but . . ." are tricky sentences. "All except water shrinks when frozen" must be changed into "All non-water things are things that shrink when frozen," since what is denoted here is not water, but everything other than water.

"Few" and "A few" have different meanings. "A few patriots were at the services on Memorial Day" is an *I* statement. "Few are called" has the double meaning of an *I* and an *O*: "Some are called, and some are not called."

3. *Immediate inferences*

Statements imply, but man infers. Inference is the psychological process of drawing a conclusion from what premises or data imply. Immediate or direct inference is the process by which a conclusion is drawn from a single premise. In some cases the inference is an equivalent statement, for example, from "If it rains then the flowers will bloom" we infer that "It is not possible that rain falls, and the flowers will not bloom," and we also infer that "Either it does not rain, or the flowers will bloom, or both." But not all immediate inferences are equivalences. The problem solver will wish not only to reformulate his hypothesis in a variety of ways, but also to discover all that can be inferred directly from the hypothesis. For example, a physician who reads in a medical journal, "We conclude, on the basis of this extensive research, that some cancers are caused by excessive use of tobacco," will want to know if he can infer from this statement that all cancers are so caused, or if he can infer that some cancers are not so caused, or if neither inference is justified.

Traditional logicians have constructed a diagram called "The Square of Opposition" in order to make clear the various relations that exist between the four inclusion-exclusion categoricals.

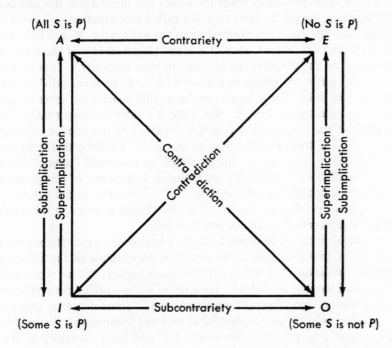

The Square of Opposition is based on the assumption that all the statements are existential; to try to make sense out of the Square of Opposition by assuming A and E to be non-existential makes for unnecessary complexities.

The easiest immediate inferences to be read from the diagram are the contradictories:

> If A is true, O is false.
> If A is false, O is true.
> If O is true, A is false.
> If O is false, A is true.
> If E is true, I is false.
> If E is false, I is true.
> If I is true, E is false.
> If I is false, E is true.

If it is true that "All plants are manufacturers of chlorophyll," then we can infer that it is false that "Some plants are not manufacturers of chlorophyll." If "Some tobacco is a thing which causes lung cancer" is false, then "No tobacco is a thing which causes lung cancer" is true.

The immediate inferences along the sides of the Square of Opposition are called subimplications when inferences are made from the universal statements to the particulars; they are called superimplications when inferring from the particular statements to the universals. If A is true, then I is true; and if E is true, then O is true. (Remember that the universal statements on the diagram are assumed to have members.) That is, if we know "All bases are things that react with acids to form salts" is true, then we can infer "Some bases are things that react with acids to form salts" as also a true statement. But if the A is false we cannot infer either the truth or the falsity of the I; and if the E is false we cannot infer anything as to the truth or the falsity of the O. If it is false that "All wars are included in the class of things caused by economic factors," we do not know whether "Some wars are included in the class of things caused by economic factors" is true or false. If "No pictures in the gallery are Rembrandts" is false, we cannot infer that "Some pictures in the gallery are not Rembrandts" is true or that it is false.

In superimplication to argue from the truth of particular statements to the truth of universal statements would be an example of the fallacy of over-generalization. Yet it is a very common fallacy: "Some women are fickle, so all women are fickle!" How many human prejudices and superstitions rest on shaky logical foundations, e.g., "Some people of that race are irresponsible, so all people of that race are irresponsible." But from the falsity of I we can infer the falsity of A; and from the falsity of O we can infer the falsity of E. If it is false that "Some birds have fur," then it is also false that "All birds have fur." And if "Some rocks are not volcanic" is false, then "No rocks are volcanic" must also be false.

The relationship of the A and the E is such that from the truth of one the falsity of the other can be inferred, and from the falsity of one the truth or falsity of the other is undetermined. If "All ink in these bottles is permanent ink" is true, then "No ink in these bottles is permanent ink" is false. But if "All ink in these bottles is permanent ink" is false, nothing can be inferred about the truth or falsity of "No ink in these bottles is permanent ink." Both A and E cannot be true.

In the case of the I and O statements both can be true, but both cannot be false. From the falsity of "Some chairs are rockers" one can infer the truth of "Some chairs are not rockers" and from the falsity of "Some chairs are not rockers," one can infer the truth of "Some chairs are rockers," but nothing can be inferred about the truth or falsity of "Some houses are not stucco" from the truth of "Some houses are stucco," nor about the truth or falsity of "Some houses are stucco" from the truth of "Some houses are not stucco." In other words, the relationship between partial inclusion and partial exclusion is alternation ($p \lor q$).

Although this exhausts the immediate inferences of the Square of Opposition, this does not exhaust the immediate inferences that can be drawn from given categorical statements. If, for example, the statement is about felines and bovines — "All felines are bovines," or "No felines are bovines," or "Some felines are bovines," or "Some felines are not bovines" — what can be inferred about the relation of bovines to felines? The carrying out of this inference is known as conversion. It consists in exchanging the positions of the two terms of the original statement. In the I statements and in the E statements we face no problems whatsoever. The conversion of "Some felines are bovines" is "Some bovines are felines," and the conversion of "No felines are bovines" is "No bovines are felines." The reason for the easy conversion is that in the I statements both terms are undistributed, and in the E statements both terms are distributed.

The A and the O give trouble because in each of these statements one term is distributed and one is undistributed. To try to convert "All felines are bovines" to "All bovines are felines" is to give more information about bovines than the original statement allows. The A, "All felines are bovines," does tell us something about all felines; the most it can tell us about bovines is that some bovines are felines. So we may suppose that the converse of "All felines are bovines" is "Some bovines are felines"; and so it is, *if we know that there are any bovines.* If the A is a conditional — as we have agreed to treat the A unless otherwise advised — there is no converse, since to convert "All felines are bovines" to "Some bovines are felines" would change a conditional to an existential. The A has a converse only if it is an existential A. The I converse of an A is called a limited converse; it is limited by the assumption that the subject term designates a class that has members.

The O has no converse of any kind. This is because the conversion of an O would entail altering the original undistributed subject class into a distributed predicate class, and this, again, would commit the fallacy of overgeneralization. An obvious example of this fallacy would be to try to convert "Some horses are not racing horses" to "Some racing horses are not horses."

The second type of question which we can ask of categorical statements has to do with the relation of the subject class to the contradictory of the predicate class, e.g., of felines to non-bovines. The inference involved is called obversion and may be illustrated by inferring from "All felines are bovines" that "No felines are non-bovines." Unlike conversion, obversion presents no special problems or exceptional cases. *A, E, I,* and *O* statements can all be obverted by following the same set of steps in each case. These steps are two: first, contradict the predicate term; second, change the quality of the statement, that is, an affirmative becomes a negative, and a negative becomes an affirmative. The quantity remains unchanged. "All felines are bovines" is obverted to "No felines are non-bovines"; "No felines are bovines" to "All felines are non-bovines"; "Some felines are bovines" to "Some felines are not non-bovines"; and "Some felines are not bovines" to "Some felines are non-bovines." Perhaps we should not say so cavalierly that obversion gives no problems; one must be careful that the denial of the predicate term is actually a denial, that is, a contradictory of the term. For example, one might be tempted to give "white things" or "non-colored things" as the contradictory of "black things," whereas the contradictory of "black things" is "non-black things." Whenever there is any doubt as to the proper contradictory, use the prefix non-.

By the alternate use of conversion and obversion, that is, by converting and then obverting the converse, etc., or by obverting and then converting the obverse, etc., five more immediate inferences can be drawn, viz., obverted converse, converted obverse (also called partial contrapositive), full contrapositive, partial inverse, and full inverse. While *A* and *E* statements have all seven of the immediate inferences — if we regard any *A* statement reached in the series of inferences as an existential statement — *I* has no contrapositives and no inverses, and *O* has no converse, no obverted converse, and no inverses. The reason for these omissions is that in the process of obverting and converting we reach a dead end every time we attempt to convert an *O*. The following list of inferences from an original *A* statement should both clarify the additional immediate inferences and stimulate an effort to discover the possible immediate inferences for the other three categorical statements:

The original *A* statement: "All weeds are plants."

> 1. *Converse*
>   Relation sought: Relation of *P* to *S*.
>   Example: "Some plants are weeds."
> 2. *Obverse*
>   Relation sought: Relation of *S* to *P'*.
>   Example: "No weeds are non-plants."
> 3. *Obverted converse*
>   Relation sought: Relation of *P* to *S'*.
>   Method used: Convert, obvert.
>   Example: "Some plants are not non-weeds."

4. *Converted obverse, or partial contrapositive.*
    Relation sought: Relation of P' to S.
    Method used: Obvert, convert.
    Example: "No non-plants are weeds."
5. *Full contrapositive.*
    Relation sought: Relation of P' to S'.
    Method used: Obvert, convert, obvert.
    Example: "All non-plants are non-weeds."
6. *Partial inverse*
    Relation sought: Relation of S' to P.
    Method used: Obvert, convert, obvert, convert, obvert.
    Example: "Some non-weeds are not plants."
7. *Full inverse*
    Relation sought: Relation of S' to P'.
    Method used: Obvert, convert, obvert, convert.
    Example: "Some non-weeds are non-plants."

Examining the Implications
of Hypotheses: Mediate
Inferences

In the last chapter we asked what can be deduced from a statement taken by itself. In this chapter we ask what can be deduced from a statement when we supply an additional or mediating statement. For example, in Chapter 10 we asked questions such as, if no large nation has ever voted to go communistic in a fair popular election, what can we infer about non-fair elections? In this chapter we ask questions such as, if no large nation has ever voted to go communistic in a fair popular election, and if some large nations have serious labor problems, what can we infer as to the relation between serious labor problems and a vote to go communistic?

1. *Nature of the syllogism*

The syllogism has been thought of as the ultimate weapon in the logician's arsenal. The syllogism should be employed in reasoning against dialecticians, and induction against the crowd, said Aristotle.[1] To change the metaphor — the syllogism is the logician's sonnet. The rules for forming syllogisms are as rigid as the rules for writing sonnets, and the contemplation of a line of syllogistic reasoning may give the logician

[1]*Topics* 157 a 20.

aesthetic satisfactions similar to the reading of a well-turned poem. The syllogism is a form of mediate inference in which there must be exactly two premises and a conclusion. The premises and the conclusion are cast in the form of categorical statements: *A, E, I,* or *O.* Although the arguments examined in Chapter 9 are sometimes called conditional, alternative, and disjunctive syllogisms, the classical syllogism is the categorical. When the term is used without qualification, it is taken for granted that it is the categorical syllogism that is meant.

The three categorical statements which make up the syllogism must contain three and only three terms — that is, refer to three and only three classes. Each term must appear twice in the syllogism. The term in the predicate position in the conclusion is called the major term. Traditionally it appears also in the first premise, and for this reason the first premise is called the major premise. The term in the subject position in the conclusion is called the minor term. Traditionally it appears in the second premise, and for this reason the second premise is called the minor premise. The other term must appear once in the major premise and once in the minor premise, and, of course, never in the conclusion. This term is called the middle term, but it might also be called the mediating term, or the vanishing term. We might say that it is through the middle term that the major term and the minor term are wedded.

Having become familiar with the nature of *A, E, I,* and *O* propositions, we need only to be reminded that a syllogism is an argument based on the inclusion and exclusion of classes. *A* statements completely include one class in another; *E* statements completely exclude one class from another; *I* statements partially include one class in another; and *O* statements partially exclude one class from another. We shall begin with an example of the simplest syllogistic form — the one in which all three statements are complete inclusions.

All the class of blue things is included in the class of round things.
All the class of smooth things is included in the class of blue things.

All the class of smooth things is included in the class of round things.

In this syllogism "the class of blue things" is the middle term, "the class of smooth things" is the minor term, and "the class of round things" is the major term. In showing the structure of a syllogism we shall use *M* as the sign of the middle term, *S* as the sign of the minor term, and *P* as the sign of the major term. *S* and *P* are used because the minor term is in the subject position of the conclusion, and the major term is in the predicate position of the conclusion. So the structure of the above syllogism may be shown as

$$\frac{\begin{array}{l} \text{All } M < P \\ \text{All } S < M \end{array}}{\text{All } S < P} \quad \text{or as} \quad \frac{\begin{array}{l} \text{All } M \text{ is } P \\ \text{All } S \text{ is } M \end{array}}{\text{All } S \text{ is } P}$$

The only difference in these two ways of writing the syllogistic form is that the first calls attention to the syllogism as the relation of classes, and the second to the terms which represent the classes.

Syllogisms are classified according to figure and mood. Figure refers to the position of the middle term in the two premises. Note that in the specimen syllogism the middle term appears in the subject position in the major premise and in the predicate position in the minor premise. This is known as the First Figure. There are four figures. In the Second Figure the middle term appears in the predicate position in both premises; in the Third Figure the middle term appears in the subject position in both premises; and in the Fourth Figure the middle term appears in the predicate position in the major premise and in the subject position in the minor premise.

First Figure: M is P Second Figure: P is M
 S is M S is M

Third Figure: M is P Fourth Figure: P is M
 M is S M is S

Mood denotes the quality and quantity of the statements, that is, whether they are complete inclusion, complete exclusion, partial inclusion, or partial exclusion when we think of the syllogism as the relationship of classes; or as affirmative universal, negative universal, affirmative particular, or negative particular when we think of the syllogism as terms designating classes. The mood of the specimen syllogism is AAA, since both the premises and the conclusion are A statements. This syllogism then would be classified as AAA in the First Figure. A very helpful way to symbolize the syllogistic form of AAA in the First Figure is to write the syllogism in this fashion

$$\frac{\begin{array}{l} M \text{ a } P \\ S \text{ a } M \end{array}}{S \text{ a } P}$$

It is wise to use lower-case letters for the A, E, I, and O statements in order not to confuse them with the terms of the syllogism which are customarily designated in capital letters. There are 256 possible ways to arrange the $A,E,I,$ and O propositions in the four figures. For example, the mood AAA theoretically could appear in all four figures:

First Figure	Second Figure	Third Figure	Fourth Figure
M a P	P a M	M a P	P a M
S a M	S a M	M a S	M a S
S a P	S a P	S a P	S a P

We say *theoretically*, because, for reasons which we shall soon discover, the *AAA* mood is valid only in the First Figure. (Deductive validity, we note again, means that the premises force the conclusion.) Beginning students in logic are always greatly relieved to be told that at least 232 of the possible syllogistic forms are invalid! There are only 24 valid syllogistic forms — 6 in each figure, if universals are assumed to be existential, and only 15 valid syllogistic forms, if universals are assumed to be nonexistential.

There is much that can be said about the nature of the syllogism which will not be discussed here, since we are interested in the syllogism chiefly as a technique in the examination of hypotheses. Anyone who enjoys crossword puzzles or chess might learn to enjoy the game of playing with the syllogism. The scholars of the Middle Ages had great fun with techniques for reducing valid moods in the last three figures to valid moods of the First Figure. We can see how it might be done by casting the premises into some of the equivalent forms we considered in the last chapter, and also by changing the order of the premises. We shall forego these mental pleasures, and shall mention but one more feature of the syllogism: its use as a method of discovery and as a method of proof. Thus far we have presented the syllogism with the two premises written first, followed by the conclusion. This suggests that the syllogism is a form of reasoning in which by relating two premises we learn something new. But is the conclusion really a discovery? Is it something new? Or was it hidden all the time in the premises? If the premises *force* the conclusion, aren't we saying that the conclusion was in the premises, and that the only novelty is the psychological novelty of discovering something of which we were initially unaware? There is no *logical* novelty — no actual discovery of new information. While this may be the case, we can go back to our illustration of Michelson and Einstein, and remind ourselves that Michelson did not see the implication of his own experiments until Einstein pointed it out to him. We ought not hastily to underrate the importance of a device for revealing the implication of premises.

There is another way of evaluating the syllogism: it also is an instrument to defend a thesis. The syllogism was invented both in ancient Greece and in ancient India. The Greeks listed the three statements in the order we have given thus far, but the Indians listed the conclusion first. That is, whereas the Greeks read their syllogisms "All *M* is *P*, and all *S* is *M*, therefore all *S* is *P*," the Indians read their syllogisms "All *S* is *P*, because all *M* is *P* and all *S* is *M*." The difference is that the Indians tend to regard the syllogism as a technique of proof, not as a technique of discovery. For them it is not so much an argument leading to a conclusion as a vindication of a position. Furthermore, the Indian logicians are not concerned about the separation of deduction and induction. Whereas the Western syllogism has three statements, the Indian syllogism has five. Here is a typical syllogism in Indian logic — it is the standard example paralleling the Western syllogism on man's mortality!

1. The Thesis to Be Established: "Yonder mountain has fire."
2. The Reason: "Because it has smoke."
3. The Example: "Whatever has smoke has fire."
4. The Application: "Yonder mountain has smoke such as is invariably accompanied by fire."
5. The Conclusion: "Therefore yonder mountain has fire."

Is the syllogism a means to explicate the implication of premises, or is it a means to defend a thesis? Perhaps it can — and should — serve both purposes.

2. *Venn diagram test for validity*

John Venn, a nineteenth-century English mathematician and logician, created a diagram which is useful in determining whether a syllogism is valid or invalid. We were introduced to the basic structure of the Venn diagram in the last chapter when we noted that the four categorical statements can be diagrammed as

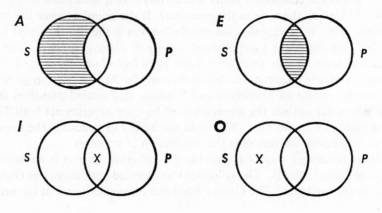

While we have diagrammed the universal statements as conditionals, they may also be diagrammed as existentials — as we noted in the previous chapter:

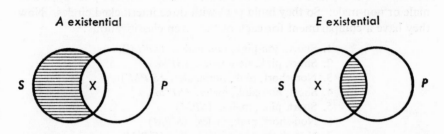

A existential *E existential*

Venn drew a third circle which interlocked with the other two circles to represent the three classes in a syllogism. The circle on the left is the class indicated by the minor term; the one on the right is the class indicated by the major term; and the third is the class indicated by the middle term.

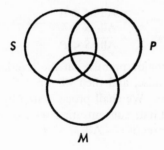

When the circles are properly drawn, there are seven separate compartments in the figure.

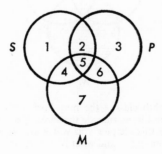

Almost any illustration one can think of to help understand this diagram is helpful. Try this one — silly though it be. Imagine a large psychological laboratory in which the psychologists wish to classify their white rats on the basis of short tails or non-short tails, pink eyes or non-pink eyes, and male or non-male. So they build pens with three interlocked circles. Now they have a compartment for each of the seven classifications:[2]

1. Short, non-pink, non-males. $(SP'M')$.
2. Short, pink, non-males. (SPM')
3. Non-short, pink, non-males. $(S'PM')$
4. Short, non-pink, males. $(SP'M)$
5. Short, pink, males. (SPM)
6. Non-short, pink, males. $(S'PM)$
7. Non-short, non-pink, males. $(S'P'M)$

As soon as you have mastered the diagram, forget the rats and get back to the syllogism.

To see how the Venn diagram works let us examine a syllogistic form in which all three statements are complete inclusions, e.g., "All mice are pink animals, and all small animals are mice, so all small animals are pink animals."

$$\text{All } M < P$$
$$\text{All } S < M$$
$$\overline{\text{All } S < P}$$

First we diagram the major premise on the interlocked circles, then we diagram the minor premise, and then we see if the given conclusion can be read off the diagram. We shall proceed step by step on this first run through the process. First, concentrating only on the M and P circles, we diagram the major premise — All $M < P$.

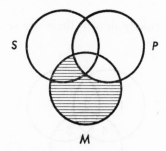

<hr>

[2]Actually there is an eighth class — the non-short, non-pink, non-males $(S'P'M')$. They will have to run around loose outside the three interlocked pens! Perhaps when you have finished studying this chapter you will know why the class $S'P'M'$ can be omitted from Venn diagramming — and what role it has in deductive reasoning.

To make sure we have made no mistake, we look at what we have drawn, and we ask ourselves "Are compartments 5 and 6, which represent all that is in the *M* class, included in the *P* class?" Since they are, we proceed to the second step.

Secondly, concentrating only on the *S* and *M* circles, we diagram the minor premise — All *S* < *M*. In order to avoid confusions make the first hatching horizontally, and the second vertically, and hatch out *all* the class that should be removed. If a compartment is removed twice, this will appear as crosshatching.

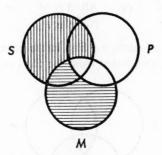

The third step is to examine the diagram to see if the given conclusion of the syllogism can be read off the diagram. Is all of the *S* class included in the *P* class? All of the *S* class is found in compartment 5. Compartment 5 is in *P*. Therefore, the syllogism is valid.

We said above that *AAA* is valid only in the First Figure. Let us try *AAA* in the other figures to see if the Venn diagram supports that authoritarian remark.

AAA in Second Figure:

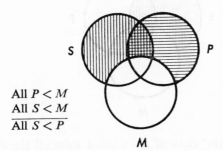

All *P* < *M*
All *S* < *M*
——————
All *S* < *P*

It is invalid because the *S* class is in compartments 4 and 5, and compartment 4 is not in the *P* class. If we draw Venn circles for *AAA* in the

Third Figure and in the Fourth Figure, we shall discover that *AAA* is invalid in these two figures. The Venn diagrams can be used to eliminate all the invalid syllogistic forms of the 256 possible ways of expressing *A, E, I,* and *O* statements as major premise, minor premise, and conclusion in the four figures.

Let us now try a syllogism which contains a complete exclusion. We shall begin with an *EAE*, e.g., "No Mandarins are pedestrians, and all Sungs are Mandarins, hence no Sungs are pedestrians."

All $M \nless P$		No M is P		M e P
All $S < M$	or	All S is M	or	S a M
All $S \nless P$		No S is P		S e P

In diagramming this syllogism we first hatch compartments 5 and 6 so that all the class of *M* is excluded from the class of *P*.

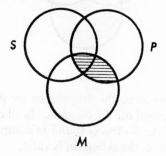

Then we hatch compartments 1 and 2 so all the class of *S* is included in the class of *M*.

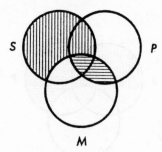

Now we ask, "Is all the class of *S* excluded from all the class of *P*?" We answer, "Since all the class of *S* is in compartment 4, and since all the class of *P* is outside compartment 4, all the class of *S* is excluded from all the class of *P*." The syllogism is valid.

Properly constructed Venn diagrams demonstrate that

$$\text{All } P \nless M$$
$$\frac{\text{All } S < M}{\text{All } S \nless P}$$

is valid, whereas *EAE* in the Third Figure and in the Fourth Figure is invalid.

The time has come to introduce the way to indicate the *I* and the *O* statements on the Venn diagram. Let us try *IAI* in the Third Figure, e.g., "Some men are punctual, and all men are sailors, so some sailors are punctual."

Some $M < P$		Some M is P		M i P
All $M < S$	or	All M is S	or	M a S
Some $S < P$		Some S is P		S i P

In Chapter 10 we saw that the *I* statement affirms the existence of at least one member of the class and that existence is marked with an X. When we had only two interlocked circles, we simply marked an X in that portion of the interlocked circles where they are interlocked.

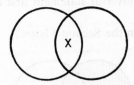

But when we have three interlocked circles, the area shared by the two circles has been bisected by the circumference of the third circle. So we must put an X in both sections of the bisected compartment. This does not change the meaning of the word "some"; it still means "at least one" — certainly it does not mean "at least two"! In diagramming the major premise of this *IAI* we place an X in compartment 5 and another in compartment 6, and then we connect the two X's to indicate that there is at least one member of the class, but as yet we do not know whether it belongs in compartment 5 or compartment 6.

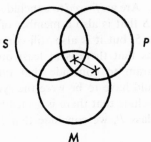

Then we indicate the minor premise — All $M < S$

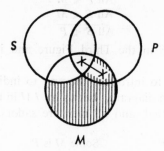

Now we examine the completed Venn diagram and ask if the conclusion can be read. Does the diagram indicate that there is at least one member of the class of S which is a member of the class of P. We note that we do have an X in compartment 5, which is a compartment shared by S and P. Therefore, the *IAI* mood in the Third Figure is valid. (Perhaps it is easier to indicate the universal statement first on the Venn circles, but this is not necessary.)

Is *IAI* valid or invalid in the Second Figure?

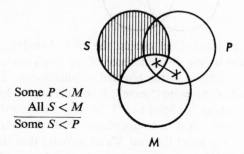

$$\text{Some } P < M$$
$$\underline{\text{All } S < M}$$
$$\text{Some } S < P$$

When we try to read the conclusion from the completed Venn diagram, we face some new problems. Are we *forced* to conclude that there is at least one member of the class of S that is also a member of the class of P? There is an X in compartment 5, but it is also still connected to an X in compartment 6. This means that there is at least one member, but we are not *forced* by the diagram to conclude that one member is in compartment 5 where it would have to be were the syllogism valid. So since we are not *forced* to conclude that there is a member of class S in a compartment shared with class P, we conclude that *IAI* is an invalid mood in the Second Figure.

Finally, we ought to examine a syllogism with an O statement in it. Let us try this AOO form:

All $P < M$		All P is M		P a M
Some $S \not< M$	or	Some S is not M	or	S o M
Some $S \not< P$		Some S is not P		S o P

First we indicate the major premise on the diagram.

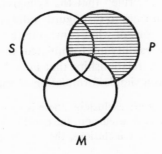

Then we mark in the minor premise: Some $S \not< M$. This O statement calls for an X in compartment 1 and an X in compartment 2 connected by a bar, but since compartment 2 has been eliminated already by the major premise, we place the X in compartment 1.

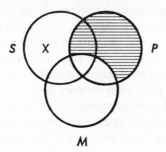

We are forced to conclude from the completed Venn diagram that there is at least one member of the class of S excluded from the class of P; so the form is valid.

This completes our introduction to the Venn diagrams. They are simple and powerful tools for determining the valid syllogistic forms. He who is progressing in critical thinking would do well to master the technique of Venn diagramming. But there are other ways to approach the problem of determining the validity of syllogisms, and we now turn to an alternate way.

3. *Rules of validity*

The rules of validity are a few clearly stated principles no one of which can be violated by a valid syllogism. There are a variety of ways to formulate the rules, but care must be exercised that the rules be rules of *validity* of syllogisms and not rules of the nature of syllogistic reasoning itself. For example, the "rule" that the syllogism must have three and only three statements and the "rule" that the syllogism must have three and only three terms are not rules to distinguish valid from invalid syllogisms; they are simply descriptions of what constitutes a syllogism.

However the rules of validity are formulated, there will be certain rules of quality which state the relationships that must hold between inclusions and exclusions. Here is a simple formulation of the rules of quality:

Rule 1. If both premises are exclusions, there is no conclusion.
Rule 2. If one premise is an exclusion, the conclusion must be an exclusion.
Rule 3. If both premises are inclusions, the conclusion must be an inclusion.

Argument for these rules would not be quite to the point. We must understand why we need these rules. If they do not appear obvious, one might try constructing Venn diagrams of syllogisms that violate the rules of quality. Soon there will come that moment of truth when one says, "Why of course! If the premises are affirmative, the conclusion must be affirmative; if there is one negative in the premises, the conclusion must be negative; and if both premises are negative, there is no conclusion."

There will also be rules of quantity in the rules of validity. These may be called rules of distribution, since they deal specifically with this aspect of the syllogism. The rules of quantity are formulated on the self-evident notion that if the premises refer to only *part* of the members of a class, the conclusion cannot state anything about *all* the members of the same class. The rules of quantity must also take account of the fact that the middle class, which we have also called the vanishing class, cannot be eliminated unless reference is made to *all* the members of the class. So we seem to take care of everything by stating that the middle class must be distributed, and that the terms undistributed in the premises cannot be distributed in the conclusion. Then two ugly questions rise in our minds: (1) How many times can the middle term be distributed? E.g., is this syllogism valid: "All vegetables are mineral foods, and all vegetables are green foods, so some green foods are mineral foods"? (2) Can a term be undistributed in the conclusion and distributed in the premises? E.g., is this syllogism valid: "All World War II airplanes are obsolete airplanes, and all DC-3 airplanes are World War II airplanes, so some DC-3 airplanes are obsolete airplanes"? If both these syllogisms are diagrammed on the Venn circles as conditional universal statements, the syllogisms are shown to be invalid. But as we have often noted, universal statements may be either conditional or existential. Common sense, general knowledge, and context — not logic *per se* — dictate whether a given universal statement is to be treated as conditional or as existential. If these two sets of premises are treated as existential, the syllogisms may be diagrammed on the Venn circles, and the conclusions can be shown to be valid deductions from existential universal premises:

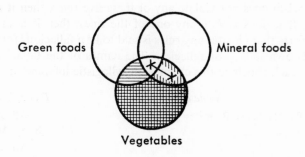

Since both the conditional and the existential interpretation of universal statements are accepted, two sets of rules of distribution are required. If this seems at first to be a bit confusing, consider the greater confusion of giving logical priority to one interpretation and of treating the other interpretation as an exception to the rule.

A. Rules for valid syllogisms which assume universal statements are *existential:*

Rule 4. The middle term must be distributed at least once.

Rule 5. Terms undistributed in the premises cannot be distributed in the conclusion.

B. Rules for valid syllogisms which assume universal statements are *hypothetical:*

Rule 4. The middle term must be distributed once, and only once.

Rule 5. Terms undistributed in the premises cannot be distributed in the conclusion, and terms distributed in the premises cannot be undistributed in the conclusion.

If a syllogism does not violate any of these five rules, then it is a valid syllogism. If it does violate any one of the rules, then it is invalid. A syllogistic form that violates any rules is said to be a fallacious form. Each rule has its own fallacy or fallacies. The names of the fallacies and an example of each conclude this chapter on syllogistic inferences:

Rule	*Name of Fallacy*	*Example of Fallacy*
Rule 1 (A, B)	Exclusive Premises	All $P \nless M$ Some $M \nless S$ —————— All $S \nless P$
Rule 2 (A, B)	Exclusive Premise to Inclusive Conclusion	Some $M < P$ Some $S \nless M$ —————— Some $S < P$
Rule 3 (A, B)	Inclusive Premise to Exclusive Conclusion	All $P < M$ All $M < S$ —————— Some $S \nless P$
Rule 4 (A, B)	Undistributed Middle Term	Some $P < M$ Some $S < M$ —————— Some $S < P$
Rule 4 (B)	Twice Distributed Middle Term	All $M < P$ All $M < S$ —————— Some $S < P$
Rule 5 (A, B)	Undistributed to Distributed Major Term	Some $P \nless M$ All $S < M$ —————— Some $S \nless P$
Rule 5 (A, B)	Undistributed to Distributed Minor Term	All $M < P$ Some $M < S$ —————— All $S < P$

Rule 5 (B)   Distributed to Undistributed Major Term   All $P < M$
                                                            All $M < S$
                                                            Some $S < P$

Rule 5 (B)   Distributed to Undistributed Minor Term   All $M < P$
                                                            All $S < M$
                                                            Some $S < P$

EXERCISES

Recognition of Assumptions

Directions: A reader of a newspaper was aroused by an editorial. He wrote a letter to the editor in which he made fifteen statements. You are to mark each of these statements as 1 or 2. Then you are to mark all 2 statements as 3 or 4. Finally, you are to mark all 1 statements as 5 or 6.

1. This statement was made by the editor, although maybe not in these words.
2. This statement was not made by the editor.
3. The editor stated something which shows that he had this in mind.
4. The editor did not state anything which shows that he had this in mind.
5. This statement was supported with evidence by the editor.
6. This statement was not supported with evidence by the editor.

The Editorial

It is often said that natural resources account for American prosperity. While this is a factor in the prosperity of any country, integrity and intelligent management of economic affairs are far more important.

In witness, we present Switzerland, a small mountainous country with little smooth, arable land, no seaports, no coal and almost no mineral resources. Nevertheless, Switzerland maintains one of the highest standards of living in the world. Switzerland has a sound fiscal system based on the gold standard.

Her gold reserve amounts to more than 143 per cent of her bank notes.

The editor visited Switzerland again last year and found government employees going to work at 7:45 in summer and working through until 6 o'clock. In winter the day began at 8:15 and continued to 6 o'clock.

Work, character, sound money, and intelligent management of economic affairs have produced prosperity in Switzerland. This has been accomplished in spite of a great paucity of natural resources.

The Reader's Fifteen Points

1. The editor believes that America's prosperity can be accounted for solely by her vast natural resources.
2. The editor believes that people want prosperity.
3. The editor believes that some people explain America's prosperity by her natural resources.
4. The editor believes that Switzerland's prosperity can be accounted for by the hard work of her citizens and by her sound financial system.
5. The editor has visited Switzerland at least twice.
6. The editor wants Americans to work until 6 o'clock each afternoon.
7. The editor thinks that America can do anything Switzerland can.
8. The editor thinks that Switzerland has a sound fiscal system.

9. The editor believes that it is possible to have a sound fiscal system based on the gold standard.
10. The editor wants America to have a sound fiscal system.
11. The editor thinks that a nation can be prosperous in spite of a paucity of natural resources.
12. The editor thinks that natural resources are a factor in the prosperity of any country.
13. The editor thinks that America ought to go on the gold standard.
14. The editor believes he knows why Switzerland is prosperous.
15. The editor believes that prosperity and a high standard of living are synonymous.

Recognizing Assumptions

Directions: Following is a list of assumptions and a list of arguments. For each of the arguments you are to select the assumption which it leaves unstated.

Assumptions

1. "Luxuries are never good for you."
2. "Some habit-forming things are good for you."
3. "Habit-forming things are never good for you."
4. "Some things which are good for you are luxuries."
5. None of these.

Arguments

1. "Luxuries are not good for you. Why, they are invariably habit-forming."
2. "Habit-forming things are not good for you. Everyone agrees they are simply luxuries."
3. "You must agree that some habit-forming things are not good for you, for you admit some of them are luxuries."
4. "Since luxuries are never good for you, it follows that some habit-forming things are not luxuries."
5. "Some luxuries are not habit-forming. This is certain because nothing which is habit-forming is ever good for you."

Immediate Inferences

Directions: Assuming that "No philosopher is practical" is TRUE, and that there are philosophers, are the following statements true, false, or undetermined?

1. Some philosophers are impractical.
2. All philosophers are impractical.

3. Some philosophers are not practical.
4. All philosophers are practical.
5. This philosopher is impractical.
6. Some practical people are philosophers.
7. No practical person is a philosopher.
8. Some philosophers are practical.
9. Some philosophers are not impractical.
10. Only impractical people are philosophers.

Directions: Assuming that "All truckers are polite" is TRUE, and there are truckers, are the following statements true, false, or undetermined?

1. Some truckers are not impolite.
2. Only impolite people are truckers.
3. Some truckers are polite.
4. All truckers are impolite.
5. Some truckers are impolite.
6. This trucker is impolite.
7. Some polite people are truckers.
8. No impolite person is a trucker.
9. Some truckers are not polite.
10. All truckers are polite.

Directions: Assuming that "Some smokers are bad husbands" is TRUE, are the following statements true, false, or undetermined?

1. Some bad husbands are smokers.
2. No smokers are bad husbands.
3. Some smokers are not bad husbands.
4. All smokers are bad husbands.
5. All smokers are not bad husbands.
6. Not all smokers are bad husbands.
7. Some smokers are not good husbands.
8. Some bad husbands are not non-smokers.
9. Some bad husbands are non-smokers.
10. Some non-bad husbands are non-smokers.

Directions: Assuming that "Some news is not good news" is TRUE, are the following statements true, false, or undetermined?

1. Some non-news is good news.
2. Some bad news is news.
3. All news is good news.
4. Some bad news is not non-news.
5. A few news is not good news.
6. Eighty per cent of the news is not good news.
7. Some non-news is not good news.
8. All good news is news.

9. Only good news is news.
10. Good news is news.

Immediate Inferences

Directions: Two students after going to a political rally are discussing the remarks of the principal speaker. They have selected four sentences from the speech and have attempted to gather implications of these sentences. You are to mark their inferences according to the following:

1. If the speaker's sentence is true, this sentence is true.
2. If the speaker's sentence is true, this sentence is false.
3. If the speaker's sentence is true, the truth or falsity of this sentence cannot be established.

The speaker said, "All tariff restrictions are unnecessary."

1. Some tariff restrictions are unnecessary.
2. Some tariff restrictions are not unnecessary.
3. Some tariff restrictions are necessary.
4. All unnecessary things are tariff restrictions.
5. Some unnecessary things are tariff restrictions.

The speaker said, "No man who wants to work will go hungry."

1. No man will go hungry who wants to work.
2. All men who want to work are included in the class of those who will not go hungry.
3. Some men who want to work will go hungry.
4. Some men who want to work will not go hungry.
5. All who want to work are excluded from the class of those who will go hungry.

The speaker said, "Some of my opponents are honest."

1. Some of my opponents are dishonest.
2. None of my opponents is honest.
3. All of my opponents are dishonest.
4. Some dishonest people are included in the class of my opponents.
5. Most of my opponents are dishonest.
6. Some of my opponents are not dishonest.
7. Some honest people are among my opponents.

The speaker said, "Some people will not enjoy my remarks."

1. Some people are excluded from the class of those who enjoy my remarks.
2. Some people will enjoy my remarks.
3. No people are enjoyers of my remarks.
4. All people will enjoy my remarks.

Material Relations

Directions: Characterize the following relations as to symmetry and transitivity.

1. Symmetrical
2. Asymmetrical
3. Non-symmetrical

a. Transitive
b. Intransitive
c. Non-transitive

1. as tall as
2. father of
3. best friend of
4. employer of
5. next to
6. blood relative of
7. envious of
8. higher than
9. cousin of
10. parallel to

11. ancestor of
12. greater than
13. married to
14. works for
15. has a greater velocity than
16. causes
17. the king of
18. part of
19. drove his car past
20. next door to

Inferences from Conditionals, Alternatives, and Disjunctives

Directions: Evaluate the following arguments as valid or invalid. If invalid, indicate why.

1. If a country is prosperous, the people will be loyal. The people are loyal, so the country must be prosperous.
2. If he had studied his lessons, he would be able to recite. He was not able to recite, so he did not study his lessons.
3. If it swims, we have it. It does swim, so we've got it.
4. If it becomes colder tonight, the pond will freeze over. Alas, it did not become colder, so the pond did not freeze over.
5. If man were not capable of improvement, his lot would be hopeless, but man is capable of improvement, so his lot cannot be hopeless.
6. If Rex is a terrier, so is Rover. But Rex is a terrier. Hence, Rover is a terrier.
7. If you answered the telephone, he heard you. Since he did not hear you, that proves you could not have answered the telephone.
8. He acted very suspiciously, and surely if he were guilty he would have acted very suspiciously. He must be guilty.
9. You will not get an answer if you write. You will be miserable if you do not get an answer. It follows that if you write you will be miserable.
10. If the postman is not late, I shall not miss my class. The postman will be late. I am bound to miss my class.
11. If the weather does not change, we shall have a picnic. The weather will not change. We shall have a picnic.
12. It is not the case that you can be in New York City and not also be in the

State of New York. You are not in New York City, so you are not in the
State of New York.

13. This is no joke, since when he is joking a dimple shows on his chin, and
this time I see no dimple.

14. Only if the U.S. gets a man on the moon before the Russians do, will the
U.S. get ahead of the Russians in the race for the conquest of space. My
favorite fortuneteller says that the U.S. will get ahead in the race for the
conquest of space. So according to her the U.S. will get a man on the moon
before the Russians.

15. When this object is made of plastic, it is too fragile. This particular one is
not made of plastic, so it will not be too fragile.

16. If one takes time, one can do wonders. The fellow at the end of our hall
never does any wonders, so I guess he never takes time.

17. It cannot both be that Mary is at the office and Mary is at home. Frank
is sure that Mary is not at the office, so Mary is at home.

18. If the light is on, they must not have gone to bed. They have gone to bed,
so the light is not on.

19. Either you dislike me or I have offended you. I know I have offended
you, so thank goodness you can't also dislike me.

20. Either this paper will change its editorial policy, or I'll not renew my subscription. The paper will change its editorial policy, so I will renew my
subscription.

21. If this lecture doesn't get more interesting, I'll get out my knitting. I
won't get out my knitting, because the lecture has gotten more interesting.

22. He cannot both marry that girl and not lose the family inheritance. He
will not lose the family inheritance. Thus he will not marry that girl.

23. I can go to Cleveland only if my allowance comes in time. My allowance
will come in time, so I can go to Cleveland.

24. I shall be glad to see him, unless you would rather see him yourself. You
say you would rather not see him yourself, so I shall be glad to see him.

25. Either this room is too hot or I'm ill. I am not ill in any way, so the room
is too hot.

26. "Education implies teaching. Teaching implies knowledge. Knowledge
is truth. The truth is everywhere the same. Hence Education should be
everywhere the same." (Robert M. Hutchins)

27. "King Solomon, according to the Scriptures, possessed the united wisdom
of heaven and earth; but King Solomon knew nothing about alchemy,
and sent his vessels to Ophir to seek gold, and levied taxes upon his subjects; ergo, alchemy has no reality or truth." (Figuier, *L'Alchimie et les
Alchimistes*)

28. An apple is better than heaven, since an apple is better than nothing, and
nothing is better than heaven.

29. A brand of mustard has this slogan printed on the label: "Keep me cold
and I'll stay hot." On the label the manufacturers interpret the slogan in

these words: "This mustard will lose strength unless refrigerated when not in use."

30. "Wealth depends upon the pursuit of wealth; education depends upon wealth; knowledge depends on education; and Religion depends on knowledge; therefore Religion depends on the pursuit of wealth." (Newman, *The Idea of a University*)

31. "Now if all positive morality rests upon genuine discernment, and if all discernment of values is itself an aprioristic perception of valuational essences, the historical relativity of morals cannot rest upon that of values, but only upon that of discernment." (Hartmann, *Ethics*)

32. During the past 150 years the population of the world has approximately doubled. If the population had doubled every 150 years, beginning with one couple living about 6000 years ago, then the present population would be reached. So mankind has been on this planet for only about 6000 years.

Inferences from Conditional Statements

Directions: Basketball coach John Hardaznales shakes his head one Saturday morning as he says to the inquiring reporter, "If we lose this game, we are out of the race for the conference title." In preparing his copy the reporter wishes to make an indirect reference to the coach's statement. He tries many ways. Mark each statement "C" if it correctly restates the meaning of the coach's statement, and mark "I" if it incorrectly restates the meaning of the coach's statement. Why are the incorrect ones incorrect?

1. The coach affirmed that losing the game will put the team out of the race for the conference title.

2. The coach believes that if the team is put out of the race for the conference title, it can only be because the team lost this game.

3. In the view of the coach, if the team is not put out of the race, that means it won this game.

4. The coach expressed his opinion that if the team wins, then it still may be in the race for the conference title.

5. In the opinion of the coach, if the team does not lose this game, then the team may still be in the race for the conference title, or the team may be out of the race for the conference title.

6. If we are in the race for the title, mused the coach, then it can only be because the team loses this game.

7. Coach Hardaznales said a number of things about the game, but they can be briefly summarized as: No win this game; no title.

8. If the team is out of the race for the title by the time the game is over, there is still a possibility that they may have lost this game, said the coach.

9. Coach's remarks boil down to this: If the team is to win the title, then it must win this game.

10. As the coach now sees it, if we don't lose this game there is a chance we may win the title.

Conditionals, Alternatives, Disjunctives

Directions: What conclusions, if any, can be drawn from the following?

1. Rainbow at morning, sailors take warning. We had a rainbow this morning.
2. If one uses bacon rind, he'll catch a lot of fish. I didn't use bacon rind.
3. If one uses bacon rind, he'll catch a lot of fish. I didn't catch a lot of fish.
4. If one uses bacon rind, he'll catch a lot of fish. I caught a lot of fish.
5. If I take the low road, I will get to Scotland before you. I take the high road.
6. He could have had the car if he had paid for the gas. He did not pay for the gas.
7. If he is the Duke of Windsor, then I'm Charlie Chaplin. And I certainly am not Charlie Chaplin.
8. If this is a sample of his work, and it is, we are not interested.
9. If you practice you will play well, but you don't practice.
10. Only if you practice will you play well. You don't practice.
11. If this is the right road, we should be about to the detour. There is a detour sign just ahead.
12. If the honor system works, all students will indicate their absences from chapel. All students do indicate their absences from chapel.
13. If the honor system works, all students will indicate their absences from chapel. Six juniors did not indicate their absences from chapel.
14. If the honor system works, all students will indicate their absences from chapel. The honor system works.
15. If the honor system works, all students will indicate their absences from chapel. The honor system does not work.
16. It's either work or relief. And we cannot get work.
17. Either he has forgotten or he is a good actor. He has forgotten.
18. Either a man produces or he is a parasite. He doesn't produce.
19. He is a Republican or a Democrat. He is not a Democrat.
20. He is at the office or on the road. He is on the road.
21. Either he has reached home or he is in trouble. His wife has just telephoned that he is home, so I guess he is all right.
22. If you can sing, so can I. I cannot sing.
23. If you can sing, so can I. You cannot sing.
24. If life is like a scrambled egg, then I've had enough of it. And I certainly have had enough of it.
25. All work and no play makes Jack a dull boy. I do nothing but work.
26. If this is my hat, I'll eat it. This is not my hat.

27. When ragweed is in the pollen stage, I get hay fever. I now have hay fever.
28. No ladies allowed. I'm here.
29. In London cars are driven on the left side of the road. We are driving on the left side of the road.
30. Either she does not know the score or she is blind and deaf, and I know she has almost perfect vision and hearing.
31. You cannot both sleep in logic class and do well in logic. Gertrude does well in logic.
32. If Adams can make a basket in one second, he is a magician. Adams did make the basket in one second.
33. Either all men are irrational beings, or all men are bipeds, or both; but certainly all men are not irrational beings.
34. Only fish swim, and all trout swim.
35. It is not possible for water to be in the gas tank and the car to start. Well, the car certainly will not start.

Conditionals, Alternatives, Disjunctives

Directions: In the following arguments "*C*" means "Canto stays in power another year" and "*W*" means "a state of war occurs within the next year." You are to indicate the valid conclusion (using these symbols) where there is a valid conclusion. Where there is no valid conclusion you are to indicate this by use of "*U*" for uncertain.

First Premise	*Second Premise*
1. $C \supset W$	1. C
2. $C \supset W'$	2. C'
3. $(C \cdot W)'$	3. C'
4. $(C \cdot W)'$	4. C
5. $C \lor W$	5. C
6. $C \lor W$	6. C'
7. $C \supset W'$	7. C'
8. $C \supset W$	8. C
9. $(C \supset W) \cdot (W \supset C)$	9. C
10. $(C \supset W) \cdot (W \supset C)$	10. C'

Conditionals

1. What clues as to the character of each girl can you deduce from these remarks of three roommates a week before the Junior Prom?
   MARY: "If I have a date, I'll have a good time."
   JANE: "Only if I have a date, will I have a good time."
   KATE: "If and only if I have a date, will I have a good time."

2. A union leader says, "Only if the steel companies pay full pension will the steelworkers go back to work." Striker Jones carries a placard which reads, "No pension means no work." Striker Smith carries a placard which reads, "No work means no pension." Which striker knew his logic?

3. A grape juice company advertised its product in 1914 with a picture of an attractive young woman holding a glass of its product and saying, "The lips that touch Welch's are all that touch mine." Under what conditions could she be kissed?

4. Prove by use of the Rules for Validity of Syllogisms given in this text (either Form *A* or Form *B*) that the following rule is unnecessary: "If both premises are particular, there can be no conclusion."

5. Express the following as conjunctives, and also as alternatives:

> If wishes were horses,
> Beggars would ride;
> If turnips were watches,
> I'd wear one by my side.

Categorical Statements

Directions: Rewrite the following using "included in" and "excluded from":

1. All that glitters is not gold.
2. Not all gold glitters.
3. Only gold glitters.
4. A few golden things glitter.
5. Few golden things glitter.
6. None but glittery things are golden.
7. All but glittery things are golden.
8. All except golden things are glittery things.
9. None except golden things glitter.
10. Golden things alone glitter.
11. All golden things are rejected unless they glitter.
12. Thirty per cent of the golden things are things that glitter.
13. Nearly all that glitters is not gold.
14. Not any golden thing glitters.
15. Only some golden things are glittering things.

Categorical Statements

Directions: The following is a list of categorical statements. There are a number of operations which can be performed upon them:

    a. Identify as *AEIO.*
    b. Rewrite using "included in" or "excluded from."

   c. Underline distributed terms after rewriting the statements.

   d. Convert.

   e. Obvert.

1. Nothing is impossible.
2. Who thinks must mourn.
3. Some must watch while some must sleep.
4. A pretty girl is like a melody.
5. All save one are out of danger.
6. Some men are not in business for profit.
7. Whatever is is right.
8. Many are called, but few are chosen.
9. Pleasure vehicles only.
10. Only cash customers get coupons.
11. Behold all flesh is as the grass.
12. Not everyone dreads the dentist chair.
13. Some shall reap that never sow.
14. In this land of plenty there are those who starve.
15. Many's the slip twixt the cup and the lip.
16. This is only a rose.
17. Whoso would be a man must be a non-conformist.
18. None but the English drink tea with milk.
19. Every woman has her price.
20. Some ignorant people are not stupid.
21. Not all freedom is desirable.
22. Whoever is not concerned, let him leave.
23. Little we see in nature that is ours.
24. Euclid alone has looked on beauty bare.
25. All except one member favor the motion.
26. Not every knock is a boost.
27. Some are born great.
28. Fifty per cent of the work is work assigned to our union.
29. Only God can make a tree.
30. Few people can stand on their heads.
31. All that sells for less than a dollar is not worth the price.
32. Conifers alone will grow in this soil.
33. All people unless they have a ticket are turned away.
34. None but thee is crazy.
35. Americans are friendly.
36. Not all dogs are gentle.
37. The whole team played splendidly.
38. No compound is an element.
39. Only clowns laugh.
40. All but those with less than a 2.0 grade average are graduated.
41. All motorists are not careful.

42. All men must serve in the armed forces unless they have a serious physical defect.
43. All except fires caused by arson are protected by this policy.
44. A few Hollywood stars are good actors.
45. Some heated metals are not non-brittle.
46. None but the wealthy will not ride motor scooters.
47. Some senators are a menace to democracy.
48. All men — and I can name several — are brutes.
49. Only Henry was out of step.
50. All's well that ends well.

Venn Diagrams

Directions: Draw two-circle Venn diagrams for the following statements:

1. All *S* is *P*, and there is an *S*.
2. Some *S* is *P*, some *S* is not *P*, and some *P* is not *S*.
3. All *P* is *S* (conditional), and some *S* is not *P*.
4. All *S* is *P* (conditional), and all *P* is *S* (conditional).
5. No *S* is *P*, and some *P* is not *S*.
6. All *S* is *P* (conditional), and some *S* is not *P*.
7. All *P* is *S*, and there is a *P*, and some *S* is not *P*.
8. All *S* is *P* (conditional), some *P* is not *S*, and there are some things that are neither *S* nor *P*.
9. All *S* is *P* (conditional), and there is a *P*.
10. No *S* is *P*, some *S* is *P*, some *S* is not *P*, and some *P* is not *S*.

Categorical Syllogisms

Directions: Which of the following syllogisms are valid, and which are invalid? What fallacy is committed in the invalid syllogisms?

1. Some brutes eat their young.
   No humans eat their young.

   Some humans are not brutes.

2. All who drink afternoon tea love the English.
   No Irishmen drink afternoon tea.

   No Irishmen love the English.

3. Some of his paintings were in the gallery.
   Some of the paintings in the gallery were destroyed by fire.

   Some of his paintings were destroyed by fire.

4. All books are interesting.
   Henry is a great reader of books.

   Therefore, Henry is interesting.

5. No dirigibles are safe.
   No airplane is a dirigible.

   So all airplanes are safe.

6. Only women are admitted.
   I'm admitted.

   Hence, I'm a woman.

7. All British planes are marked with concentric circles.
   This plane is marked with concentric circles.

   This plane is British.

8. Some paint is rubber-based paint.
   No rubber-based paint is successful when painted on cement.

   Some paint is not successful when painted on cement.

9. Some artists' paints are casein; all artists use oil paints; so some oil paints are casein.

10. Spiders are not insects because no insects have eight legs, and spiders do have eight legs.

11. All good lessons develop initiative, and some things that develop initiative are not easy, so it follows that some easy things are good lessons.

12. No valid syllogism has an undistributed middle.
    This syllogism does not have an undistributed middle.
    Hence, this syllogism is valid.

13. All wild canaries are migratory birds.
    All wild canaries are songsters.
    Therefore, all migratory birds are songsters.

14. Not to vote is to neglect your duty.
    Not to register is not to vote.
    Hence, not to register is to neglect to do your duty.

15. All Bronxites are Easterners.
    All Easterners are Americans.
    Some Americans are Bronxites.

16. Every *a* is *b*.
    Every *b* is *c*.
    Every *c* is *a*.

17. All birds fly.
    All geese fly.
    Therefore, all geese are birds.

18. Every Nazi favors racism.
    No loyal American is a Nazi.
    Hence, some loyal Americans do not favor racism.

19. All *d* is *e*.
    Some *f* is *e*.
    Therefore, some *f* is *d*.

20. All men are rational beings.
    All rational beings are bipeds.
    Therefore, all bipeds are men.

21. All men are rational beings.
    All rational beings are bipeds.
    Therefore, men are rational beings.

22. No dogs are bipeds.
    Some bipeds are not rational beings.
    Hence, some rational beings are not dogs.

23. Some dogs are rational beings.
    No rational beings are six-legged.
    So some dogs are not six-legged.

24. Some church steeples have belfries.
    This is a church steeple.
    Therefore, it has a belfry.

25. All followers of Plato are idealists.
    He is an idealist.
    So he is a follower of Plato.

26. Some rocks are sedimentary; granites are not sedimentary; therefore, some
    rocks are not granites.

27. No cat has nine tails.
    Every cat has one more tail than no cat.
    Therefore, every cat has ten tails.

28. Man is studied by psychology.
    John is a man.
    Therefore, John is studied by psychology.

29. Every cow is cloven-footed.
    Every cow is ruminant.
    Therefore, every ruminant is cloven-footed.

30. All gold is metal.
    Something that glitters is not gold.
    Hence, all that glitters is not metal.

31. Every Communist is pro-labor.
    No member of the N.A.M. is Communist.
    Hence, no member of the N.A.M. is pro-labor.

32. No *a* is *b*.
    No *b* is *c*.
    Hence, no *c* is *a*.

33. All British planes are marked with concentric circles.
    Some of these planes are marked with concentric circles.
    Hence, some of these planes are British.

34. No cows are used for dairy purposes in China.
    No cows are used for meat in Norway.
    Nothing used for meat in Norway is used for dairy purposes in China.

35. All Indians are semibarbarians.
    No white people are Indians.
    Therefore, all white people are semibarbarians.

36. All beverages containing more than 5 per cent of alcohol are intoxicating.
    No beer contains more than 5 per cent of alcohol.
    No beer is intoxicating.

37. All airplanes are lightly constructed.
    All airplanes are speedy vehicles.
    All speedy vehicles are lightly constructed.

38. No teachers are bigots, since no teachers are prejudiced, and only bigots
    are prejudiced.

39. There are no insincere reformers; therefore, no reformers are hypocrites,
    since none but the insincere are hypocrites.

40. Some ideas are harmless; so not all weapons are harmless, since ideas
    are weapons.

41. No one present is out of work. No members are absent. So all members
    are employed.

42. All flies are dangerous. Some dangerous things are caught between second
    and third. So some flies are caught between second and third.

43. It follows that the Sahara desert is overpopulated, since some areas of the
    earth are overpopulated, and the Sahara desert is an area of the earth.

44. No dogs are allowed. This we know because only those things that bark
    are allowed, and everyone knows that every single dog barks.

45. Some wild flowers are beautiful, and no beautiful flowers are perishable.
    Thus, some perishable things are not wild flowers.

46. All Republicans are protectionists. Therefore, some protectionists are not
    conservatives, since some Republicans are conservatives.

47. Some of the students in college are not in the classes in Latin, and all of
    the students in college are in classes in speech. So it follows that some of
    the students in classes in Latin are not in the classes in speech.

48. Since all bankers are golfers, and all middle-aged men are golfers, it follows that all bankers are middle-aged men.

49. Some Hindus are vegetarians, and all Brahmins are Hindus. So don't you see that some Brahmins are vegetarians?

50. All weeping willows are weepers, and some women are weepers, so some women are weeping willows.

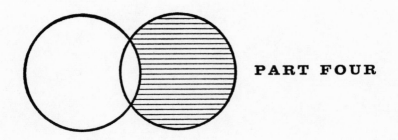

PART FOUR

The Testing
of Hypotheses

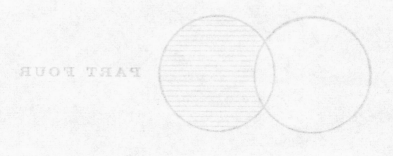

Interpreting Observations

In Part Three we considered what John Dewey calls the mental elaboration of hypotheses. We studied the importance of identifying hidden assumptions, of rephrasing the hypotheses in every conceivable equivalent form, and of determining what can be rationally inferred from hypotheses by assuming the truth or falsity of the component statements, or by assuming the existence or non-existence of the component classes or members of classes. The next aspect of critical thinking is the testing of hypotheses both by observations alone and by observations in the framework of experiments. We shall confine ourselves to the former in this chapter; in the next chapter we shall consider experiments.

1. *Fallibility of observations*

In Chapter 5 we noted that the three most common errors in observation are those resulting from non-observation, from mal-observation, and from faulty memory. A well-known parlor trick is built on the first of these errors. In this trick a pair of scissors is passed from person to person around the room. As the scissors are passed the person says either "I receive them crossed, and pass them uncrossed" or "I receive them uncrossed, and pass them crossed." The few that know the trick inform the others whether they did it correctly or incorrectly. A good many minutes lapse before everyone discovers that "crossed" and "uncrossed" refer to the legs of the person receiving and passing the scissors, and not to the scissors. W. I. B. Beveridge reports an incident in an English medical school in which the professor pulled a similar trick based on non-observation to remind his students of the importance of accurate observations.[1] While teaching a class, the professor took a sample of diabetic urine and dipped his finger in it to taste it. He then asked the students to repeat his action. They did — reluctantly. After they had all tasted the urine, and agreed that it tasted sweet, the professor said, "I did this to teach you the importance of observing detail. If you had watched me carefully you would have noticed that I put my first finger in the urine but licked my second finger!" An experiment in observation which exemplified all three errors was conducted first at a conference of psychologists in Germany, and has been repeated many times in psychology classrooms. In the midst of one of the meetings a man rushed into the room chased by another man brandishing a revolver. After a brief scuffle in which one shot was fired, the men rushed out of the room. The chairman of the meeting at once asked each man in the room to write down exactly what he had seen. "Of the forty reports presented, only one had less than 20 per cent mistakes about the principal facts, fourteen had from 20 to 40 per cent mistakes, and twenty-five had more than 40 per cent mistakes. The most noteworthy feature was that in over half the accounts, 10 per cent or more of the details were pure inventions."[2] And this was the record of scientifically trained psychologists! Yet many times a man's life in a court trial depends upon what someone remembers about what he saw or heard.

What people see depends not only upon their immediate interests, but also upon their fundamental values and prejudices. The last-mentioned experiment in observation has sometimes been performed by men of different races, and the reported observations follow the line of the observers' prejudices. A group in the United States organized to promote better race relations has prepared a few slides to test race prejudices. One of the more effective slides is a cartoon of the inside of a trolley car in which a white man is shown in the act of threatening a Negro with a knife. The slide is projected on the screen for only a few seconds, and then the members of the audience are asked questions about what they saw. If the audience is composed of white people, about 25 per cent will indicate that they saw the knife in the hand of the Negro.

In many ways we do not "see" what we see! Ernst Mach has a drawing in his *The Analysis of Sensations* of what he sees with his left eye while lying on a sofa in his study looking down his body to the opposite end of the room. This eerie drawing — one which, if once seen, will never be forgotten — does, when one thinks about it, accurately represent what

---

[1] *The Art of Scientific Investigation* (New York: Random House, Vintage Books, n. d.), p. 133.
[2] *Ibid.*, p. 131.

one sees in this position. Many an amateur photographer learns through experience that the camera does not allow for perspective as does the human organism.

Man is endowed with the power to determine what he sees. Of course he cannot see just what he wishes; no one can call up sensations completely at will, although one can disregard the obvious, and concentrate on the most minute. A technique used in training neophytes in yoga in Buddhist monasteries of Southeast Asia is designed to develop this native ability. Young monks are asked to sit cross-legged before a yellow disk about the size of a hockey puck and to look steadily at it for several hours. After the monks have developed the ability to cut everything out of attention except the disk, they are then asked to sit in meditation before the disk and consider only the color. On another day they will be asked to disregard color, and concentrate only on the form. Thus is developed what Buddhists call pin-point concentration.

All men make a distinction between things as they are and things as they are observed. Philosophers call this the difference between appearance and reality. The railroad rails are "really" parallel, although they are seen as though they meet about one-half mile down the track; the oar resting in the water from the side of the boat appears to be broken, although it is "really" straight; the pitch of the automobile horn seems to be higher when the car is coming rapidly toward the person standing beside the highway, and seems to be lower when the car is moving rapidly away. But why is not one experience as "real" as another? What justification can be given for these distinctions? Why are not things as we *see* them, and why do we not see them as they *are*? From the point of view of a person standing in the middle of a railroad track, the rails do meet in the distance; and from the point of view of a person in a boat, oars are broken in water. But when a second sense can be used to verify the observation, the appearance may vanish. For example, the person in the boat may run his hands down the oar and discover that the oar does not feel as if it were broken. The following conditional syllogism is then used:

If the oar were broken as vision suggests, then it would feel as if it were broken. But it does not feel broken.

Therefore, the oar that looks broken is not broken.

The parallelism of the rails cannot be established by touch, but one might walk down the track with a measuring stick and measure the spread of the rails one-half mile away, but then one would discover that the rails now converge at the original spot! The statement "Rails converge one-half mile down the track" is still true! In this case a more satisfactory handling of the situation might entail shifting from induction to deduction by arguing:

> If trains move down this track, then the rails do not converge.
> Trains move down this track.
> _____
> Therefore, the rails do not converge.

The case of the varying pitch of the automobile horn is solved in another manner. Without going into details, we shall only say that in this case a distinction does have to be made between the vibrations of sound waves of the moving horn as received by the observer and as originating at the moving source. The Doppler effect principle explains this phenomenon. Sound *vis-à-vis* observer does vary in tone; sound *vis-à-vis* sender does not.

Sometimes appearance is of more utilitarian value than reality. Although lines A and B are the same length, they appear to be of different length. This optical illusion has many significant uses in architecture,

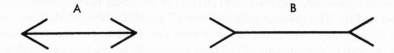

automobile design, hairdressing, theatre staging, furniture design, landscaping, and other activities and occupations concerned with form.

Besides these common universal errors in human observation, each individual is unique in his observing; as Bacon would say, each has his cave. Since each man's cave is his own and he can experience no one else's, a man may never realize the limitations of his own cave. Most color-blind or tone-deaf people make the discovery through some chance event. Medical history records cases of people almost blind or deaf who did not seek medical attention because they thought everyone saw or heard as they did. The remarks of people who are fitted with glasses are often revealing: "Why trees do have leaves!" "Neon signs aren't fuzzy after all!" "How long have those cobwebs been on the ceiling?"

Observation is subjective. Yet observation — subjective though it be — is the foundation of objective science. "I see it. Don't you?" is the form by which many profound scientific hypotheses become established as conclusions of a scientific problem. The socially unshareable, linguistically inexpressible, and quantitatively unmeasureable sense data of individual men and women are foundations for the socially shareable, linguistically expressible, and quantitatively measureable knowledge of the sciences. Even if the object of the sciences, as Eddington once said, is to reduce reality to pointer readings, the fact remains that a man is needed to observe the pointer and to interpret what the reading means. No one has yet suggested that scientific hypotheses can be created and tested by automation. The scientist tries in every way to eliminate the possibility of human error, for he is well aware that man's observations are notoriously fallible.

The fallibility of the human senses is of two types: one is the inherent fallibility of sensing; the other is the fallibility of interpreting what is sensed. The former denotes all the errors of perception of which we are aware as well as others which the psychologist calls to our attention. For example, Colin Cherry of the University of London has made many studies of a phenomenon he calls Biaural Gestalten, that is, the psychological fact that man has the problem of fusing aural data from two ears into one experience. He has conducted experiments in which the subject receives in one ear "stochastic" signals, that is, sounds for which the brain cannot know in advance exactly what is next coming to the ears, for example, human speech, and in the other ear, "non-stochastic" signals, for example, a steady buzzing sound. Cherry has established that if the speech signal is set earlier in time than the noisy signal, the fusing of the signals takes place without difficulty; but if the noisy signal is earlier in time, then the fusion is varied and uncertain.[3]

Fallibility of interpretation is evidenced in all those cases in which we take for granted that the person in the blue coat fifty feet ahead of us is our friend Jack, or hastily conclude that the loud noise is a revolver shot, or believe that the people across the room are talking about us. Robert Nathan has written a short story called "Digging the Weans"[4] in which a people living thousands of years in the future reconstruct from archaeological remains a long-forgotten civilization. "I call these people the Weans," says the author, "because certain archaeological findings incline us to the belief that they called their land the We, or the Us." The chief mounds are Cha'ago, n. yok, Oleans, Boxton, and above all the rich mound called Pound Laundry. In the last mound they find sections of an inscription, "Nor (north?) rain nor hail nor snow ... their appointed rounds." The full inscription, according to the archaeologists, may have been: "The north rain, the hail, and the snow (also from the north) have accomplished their appointed rounds (or tasks)," namely, have annihilated the inhabitants. As one reads this delightful story one wonders how much

[3] Colin Cherry, "Two Ears — But One World," in *Sensory Communication*, ed. Walter A. Rosenblith (New York and London: John Wiley and Sons, Inc., and The Massachusetts Institute of Technology Press, 1961), pp. 99–117.

[4] *Harper's Magazine*, November 1956, pp. 46–49.

archaeologists malign ancient peoples by reconstructing civilizations on the basis of fragments of stone, iron, and bronze which happen to have survived.

2. *The nature of fact*

When the problem solver comes to the stage which we have called the testing of hypotheses by observation, he may say, "Let us look at the facts," or "Let the facts speak for themselves," or "Theories must be rooted in facts." The term "fact" has a variety of meanings. We shall mention only two. Sometimes the term is used to designate statements that are true, e.g., "A book is in my hands" and "My desk lamp is on" may be two facts. A fact in such instances may also be called a truth. Sometimes the term is used to designate that which makes a statement true, e.g., the presence of a book in my hands is what makes the statement "A book is in my hands" a true statement, and the desk lamp casting light on my book is what makes the statement "My desk lamp is on" a true statement. Fact, in the second sense, is also that which makes a false statement false; e.g., the desk lamp casting light on my book is also the fact that makes the statement "My desk lamp is not on" a false statement. The second meaning of fact is the one which we have in mind in this section.

A reality and a fact are not the same. A fact must be a reality, but a reality need not be a fact. As we are using the term here, a fact is a reality in the context of a problem. A reality is independent in a manner in which a fact is not. Facts are dependent upon inquiry. Problems generate the search for facts, and problems confer factuality upon realities. If there were no problems, there would be no facts. Facts are those specific aspects of reality singled out with reference to a specific inquiry. If the problem is "Is there a book on the table?" the fact is the presence or the absence of a book on the table. The term "non-facts" may be used to denote those aspects of existence which are not singled out with reference to this inquiry. In the problem regarding the presence or absence of the book on the table, the cat sleeping on the hearth is a non-factual reality. We might note in passing that facts may be positive or negative; that is, the presence of the book on the table is as much a fact as is the absence of the book on the table in the context of seeking to know whether there is a book on the table.

Facts are selected from reality. In studying data with a galvanometer the bands of shadows are the facts; the glass of the dial is real, but non-factual — it is not relevant to the inquiry. When a motorist glances at the speedometer of his car while driving on the highway, the needle and the numbers on the speedometer are the facts, if his problem is "Am I exceeding the legal speed limit?" The glass of the speedometer face is not a fact in this context. However, if the glance at the speedometer is in the context of another inquiry, e.g., "Why is my speedometer stuck?" the glass of the face of the speedometer might very well be a fact to be considered. If the glass is broken, or loose, or strangely discolored, these conditions must be considered in the context of a stuck speedometer. Facts are subjective, but they are not merely subjective. If they were, the snakes which have no foundation other than the delirium of the drunkard would have to be designated as facts.

Facts depend upon a point of view. Facts are realities singled out for attention. They are realities in a frame of reference, and that frame of reference is a problem. Lawyers speak of "the facts in the case." That is the only place where there are facts — in a case. The glass of a dial is always real, but it is a fact only when relevant to a problem. Facts are realities for a subject who is confronted with a problem. In the absence of problems — and of beings who have problems — there are realities, but no facts.

As an illustration of facts and realities, imagine a woman looking in a dress shop window. When her husband arrives, he notices that she is looking in the window, and he asks, "What facts have you noticed?" His wife (who happens, like himself, to be a philosopher) replies, "None — I had no inquiry, so I was merely observing." "Well, what did you observe?" persists her husband. "Realities — blue dresses, price tags, manikins, artificial palms," replies his wife. But to lend a feeling of authenticity to this little skit, we probably should add that the philosophical wife is still a lady very much interested in stylish clothes. Hence, she would more likely reply to the first question, "What facts have you noticed?": "Twilight blue is coming back in style. The hem lines are a bit higher. Belts are a little wider. Hips are fuller again. These are bargains considering their quality. Do you think we have time for me to try on that darling number on the manikin leaning against the tree?" In this more probable husband-wife conversation, the realities in the window become facts in the context of a problem, e.g., "What can I wear at the party Saturday night?"

3. *Observation as evidence*

"How odd it is that anyone should not see that all observation must be for or against some view, if it is to be of any service," said Darwin. There is a vast difference between "just looking" and "looking for something." A university student looks up from his book and gazes at the campus green outside his window, yet sees nothing for he is looking for nothing; but when he goes to his mailbox to see if a letter has finally arrived from home, or when he seeks out a particular girl that evening at the college dining room to invite her to the dance next weekend, he does a different sort of looking. Men had watched the flight of birds probably for thousands of years before some shaman decided that fortunes could be told by studying these flights. In ancient Athens birds were purchased in the Agora, to be released later in order that from their flight men could learn auspicious times and places for personal business undertakings. In fifteenth-century Milan there was a man who bought birds in the marketplace to study their flight for another purpose. Leonardo da Vinci believed that by the study of the flight of birds he could devise a technique for human flight. Observation is evidence when it is for or against something. When realities are observed, not just looked at, they become facts which support or weaken hypotheses.

Sometimes the observation is direct observation. We look to see if the book is or is not on the table, the expected letter is or is not in the mailbox. Sometimes the observation is indirect. A red line in the thermometer indicates the heat of the room; a furrowed brow may be the symptom of another's headache; a busy signal on the telephone indicates the line is in use; a dial on the dashboard of an automobile shows the amount of gas remaining in the gas tank. Rarely is direct observation used in the sciences. Even the simplest sort of observation in the sciences is indirect. For example, when one uses the litmus paper test for acidity, one does not *see* the acid; one *sees* the change that takes place in the litmus paper, and infers that acid caused the change. Auguste Comte once said, "If it is true that every theory must be based upon observed facts, it is equally true that facts cannot be observed without the guidance of some theory. Without such guidance, our facts would be desultory and fruitless; we could not retain them: for the most part we could not even perceive them."[5] Without the theory regarding the effect of acid on litmus, the change in color would have no meaning. This was Michelson's difficulty; he had no theory to give meaning to the non-appearance of signs of acceleration or retardation of either beam of light in the interferometer

---

[5] *The Positive Philosophy*, Vol. I, Chap. 1.

experiment. He saw, but did not understand what he saw. Darwin once said that nature tries to hide herself; but this blames nature for difficulties largely of the scientist's own making. Scientists observe indirectly chiefly as a result of their endeavor to transmute psychological data into physical data, quality into quantity. Rarely are scientists interested in the fact that a certain liquid feels warm; they want to know how far on a thermometer the liquid will raise a column of mercury. Eighty-four degrees centigrade is an indirect way of saying that the liquid feels warm. One of the problems peculiar to the science of psychology is that most of its data are non-quantitative data (sensing, feeling, thinking, valuing, etc.) which must be transformed into quantitative data (heart beat, changes in temperature, verbal responses, color flushes, etc.) before they can be accepted. There is always the suspicion that something is lost in the transformation.

The type of observation of most interest to the scientist is the *crucial* observation. After a wealth of observational material has been collected, a hypothesis may hinge upon one experiment. One of the most exciting crucial observations in the twentieth century was that which grew out of Einstein's prediction of the effect of gravitation on light. Einstein had formulated gravitational laws alternative to the Newtonian laws which described in terms of geometry the field properties of the space-time continuum. Already his hypothesis had proved successful in predicting the rotation of Mercury's elliptical orbit — the ellipse advances only 43 seconds of an arc per century! — and this Newton's laws could not explain. But still the scientific world was not completely willing to accept Einstein's General Theory of Relativity. Einstein also calculated that the mass of the sun was such that it would cause a deviation of about 1.75 seconds of an arc in the light beams from stars closest to the sun as observed from the point of view of earth. Einstein proposed that photographs be taken of the stars bordering the darkened face of the sun during an eclipse, and that these photographs be compared with the location of these stars as established by celestial charts. But there were no photographs of the stars bordering the sun during an eclipse. Arthur Eddington led an expedition to the south Atlantic to photograph a total eclipse of the sun on May 29, 1919. This was a crucial observation. Einstein's General Theory of Relativity of 1915 hung in the balance. Einstein, himself, had recommended the technique of observation. When the photographs were examined, the deviation of the light from the stars in the gravitational field of the sun was found to be 1.64 seconds! Allowing for instrumental inaccuracy, Einstein's predictions were completely vindicated. The General Theory of Relativity was accepted by the scientific world.

There is one more problem about observation as a source of evidence which should be noted: What constitutes a sufficient number of observations? We said on the first page of the Introduction to this book that an American Council of Education study of the improvement in thinking made by college students in logic classes was made of too few students to justify reliable generalizations. Some educational testing experts say that a study of at least 25,000 students must be made before the norms of an educational test can be reliable. One of the early tests of Salk vaccine for polio included some 10,000 school children. There is nothing magical about either 10,000 or 25,000. The sad lesson of the *Literary Digest* public opinion poll of 1936 is that it is not the number of observations, but the selectivity of the observations that counts. By selecting for polling those whose names they found in telephone directories, the *Literary Digest* pollsters predicted a landslide for Landon. And well it might have been — if those who did not have telephones had stayed away from the polls! Public opinion polls today are conducted with a smaller number of people polled, but the selectivity of people asked is very precise. Should there be few or many observations? For Eddington's problem one observation was sufficient; for the *Literary Digest* poll hundreds of thousands were too few. The homogeneity of the subject matter, the importance of varying contexts, and the number of possible variations are all matters to be considered. Each critical thinker must decide whether the solution of his problem rests upon one or many observations. There are no rules.

4. *New perspectives in observation*

If man had relied solely upon his unaided sense organs to observe his world, he would never have developed the knowledge of the world he now has. Instruments of observation such as the telescope and microscope were designed to assist man to see great distances and to see smaller objects than the normal human eye can see. Stethoscope, telephone, and radio extend the human ear. Sometimes that which was designed for another purpose also gives unexpected observational extensions. The airplane, for example, was not designed chiefly for the extension of the eye, yet by means of aerial photography the sites of medieval castles have been discovered in England, heretofore unknown ancient cities have been located in Italy, oval craters in South Carolina, and serpentine mounds in Ohio. The airplane has also opened up new vistas of aesthetic value, as anyone will testify who has witnessed a sunrise from above the clouds.

These new perspectives in observation have not always been received with enthusiasm — even by the scientists. The professors of natural philosophy at Florence and Padua refused to look through Galileo's telescope. Churchmen warned Galileo not to investigate the heavens, for it was the throne of God. Galileo wrote on one occasion to his friend Kepler: "What would you say of the leading philosophers here to whom I have offered a thousand times of my own accord to show my studies, but who, with the lazy obstinacy of a serpent who has eaten his full, have never consented to look at the planets, or moon, or telescope? Verily, just as serpents close their ears, so do men close their eyes to the light of truth. To such people philosophy is a kind of book, like the Aeneid or the Odyssey, where the truth is to be sought, not in the universe or in nature, but (I use their own words) by comparing texts!"

The microscope did not arouse opposition, for it was regarded as a toy and source of amusement. When Anthony van Leeuwenhoek discovered "little animals observed in rain, well, sea, and snow water" in 1676, his discoveries were regarded as useless — and so, as unharmful. The Church did not regard observations of the microcosmos to have the theological implications that observations of the macrocosmos did. God was associated more with the stars and planets than with drops of water.

Lest we smugly suppose that in our enlightened times we have learned to accept new instruments of observation and new perspectives, we might look at the history of parapsychology. In 1882 the Society for Psychical Research was established in England for the scientific examination of reported cases of presences, witches, seances, and other phenomena claimed to transcend the usual forms of sense and communication. In 1884 the American Society for Psychical Research was founded. William James joined the society, much to the disgust of many of his friends and colleagues. In 1927 research began in parapsychology in the Department of Psychology at Duke University. The research was primarily in extrasensory perception (usually called ESP) to determine if there are some persons who can consistently manifest telepathic abilities beyond that which might be accounted for by chance. By 1934 the work at Duke University under Rhine had touched off a wave of criticism among professional psychologists. The first attack was on the correctness of Rhine's statistical methods, but many of these criticisms came to an end when the Institute of Mathematical Statistics in 1937 approved the methods used. In 1938 the American Psychological Association scheduled a symposium on ESP. Three types of criticism were raised: (1) some criticized Rhine's mathematical and statistical methods, (2) some the experimental methods, and (3) some the approach and conclusion of the research. In that same year questionnaires were sent to 603 members of the American Psychological Association asking each psychologist to answer a number of questions about ESP research. There were 352 replies; 76 per cent of those who replied said that parapsychology belonged in academic psychology. The year before (1937) the *Journal of Parapsychology* began quarterly publication, and in 1957 the American Parapsychological Association was founded. Thus parapsychology, with journal and association, finally entered the ranks of approved approaches to man and his world!

Another perspective in observation which is very ancient, and which is now being revived, is the use of drugs to enhance man's powers of sensing. The Indo-Aryans who moved into Iran and India in the second millennium B.C. made a drink from a plant called soma or haoma which seemed to intensify man's sensations. "We have drunk Soma and become immortal" sang a poet of the *Rig Veda*. In various cultures opium, hashish, marijuana, ether, nitrous oxide, alcohol, and tobacco have been used to enlarge man's normal powers of seeing, hearing, tasting, touching, and smelling. Medieval mystics sometimes experimented with drugs to stimulate the mystic experience, although usually with little encouragement from the Church. Recently among Western intellectuals there has been new interest in the use which the Indians of Mexico and southwestern United States have made of the root peyote or peyotl. The drug mescalin has been discovered to be the active ingredient in the root. Some claim that when the drug mescalin is properly administered, the result is more potent than any known drug in changing the quality of consciousness. Furthermore, it has no disagreeable aftermath. Aldous Huxley reports that while under the effect of mescalin he was obsessed with the beauty of the form of the crease in his trousers.[6] R. C. Zaehner saw stained glass windows in a cathedral at the University of Oxford as expanding and contracting rhythmically.[7] Harry Asher saw a spectrum down the edge of a factory chimney.[8] Two additional drugs have now been added to the psychedelic ("mind-manifesting") substances: lysergic acid (usually called LSD) and psilocybin. Some research is now being conducted in the alteration and expansion of consciousness in psychological laboratories in a few American universities, but most of this research has had little publicity, since it is as yet looked at askance by university administrators and the general public. Nevertheless, the inevitable organizing of new ideas is underway! The organization fostering such research is called The International Federation for Internal Freedom; and the journal is

[6] *The Doors of Perception* (London: Chatto and Windus, 1954).
[7] *Mysticism, Sacred and Profane* (New York: Oxford University Press, A Galaxy Book, 1961), pp. 212–226.
[8] "They Split My Personality," *Saturday Review*, June 1, 1963, pp. 39–43.

The Psychedelic Review. Thus far the psychedelic substances have enhanced religious and aesthetic experiences. Someday these substances may be used to assist in the invention of scientific hypotheses. But for the present they are controversial ways of increasing the range of human observations.

Perhaps the most amazing new instrument for achieving new perspectives in observation is the radio telescope which collects radio waves from distant heavenly bodies rather than the light which is collected by the regular telescope. Only a few years ago astronomers were predicting that with the largest telescopes man was going to push one billion light years into space; but the radio telescope, which has been developed since World War II, has already studied galaxies seven billion light-years distant from the earth, which means that man is now recording observations of galaxies so far away that a beam of light from these galaxies reaching us today left the galaxies before the planet Earth was formed! When such thinking causes us to ask what is the significance of man in the midst of the universe, we need to remember that it is man who makes the instruments to aid his own observations, and it is man who interprets his augmented observations.

13

Controlling Observations

Descartes begins his Third Meditation with these words: "I will now close my eyes, I will stop my ears, I will turn away my senses from their objects, I will even efface from my consciousness all the images of corporeal things; or at least, because this can hardly be accomplished, I will consider them as empty and false; and thus, holding converse only with myself, and closely examining my nature, I will endeavour to obtain by degrees a more intimate and familiar knowledge of myself." Recently in a Canadian university a young man also closed his eyes, stopped his ears, and turned his senses from objects that he might have a better knowledge of himself. But the similarity ends there. Descartes, pursuing a deductive method, sought to cut himself from all external stimuli in order that he might through clear and distinct ideas establish his own existence and nature. The Canadian university student was the subject of an experiment to see what happens when a person lives in a dark, silent chamber for several days. Descartes stood on the threshold between the Age of Scholasticism and the Age of Experimental Science; his meditation cannot be termed the record of an experiment. He was introducing a change into his usual behavior, which is a *sine qua non* of an experiment, but his entire approach was in the context of rationalism. Descartes might be described as one who was examining a hypothesis; he was not testing a hypothesis. In the words of Diderot, the editor of the French *Encyclopédie*, there are "two kinds of science, experimental and rational. The one has its eyes bandaged, proceeds feeling its way, seizes everything that falls into its hands, and at last finds precious things and seeks to form from them a torch. . . . Experiment infinitely multiplies its movements; it is always in action; it sets about seeking phenomena all the while that reason looks for analogies. Experimental science knows neither what will come nor what will not come of its work, but it never ceases working."

1. *The nature of experiment*

This chapter is about experiments, the other half of the testing of hypotheses. It might have been titled "Experimental Testing of Hypotheses," but the selected title reminds us of the close relation between sheer observations and controlled observations. Perhaps observations can be classified into the natural and the artificial. Natural observations are those man makes of objects which he finds and which he observes without introducing any change into the objects. No matter how much he extends and refines his instruments of observation, if no change is introduced into the observed objects, the observations remain natural. Artificial observations are those in which the observer has introduced something into the object, or placed the object in a different environment, or in any way made a change in the object. This is an experiment. There can be observations that are not experiments, but there cannot be experiments in the absence of observations. Ronald A. Fisher of the University of Cambridge distinguishes observations and experimental observations, and defines the latter thus: "Experimental observations are only experience carefully planned in advance, and designed to form a secure basis of knowledge; that is, they are systematically related to the body of knowledge already acquired, and the results are deliberately observed, and put on record accurately."[1]

According to John Stuart Mill the "first and most obvious distinction between Observation and Experiment is, that the latter is an immense extension of the former."[2] Mill goes on to say that experiment has two advantages over observation. One is that experiment enables man to produce a greater number of variations than nature offers, and in addition to produce the precise sorts of variations which he may want. For example, adds Mill, if we wished to find which element of the atmosphere is necessary to sustain life, we could experiment by putting animals in an artificial environment which contains only one of the elements. The second advantage is that we can produce a phenomenon artificially, or as Mill says, "We can take it, as it were, home with us, and observe it in the midst of circumstances with which in all other respects we are accurately ac-

[1] *The Design of Experiments*, fifth edition (New York: Hafner Publishing Company, 1949), p. 8.
[2] *A System of Logic*, Bk. III, Chap. 7, Sec. 3.

quainted." If scientists today had to depend upon nature's lightning in order to do research in electricity, as did Benjamin Franklin, there would be very limited research in electricity! Mill attempts to describe a situation in which observation is to be preferred to experiment, but he is not very convincing.[3] He contends that in those cases in which we wish to establish the cause of known effects, and we have no suspicion of the cause, we are forced to observe instances in which the effect has appeared and compare them with observed instances in which the effect has not appeared, until we discover what is the cause. His example is the quest for the cause of the blackening of chloride of silver. However, it seems unlikely that scientists facing this problem would not set up a number of experiments including that of both exposing and not exposing the substance to light.

An experiment is a question addressed to nature. It is a problem contrived to force nature's hand. When man depends solely on the observance of occurrences in nature, too many factors contribute to the production of the events to be singled out as contributing causes. An experiment is a means of singling out the contributing factors. When man is able, through his manipulating of nature's activities, to see one factor at work isolated from the others, he gains a better idea of how nature works without his interference.

Experimentalism is usually thought to have been the innovation in seventeenth-century Europe which turned the tide from mathematical rationalism and scholastic authoritarianism and launched man into the scientific revolution of the nineteenth century. The new ideal of science was called empiricism, or positivism, or phenomenalism, depending upon whether one emphasized the methods or the objects of the quest for new understanding of man and his world. Between the death of Aristotle in 322 B.C. and the rise of modern experimental science in the seventeenth century, a great tragedy in human intellectual history had taken place. The experiential approach to the natural world had been prostituted into an authoritarian approach with Aristotle as the final authority. Aristotle's method of study was to begin with the commonly accepted and observed features of the object of study and advance to what is "more knowable by nature." While dissection and observation had been his usual method of studying flora and fauna, he seems on occasion to have engaged in simple experiments: he cut insects and animals in two to see if they would continue to live,[4] and he may have cut out the eyes of young swallows to see if they could regain their sight.[5] In his writings on methodology he

[3] *Ibid.*, Bk. III, Chap. 7, Sec. 4.
[4] *On Breathing*, 479 a 2–7.
[5] *On the Generation of Animals*, 774 b 31–33.

discussed the use of methods later to be identified by Mill.[6] Sometimes even his words are remarkably similar to those used two thousand years later by Mill; for example, Aristotle says the following about what Mill was to call the Joint Method of Agreement and Difference: "For instance, when investigating the external marks of courage, we ought to collect all brave animals, and then to inquire what sort of affections are natural to all of them but absent in all other animals. For if we were to select this or that as the signs of courage in the animals chosen in such a way as not to exclude the possibility of the presence in all these animals of some other mental affection, we should not be able to tell whether our selected marks were really signs of courage or of this other character."[7] Yet he who held that only "observed facts" are the final authority, and who, according to Plutarch, "gave up some of the opinions that formerly satisfied [him] without fuss or chagrin and even with pleasure,"[8] became "the master of them who know." Not only did men treat the writings of Aristotle as final authorities about the natural world, but they also contended that if Aristotle did not know, men would never know. One group of monks, finding that Aristotle neglected to state how many teeth there are in a horse's mouth, noted the fact in the ledger of their monastery and added that until God deemed it wise to reveal this information to man, man must remain ignorant of the number of teeth in a horse's mouth! Seventeenth-century scientists such as Bacon, Galileo, Descartes, Newton, and Boyle recognized the need for experimentation and prepared the way, either by precept or example, for the revolution of thought soon to come.

An experiment has three essential characteristics: (1) an induced change, (2) a measurable variable, and (3) repeatability. The first characteristic is a modification of either the object studied, or of its environment, or of both. Mill says it is "the very nature of an experiment to introduce into the pre-existing state of circumstances a change perfectly definite."[9] The environment might be changed in temperature, moisture, luminosity, chemical content, geographical location, altitude, etc. The object upon which the experiment is performed might be modified by blocking a sense organ, injecting a serum, adding a chemical, changing some characteristic, etc. Sciences differ in the degree to which experimentation is possible; astronomy is a science in which the method of study must be chiefly

[6] See W. M. Dickie, "Anticipation in Aristotle of the Four Experimental Methods," *The Philosophical Review*, Vol. 32, No. 2, 1923, pp. 401–409.
[7] *Physiognomy*, 805 b 31–806 a 4.
[8] *De Virtute Morali*, C. 7.
[9] *Op. cit.*, Bk. III, Chap. 8, Sec. 3.

observation, whereas zoology and chemistry are chiefly experimental sciences.

Secondly, an experiment must have a variable that can be measured. The variable is that aspect of the experiment, either in the object or in the environment, which can be altered while everything else remains reasonably fixed. A florist who is having difficulty raising a certain species of flower will try some plants with varying degrees of moisture, some with varying amounts of fertilizer, some with varying temperatures, etc. In these plants in which he varies the moisture, he keeps all other factors constant.

Thirdly, an experiment is repeatable. All experiments must be open to the public test, that is, experiments must be such that anyone qualified by information and apparatus should be able to duplicate the operations of the experiment and achieve the same results. Any scientist who would contend that his experiment will work only for experimenters of a certain race, or who holds that his experiment is so esoteric that it cannot be repeated by anyone other than himself, would obviously have made himself ridiculous. Experiments are exoteric. They are always open to repeated testing by anyone.

There is such an entity as an uncontrolled experiment, although the title may be misleading. Sometimes without anyone's planning there may occur a series of events which, when reflected upon after they have taken place, do have the characteristics of an experiment. They would have been an experiment, if they had been planned, but they were not planned. Thalidomide, a tranquilizer, has been discovered to cause malformation of fetuses during early pregnancies, but only after obstetricians began to reflect on what might be the cause of many grotesque malformations of babies at birth. In West Germany alone within a few months over 3000 babies were dead shortly after birth and another 3000 seriously malformed but living. What had happened might be described as an experiment, but obviously no one planned this experiment. Humanitarian concerns would have dictated that such an experiment be first tried on subhuman mammals.

2. Kinds of experiments

Before examining John Stuart Mill's classification of the kinds of experiments, we shall consider three special functions of experiments. Two of these may be called *preliminary experiments*; the third is the *crucial experiment*. Sometimes before conducting the main experiment, for reasons of cost, or time, or effort, a series of preliminary experiments may be advisable. One type of preliminary experiment is the *pilot experiment*. It is a small-scale experiment conducted under limited conditions to see if a full-scale experiment is warranted. A florist, for example, who suspects that his azaleas need more acid in the soil, will experiment first with a few azaleas to determine their reaction to the addition of acid, rather than adding acid to the soil of all the azaleas in his greenhouse. An airplane factory will carry out a series of extensive experiments with small model planes in a wind tunnel before building a full-size plane of a new design. A department store chain will try a new arrangement of display in one of their stores before ordering the new arrangement in all their stores. Mice and dogs were sent into orbit around the earth before a man was launched in a space capsule.

A second form of preliminary experiment is the *screening experiment*. This is a test to determine which of many possible subjects warrant a full-fledged experiment. Rhine at Duke University has discovered that only one person out of every 125 shows sufficient evidence of psi (mental telepathy) to justify the hundreds and hundreds of hours that must be spent in experiments with each person. Therefore, he screens his candidates to eliminate the 124 out of each 125 with whom it would be unprofitable to work.

The third functional type of experiment is the *crucial experiment*. We have already noted a crucial observation: Eddington's observation of the eclipse of the sun which supported Einstein's prediction that light beams bend in gravitational fields. A crucial experiment serves the same function. A good example is that of Foucault who in 1850 established by experiment that light moves with less speed in water than in air, thus refuting the corpuscular theory of light and causing the wave theory to be generally accepted.

Mill distinguishes four types of experiments in his *A System of Logic* (1843) which he believes to be "the only possible modes of experimental inquiry — of direct induction *a posteriori*, as distinguished from deduction."[11] He regarded his methods as fulfilling the hopes of Francis Bacon for a method of acquiring knowledge which "leaves but little to the acuteness and strength of wits." If Bacon thought of himself as the John the Baptist of experimental science — as we have suggested — Mill thought of himself as the messiah! How more definitely could a logician say "I came not to destroy, but to fulfill" than this from the opening page of his preface to the first edition: "This book makes no pretence of giving to the world a new theory of the intellectual operations. Its claim to attention, if it possess any, is grounded on the fact that it is an attempt

[11] Bk. III, Chap. 8, Sec. 7.

not to supersede, but to embody and systematise, the best ideas which have been either promulgated on its subject by speculative writers, or conformed to by accurate thinkers in their scientific inquiries."

Mill thinks that his methods are both methods of discovery and methods of proof. Today logicians regard these methods as methods for the identification of a satisfactory hypothesis by eliminating unsatisfactory hypotheses. He makes two general assumptions. One is the "Law of Universal Causation" which is the assumption that everything that happens in this world is caused; there are no uncaused, or chance, events. The second assumption is an extension of the first: the natural world is so homogeneous that the same causal relationship holds throughout. This he calls the "Uniformity of Nature." Some logicians have criticized the notion of the uniformity of nature because it is a notion which cannot be proved without assuming that which one is trying to prove. But that is just what is meant by calling it an assumption. Mill correctly realizes that without the notion of universal order there can be no testing of hypotheses. The question of whether there is complete and uniform causality throughout the natural world is itself an assumption whose confirmation depends upon the fruitfulness it exhibits when action is based upon it. Attempts to establish universal causality or the uniformity of nature by rational or empirical means reveal a misunderstanding of their nature in the methodological system. This Mill understood.

The first of Mill's methods is called the Method of Agreement. Mill states it in this fashion: "If two or more instances of the phenomenon under investigation have only one circumstance in common, the circumstance in which alone all the instances agree is the cause (or effect) of the given phenomenon."[12] Consider as an example that three people have become seriously ill with the same symptoms. The physician in charge suspects that the illness has been caused by some form of liquid. This is the hypothesis to be tested. The county health official and the local physician question the patients about what they have been drinking in the last two weeks. If they can establish that all three have drunk at the town pump whereas only one or two of the patients have drunk from Jones Dairy, Smith Dairy, the local soft drink shop, and Hank's Bar, then according to the Method of Agreement the cause of the illness is the water from the town pump.

The second method is the Method of Difference: "If an instance in which the phenomenon under investigation occurs, and an instance in

---

[12] This and all the following quotations from Mill are from *A System of Logic*, Bk. III, Chap. 8.

which it does not occur, have every circumstance in common save one, that one occurring only in the former; the circumstance in which alone the two instances differ is the effect, or the cause, or an indispensable part of the cause, of the phenomenon." This method was used in the early testing of the Salk vaccine for poliomyelitis. One year thousands of children in a selected grade in the public schools were given injections of the vaccine, but in each classroom half of the children were given the vaccine and half were given an injection of distilled water. No parent knew whether his child had received the real vaccine or the water. The recorded poliomyelitis cases among this group in the following year were studied to determine if there were fewer cases and milder cases among those who had the genuine Salk vaccine.

The third method is the Method of Residues: "Subduct from any phenomenon such part as is known by previous inductions to be the effect of certain antecedents, and the residue of the phenomenon is the effect of the remaining antecedents." The planet Neptune was discovered by Adams and Leverrier by the use of this method. They concluded that only another planet at a certain location and of a certain size could account for the variation between the calculated positions of the planet Uranus and the observed positions of Uranus. When telescopes were turned to the designated portion of the sky, the planet was observed.

The fourth method is the Method of Concomitant Variations: "Whatever phenomenon varies in any manner whenever another phenomenon varies in some particular manner, is either a cause or an effect of that phenomenon, or is connected with it through some fact of causation." A woman who thinks that perhaps her breakfast tomato juice has been causing an itching rash on her arms may cut the size of her glass to half and observe if that decreases the rash, or she may take more juice and observe if that increases the rash.

These are the four methods. Now we can examine them briefly. First of all, they do cover the basic forms of experiments. Any experiment in the sciences or in the problems of everyday life will fit into one of these four types of experiments, or into some combination of them. Each has its individual virtues and difficulties. Agreement and Residues are not as experimental as Difference and Concomitant Variations. Agreement is primarily a method of observation, or in Mill's words, "the method of investigation on those subjects where artificial experimentation is impossible." Mill recognized how rarely we find two or more instances of a phenomenon that are unlike save in one respect. Another difficulty in the Method of Agreement is that there is the possibility of several causes of the phenomenon. In our example of the three men with the serious illness, the hypothesis was that their illnesses were due to something they had drunk, and there was the possibility that the milk from *both* dairies as well as water from the town pump were causes. On the Method of Agreement the dairies were exonerated because not all the men had drunk milk from any one dairy, but perhaps the illness was caused by milk whether from the Smith dairy or the Jones dairy. There is also the possibility of a secondary common feature being selected and the primary common feature being neglected; the drunkard who blames water for his hangovers because he drinks gin and water on Monday nights, scotch and water on Tuesday nights, rum and water on Wednesday nights, rye and water on Thursday nights, vodka and water on Friday nights, bourbon and water on Saturday nights, and brandy and water on Sunday nights is an excellent example of this fallacious identification of a common, although innocent, factor! Because of these limitations of the Method of Agreement, Mill recommends the use of both Agreement and Difference. The former, he says, may lead only to uniformities which suggest applications to the Method of Difference. This method, which he calls "the Indirect Method of Difference, or the Joint Method of Agreement and Difference," is stated as follows: "If two or more instances in which the phenomenon occurs have only one circumstance in common, while two or more instances in which it does not occur have nothing in common save the absence of that circumstance, the circumstance in which alone the two sets of instances differ is the effect, or the cause, or an indispensable part of the cause, of the phenomenon."

Mill is especially enthusiastic about the Method of Difference; when he turns from Agreement to Difference he says, ". . . we proceed to a still more potent instrument of the investigation of nature." Usually in order to have a situation in which two or more instances are precisely alike save for the presence or the absence of one item man has to enter and bring about the change. Difference is clearly a method of experiment. A woman bakes one batch of cookies with cinnamon, and one batch without cinnamon; but are the two batches *exactly alike* otherwise? Strictly speaking, no two things in the world are exactly alike. Induction in many ways has to be satisfied with probabilities.

Mill is apologetic about the Method of Residues, for he recognizes that it is primarily a deductive method: ". . . the Method of Residues . . . is not independent of deduction; though, as it also requires specific experience, it may, without impropriety, be included among methods of direct observation and experiment." It is a rational, rather than an empirical, method, but it subducts on the grounds of previous observations and experiments. There is, however, a tremendous merit in listing this method among the more experimental methods, for it clearly reveals the eliminative function of all the methods. The methods are not ways of discovering causes, as Mill believed them to be; rather they are methods of eliminating hypotheses. Assuming that the satisfactory hypothesis is listed among the hypotheses to be tested, the satisfactory one will be disclosed as the unsatisfactory ones are eliminated. But if the satisfactory hypothesis is not listed among those to be tested, then the four methods are of little use. In our first example, if the illness was food poisoning caused by tainted meat, the methods would not discover the real cause until it was listed as one of the hypotheses.

The Method of Concomitant Variations, like the Method of Difference, is experimental. This is a quantitative method, and as such is distinguished from the other three. It requires that the cause be one that can be quantitatively varied and quantitatively measured. It also has the advantage of being more nearly a method of discovery than any of the other four. If one did not know what was the cause of his allergic condition, he could start almost blindly by increasing or decreasing foods, drinks, exposure to sun, cosmetics, etc. But there is always the chance that two entities may show concomitant variations, yet have no impact upon each other. A remarkable correlation might be established between the rainfall of New York City and the death rate in China!

Mill's four methods, as we have said before, are ways to eliminate hypotheses. If we have three hypotheses (A, B, C) to account for a certain phenomenon (P), we are to take the hypotheses one by one and try to eliminate them by showing instances of P when A is not present, by showing A is present when P is absent as well as when P is present, by showing a quantitative variation of A is not paralleled with a quantitative variation of P, and by showing P can be accounted for without the presence of A. Then we put hypotheses B and C through the same testing. If all but one of the three is eliminated, then that one is presumably the cause of P; but if all three are eliminated, then we know that the satisfactory hypothesis will have to be found elsewhere. Mill would have made a greater impact on modern scientific thought if he had presented his methods as eliminative techniques rather than as ways to discover and to prove cause-effect relationships.

3. *Problems of induction*

If there is a "seductive fallacy" in critical thinking, it is the temptation to make induction into a form of deduction, to claim for induction the logical certitude found in deduction. Both Bacon and Mill believed that induction was a method of demonstrative proof. Both aimed to extend deductive thinking to make logic both inductive and deductive, but what they did was to turn induction into deduction. Mill correctly pointed out that the so-called "perfect induction" is really deduction. (Perfect induction is that form of reasoning which proceeds by enumerating a finite number of objects and reaches a conclusion about each of the objects, for example, "There are fifty chairs in this room; chair 1 is brown, chair 2 is brown, chair 3 is brown, ... chair 50 is brown; therefore all the chairs in this room are brown.") Mill argued that perfect induction is deduction, since the conclusion is forced by the premises, and nothing is added in the conclusion that is not found in the premises; yet Mill did not see that his own analysis of induction turned induction to deduction because of the certainty of the conclusion which he demanded of all induction. Mill thought that when a hypothesis is established *via* his methods, the hypothesis is no longer a hypothesis — it is an established truth. But scientific hypotheses are not demonstrated as the Pythagorean theorem is demonstrated. In deduction Q.E.D. (what was to be demonstrated) may be added to the conclusion; in induction only U.F.N. (until further notice) may be added! A deductive conclusion cannot be made more certain than it is; absolute certainty cannot be made more certain! An inductive conclusion is never so certain that it cannot be made more certain. The principle of induction is not the attainment of valid conclusions inferred from premises with logical certitude, rather it is the increasing of the probable truth of the conclusion. Hume was the first Western philosopher to understand clearly that inductive conclusions are always probable and never certain, but because he had nothing constructive to offer, many scientists and philosophers were slow to recognize the significance of Hume's observations on induction. Mill, on the other hand, offered so much that was constructive, although misleading! He held that the assumption of the uniformity of nature was the unstated major premise of all his four methods of experimental inquiry. The very language — "major premise" — inclined Mill to affirm that the conclusion reached by his methods was a valid, i.e., forced, conclusion.

If there is doubt about the distinction between induction and deduction, one clear basis of difference lies in the fact that while it is nonsense to affirm the premises and deny the conclusion in deduction, this is the heart of induction. Induction, in other words, is a form of reasoning in which the conclusion is never forced. It is always probable. An inductive conclusion lies between logical impossibility (e.g., A is greater than B; B is greater than C; therefore C is greater than A) and logical necessity (e.g.,

A is greater than *B*; *B* is greater than *C*; therefore *A* is greater than *C*). In other words, an inductive conclusion is never absolutely certain; it is always probably true — and probably false. Hume thought that the probability of the truth of an inductive conclusion was a psychological probability. The subjective element in induction cannot be eliminated, but to rest inductive conclusion on psychological probability alone would throw us back into the relativism of Protagoras who declared that each man is the measure of all things. Some logicians in reaction against the psychological interpretation of inductive probability have attempted to interpret this probability in some form of mathematical or statistical probability. Mathematical probability plays an important role in inductive procedures. For example, it is needed to show the percentage possibility of chance in inductive sampling. But it is a misunderstanding of the nature of the probability of inductive conclusions to examine them in the framework of mathematical probability alone. Some form of the truth-frequency interpretation of probability is needed to deal adequately with the probability of inductive conclusions. Truth-frequency refers to the ratio of true statements to all the statements of a class examined, if the class is finite, or to all the statements of the same type in the long run, if the class is infinite. This is as far as we ought to go in discussing probability in an elementary volume on critical thinking.

A second problem of induction is the problem of sampling. Except in the case of perfect induction — which we have said is not induction anyway — inductive thinking moves from a sample of a population to the population as a whole, from particulars to generals, from some to all. As we have seen, all induction commits the fallacy of overgeneralization. The data is always inadequate in the sense that the conclusion goes beyond the evidence. So one of the central problems of induction is the problem of getting a fair random sample. For example, if the trustees of a university wished to know what would be the reaction to the hiring of a dedicated Communist to teach in the Department of History, how should they sample the opinion of students, faculty, alumni, and townsmen? If they ask people to write their opinions, that would get only the opinions of those who were extremely for or extremely against the hiring. Should they contact only student and civic leaders? Should they ask for the opinion of every tenth person met on campus and street in a two-week period? Should they send a questionnaire to people whose names appear on the pages of the telephone directory? How about getting the opinion of one group of women (e.g., Daughters of the American Revolution) and one group of men (e.g., Rotary Club)?

A third problem about induction is the problem of establishing induction as a valid method for the testing of hypotheses. The efforts to prove induction are quite unsuccessful, because inductive principles must be assumed in order to establish induction itself. Consider the folly of trying to prove that man learns from generalizations by generalizing from instances of man's learning from generalizations! Induction as a way of testing hypotheses can only be shown to be dependable by the pragmatic test of putting it into operation. In the working is the proof. Any proof more certain than this is impossible. The maxim "Life is more than logic" has meaning if it means that the problems to which man addresses himself need to be solved in part by procedures whose only justification is in terms of the success with which the problems are settled. The principle of induction has been stated by one philosopher of science as follows: "Seek to achieve a maximum of order by logical operations upon elementary propositions. Generalize this order (whatever its form be: causal, statistical or other), with a minimum of arbitrariness, that is, according to the principle of simplicity."[13] The phrase "with a minimum of arbitrariness" beautifully suggests the relativism, subjectivity, and probability implicit in induction.

If induction is so hedged with uncertainties, why don't we combine induction and deduction? That is exactly what we have been doing in this volume. Deduction needs induction to supply reliable premises; and induction needs deduction to show the implication of assumptions, hypotheses, and conclusions. Deduction is a recipe for pheasant-under-glass which begins with "First shoot a fat wild cock." Induction is the method for shooting the pheasant.

Einstein was a great scientist for many reasons; perhaps one of his outstanding claims to greatness was the way in which he combined in his own work the inductive and the deductive procedures. Although many of his contributions to twentieth-century physics were the result of his marvelous powers of rational thinking, his speculations were never far removed from the laboratory. The dual role of induction — it may verify hypotheses with increasing degrees of probability without ever reaching certainty, and it may in one crucial experiment disprove a deductive conclusion — was once described by Einstein in one pregnant statement: "No amount of experimentation can ever prove me right; a simple experiment may at any time prove me wrong."

[13] Herbert Feigl, "The Logical Character of the Principle of Induction," *Philosophy of Science*, Vol. I, No. I, January 1934, p. 28.

EXERCISES

Sampling

Directions: Describe a technique for securing a good random sample in order to establish by induction each of the following statements:

1. "The books on my shelves average between 400 and 500 pages each."
2. "The family that prays together, stays together."
3. "Zingo gets your clothes 35 per cent cleaner than any other soap."
4. "The eggs in this truck load of eggs are fresh eggs."
5. "The taxpayers in my district do not cheat on their real estate taxes."
6. "Television does not influence the reading habits of children."
7. "The English are slow to see a joke."
8. "It's not the heat, it's the humidity that gives people headaches in hot weather."
9. "The grass seed from that dealer is free from weed seed."
10. "Hens lay more eggs when lights are turned on at 3 A.M."
11. "Stocks and bonds rose in this morning's trading."
12. "Most of the students in our dorm like cream in their coffee."
13. "Only the blue gills are biting in the lake today."
14. "The average temperature of the water in the oceans of the world is below 70 degrees F."
15. "Gentlemen prefer blondes."

Application of Mill's Methods

Directions: Apply two or more of Mill's Methods of Experimental Inquiry to test each of the following hypotheses:

1. A man thinks that a certain brand of fertilizer will improve the grass on his lawn.
2. A college student wonders if a quick review of the lesson for the day just fifteen minutes before class will help him improve the quality of his work.
3. A paint company believes that its new paint will be more resistant to light than any of its previous paints or any of the paints of its competitors.
4. A dentist contends that soft drinks cause tooth decay. The local soft drink dealer does not believe this.
5. A young man who has been unsuccessful in winning the love of a young lady speculates that flowers will accomplish what he has thus far been unable to accomplish.
6. The city council wishes to improve the movement of foot traffic and automobile traffic at a busy corner. One of the members argues that a light

which will allow people to move in any direction while cars from all four directions are stopped will be safer and will move traffic quicker than the old system of stop-go lights.

7. A college chaplain is convinced that purple lights and soft music are the best ways to dispel homesickness in the student body.

8. A contractor wishes to use aluminum rather than fiberglass as insulation in a new home. He wants to establish by test that the aluminum is better.

9. "A lemon a day keeps the colds away," says a food faddist.

10. "Wars stimulate the arts," claims a militarist.

Identification of Mill's Methods

Directions: Which of Mill's methods is illustrated in each of the following?

1. A housewife buys several different brands of butter. They vary in size, color, and shape. She puts some of each brand in the pantry, some of each brand in the cupboard, and some of each brand on the kitchen table. Within a few hours all the butter is soft. Since it is an August day, she decides that heat is the cause of the melting of the butter, rather than differences in brand, size, color, and shape.

2. To make sure that it is heat that caused the butter to melt, she cuts two pieces of butter from the same pound, and puts one piece on the table, the other piece in the refrigerator.

3. Still not satisfied, she leaves a piece of butter on the table all night. She discovers that during the cool night the butter stayed firm, but the next day as the temperature rises the butter becomes softer and softer.

4. During the afternoon our housewife bakes a pan of rolls. After the rolls are baked, she finds that they do not come out of the pan easily. She checks the ingredients: flour, sugar, salt, water, yeast, butter. She knows she put in the proper amounts of the first five ingredients, and she knows they could not cause the rolls to behave in this improper manner. But the butter — now she recalls that she forgot to butter the pan. She decides that it is the absence of the butter which caused the rolls to stick.

5. A student gave up and went home from college because, as he said, "The harder I worked, the more poorly I recited in class."

6. The ice on the sidewalk melts in the sun. Lard melts in a hot skillet. Cast iron melts in the great heat of a foundry. Heat, therefore, is the cause of liquefaction.

7. Two pieces of iron are taken, of the same weight and shape. One is allowed to retain its ordinary temperature; the other is subjected to great heat. The former remains rigid; the latter becomes molten.

8. A woman contends that she can determine by the taste whether in making *café au lait* the coffee is added to the milk, or the milk is added to the coffee. Five cups are prepared in each manner. The ten cups are placed before her, and she is asked to identify how each cup was made.

9. If a coin and a feather are dropped at the same instant in the receiver of an air pump when the receiver is full of air, the coin falls more quickly. If, however, the air has been removed, they will reach the bottom together.

10. A man who wishes to keep an accurate account of his weight weighs himself each week on the same scales in the drugstore and in order to find his exact weight always subtracts five pounds for the weight of his clothes.

11. Johnny has discovered that the faster he pumps his bicycle the warmer he becomes, even though fast pumping makes him move more quickly through the cool air.

12. In the recent tests of the effectiveness of the Salk vaccine for poliomyelitis, half of the children who were vaccinated were given the real vaccine; half were given a harmless liquid.

13. Now there is some question about the amount of vaccine needed to give full protection from the disease. If a test is made by using various quantities of vaccine, that would be using which method?

14. If a man seeks to prove that a full beard is conducive to success in the military profession by pointing out that most of the generals in the Civil War wore full beards, what method would he be using?

15. Pliny the Elder disproved the claims of the astrologers as follows: "If a man's destiny is caused by the star under which he is born, then all men born under that star should have the same fortune. But masters and slaves, and kings and beggars are born under the same star at the same time."

16. A nurseryman suspected that the fertilizer he was using was causing his plants to turn brown. Therefore, the next season he used only half the usual amount of fertilizer.

17. The same nurseryman, desiring further to confirm his suspicion, used a different brand of fertilizer the next season.

18. A grocer who wished to measure two quarts of dry beans reasoned that by filling a five-quart measure with beans and by pouring from this measure into a three-quart measure he would have exactly two quarts left in the five-quart measure when the three-quart measure was filled.

19. Eijkman knew that beri-beri occurs much more among eaters of polished rice than among eaters of unpolished rice. He also knew that among chickens around a certain prison in Java, those who got their meals in the garden (eating unpolished rice) did not get beri-beri, while those kept inside and fed food given prisoners (which included polished rice) did get the disease. He began to suspect that polished rice was a cause of beri-beri.

20. Eijkman fed a group of chickens exclusively on polished rice. They all developed beri-beri and died. He fed another group of chickens unpolished rice. Not one of them got the disease.

21. Suppose he had performed another experiment in which he fed one group of chickens a mixture of one-fourth polished rice and three-fourths unpolished rice, and a second group he fed one-fourth unpolished rice and three-fourths polished rice.

22. An ancient Greek, upon being shown the offerings of sailors who had prayed to the goddess and been rescued from shipwreck, asked, "Where are the offerings of those who prayed and were lost at sea?"

23. A truck driver reasons that in order to determine the weight of his cargo he can weigh the loaded truck and subtract from this total weight the known weight of the truck.

24. A girl tries the effectiveness of a suntan lotion by using lotion and by using no lotion on alternate days of her vacation.

25. Scientists have tested the relation of coal tar and cancer by painting the ears of rabbits with coal tar, and then have watched the appearance of cancerous growths on the ears.

26. "The sutures in the skulls of young mammals have advanced as a beautiful adaptation for aiding parturition, and no doubt they facilitate, or may be indispensable for this act; but as sutures occur in the skulls of young birds and reptiles, which have only to escape from a broken egg, we may infer that this structure has arisen from the laws of growth, and has been taken advantage of in the parturition of the higher animals." (Darwin)

27. Hume states that "every simple idea has a simple impression, which resembles it, and every simple impression a correspondent idea." To support this statement, he says, "That the case is the same with all our simple impressions and ideas, it is impossible to prove by a particular enumeration of them. Everyone may satisfy himself in this point by running over as many as he pleases. But if anyone should deny this universal resemblance, I know no way of convincing him, but by desiring him to show a simple impression that has not a correspondent idea, or a simple idea that has not a correspondent impression."

Induction and Deduction

Directions: The following twenty characterizations are to be marked as follows:

It applies to *induction* but not to deduction.
It applies to *deduction* but not to induction.
It applies to *both* induction and deduction.
It applies to *neither* induction nor deduction.

1. May be defined as the process of following the network of relations which binds truths together.

2. Starts with sense experiences.

3. Gives results which are characterized by logical necessity.

4. Depends upon sensation.

5. Used by the social scientist.

6. May be defined as the process of transition from particular facts to a general knowledge about these facts.

7. For the most part it is the method of mathematics.

8. Does not depend upon sensation.
9. Claims to increase man's knowledge.
10. Starts with premises.
11. May be described as the method of making generalizations.
12. The complete method of the natural scientist.
13. For the most part it is the method of experimentation.
14. Gives results which are characterized by probability.
15. Emphasized by the rationalist.
16. An infallible way of gaining knowledge.
17. May be described as the method of drawing implications.
18. Used by the physical scientist.
19. Emphasized by the empiricist.
20. Can give true conclusion, even when it starts from false premises.

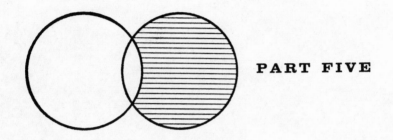

The Drawing
of Conclusions

PART FIVE

The Drawing
of Conclusions

14

Applying the Conclusion

1. *Statement of the conclusion*

The conclusion is the hypothesis which survives examination and testing. In all inductive procedures the selected hypothesis remains hypothetical in nature even though it be the conclusion. It is the best answer at the present time to the problem that generated the inquiry.

Sometimes the conclusion remains the same, although the problem radically changes. The huge, dusty mounds of brick and broken pottery near the village of Harappa were in 1856 the solution to engineer John Brunton's problem. John and his brother William were building a section of the East Indian Railway from Karachi to Lahore, and were in need of ballast for the bed of the railway. John found the remains near Harappa ideal for his purposes, but his plundering of the mounds was an archaeological catastrophe. In the 1920's the mutilated tell at Harappa and its twin at Mohenjo-daro were conclusions to a set of problems quite different from the Bruntons': Where is to be found the remains of the earliest penetrations of the Indo-Aryans into the Indian subcontinent? What can be found to give light on the life of the peoples of the Indian subcontinent two or three millennia B.C.? Can archaeological support be found for the earliest hymns of the *Rig Veda*? Harappa provided answers to these questions. What remained of Harappa is being carefully searched for each scrap of brick and pottery.

Sometimes the statement of the conclusion must be refined, not because a different problem is raised, but because an assumption is discovered to be false. Karl Marx assumed in his economic determination theory of history that human history moves through four stages before reaching the Utopia of the Classless Society: Primitive Communism, Slave Economy,

219

Feudalism, and Capitalism; and he also assumed that as a democratic revolution was needed to end Feudalism, so nothing less than a socialistic revolution would end Capitalism. The Manifesto of the Communistic Party (1848) declared: "The Communist revolution is the most radical rupture with traditional property relations; no wonder that its development involves the most radical rupture with traditional ideas.... the first step in the revolution by the working class is to raise the proletariat to the position of ruling class, to win the battle of democracy." Communism proposed to fulfill the broken promises of the French Revolution; its proponents assumed that the same revolutionary techniques would be required. In 1928 the Sixth Congress of the Communist International restated the Manifesto in application to what the Communists regarded as the imperialistic stage of Capitalism; but since the timetable of revolution had not been as anticipated, the Sixth Congress said, "... the international proletarian revolution cannot be conceived as a single event occurring simultaneously all over the world. At first socialism may be victorious in a few, or even in one single capitalistic country.... Like the feudal nobility of the past, the bourgeoisie cannot abandon its historical position to the new class without a desperate and frantic struggle." The unexpected events that took place in the economies of the leading capitalistic countries have necessitated a new conclusion in Communistic ideology. The revolution did not take place in England as Marx had predicted; and, even more surprising, in America tax reforms were instituted to equalize incomes, unemployment compensations were introduced, and the laboring man's situation was improved in every way; furthermore, the proletariat owned so many stocks and bonds that the distinction between bourgeoisie and proletariat became increasingly meaningless. The Russian leaders, not being able to revamp the conclusions of 1848 and 1928 to account for the evolutions in capitalistic countries, dropped an Iron Curtain in an effort to keep the Russian people ignorant of innovations in capitalistic lands. A new conclusion is now in the making; it may be a denial of the necessity of revolution. One of the straws in the wind is the opposition to revolutionary ideas in art. Ex-Premier Khrushchev expressed this new Puritanism, this anti-revolutionary Communism, in a visit to an exhibition of Soviet modern art in Moscow: "I would say this is just a mess.... I don't like jazz. When I hear jazz, it's as if I had gas on the stomach.... Or take these new dances which are so fashionable now. Some of them are completely improper.... We won't spare a kopeck of government money for any artistic daubing.... For the time being history has put us at the head of this state, and we have to answer for everything that goes on in it. Therefore we are going to maintain a strict policy in art."

Sometimes the statement of the conclusion can be improved by substituting terms whose connotations are more acceptable. For example, the ideas Darwin expressed in *The Descent of Man* were much more palatable when they appeared in Henry Drummond's book, *The Ascent of Man*. William James regretted that he had not named his essay "The Will to Believe" by the more acceptable title "The Right to Believe." Rudolf Bultmann, a New Testament scholar, argues for "the demythologizing of the New Testament." "Demythologizing" suggests the removal of myths from the New Testament, yet, as he has said, this is not his purpose: "whereas the older liberals used criticism to eliminate the mythology of the New Testament, our task today is to use criticism to interpret it."[1] Bultmann would probably get a better reception for his ideas — at least among laymen — were he to use a term less negative than "demythologizing."

2. Implications of the conclusion

Conclusions have implications relating them to other knowledge, to values, and to other problems. A conclusion may be consistent or inconsistent with current knowledge. Some conclusions may be of such a nature that they are not even consistent with themselves. A man who has had confidence in his fellow men shaken several times may exclaim in disgust, "All men are liars." But he, being a man, lies when he says "All men are liars"! A modern scientist has said, "It seems plain and self-evident, yet it needs to be said: the isolated knowledge obtained by a group of specialists in a narrow field has in itself no value whatsoever, but only in its synthesis with all the rest of knowledge."[2] Perhaps this statement should be refined, since fully isolated knowledge would not be knowledge at all. Knowledge involves connectedness. Isolated knowledge defies the imagination.

At the same time Whitehead believes that we ought to be concerned lest we discourage originality in thinking by insisting too rigorously on the relatedness and classification of knowledge: "Unless we are careful, we shall conventionalize knowledge. Our literary criticism will suppress initiative. Our historical criticism will conventionalize our ideas of the springs of human conduct. Our scientific systems will suppress all

[1] Rudolf Bultmann and others, *Kerygma and Myth* (New York: Harper and Brothers Torchbook, 1961), p. 12.

[2] Erwin Schrödinger, *Science and Humanism* (London: Cambridge University Press, 1951), p. 5.

ways of the universe which fall outside their abstractions. Our modes of testing ability will exclude all the youth whose ways of thought lie outside our conventions of learning. In such ways the universities, with their scheme of orthodoxies, will stifle the progress of the race, unless by some fortunate stirring of humanity they are in time remodeled or swept away."[3] Granted that there is always the danger of new orthodoxies arising in educational institutions, there does not seem much likelihood that another Michelson will soon declare that we have learned all we can about both our exterior and interior worlds. There is probably greater danger that logic with its rules may so mechanize a person's thought that he ceases to engage in adventurous critical thinking. This was what Heidegger had in mind when he said, "Reason, glorified for centuries, is the most obstinate adversary of thinking."

A second implication of conclusions is the implication with reference to values. We might suppose that once we have found a conclusion to a problem, all that remains is to apply the conclusion. But seldom are things that simple. Man is a valuer as well as a knower. A proposed conclusion might solve a given problem, but it may never be applied because it is in conflict with moral ideas, religious concepts, political commitments, national ideologies, etc. For example, the United States is faced with a surplus of farm stuff. A simple solution would be for the government to seize all farms, and then determine which land should be cultivated. But this solution is in complete violation of the constitutional right regarding private property. So we suggest another solution: Send all surplus food to starving peoples in other lands. This humanitarian ideal, unfortunately, runs into the most complicated problems of international balance of trade, economic agreements, each nation's internal politics, etc. Overpopulation and war are two world problems which must be settled — and they can be settled *on paper*! To hold down population, set up an International Committee on Births to determine who shall live and who shall not — assuming that birth is no claim on life. To end war destroy all instruments of warfare. But both these conclusions run into serious moral snags: the sacredness of human life, and the right of a people to defend itself.

A third dimension of implications of conclusions lies in the curious way in which the solving of one problem creates new problems. Insecticides kill the insects that spread disease and destroy crops, but insecticides also kill fish and birds. Airplanes are designed that fly faster than the speed of

---

[3] A. N. Whitehead, *Essays in Science and Philosophy* (New York: Philosophical Library, 1947), p. 26.

sound; and the boom caused by breaking the sound barrier becomes a problem to man and beast — two gazelles in the St. Louis Zoo became so startled one night by sonic booms that they killed themselves in an effort to escape. The Eighteenth Amendment made illegal the sale and consumption of alcoholic beverages — and created the bootlegger, the speakeasy, and the gin runner, and turned millions of moderate drinkers into lawbreakers. Consider in more detail an amazing problem growing from an equally amazing solution. While making plans for the sending of American astronauts into space, geneticists pointed out that there was the possibility that the ionizing radiation would so affect the men that any issue conceived after a trip into space might be seriously mutated. A solution to the problem came from a physiologist who proposed that there be established a sperm bank. Thus future children of the astronauts can be conceived by use of the frozen sperm from the bank. A professor of law now raises a very intriguing question. Assuming, as we certainly can without any stretching of the imagination, that a future astronaut is killed on a space flight, that his wife wishes to have a son by him, and that she is impregnated from his sperm after his death — what standing will this posthumously conceived child have under the inheritance laws now in force?[4] Thus, a fine solution to one problem raises a new and puzzling problem.

David Riesman argues that there is evolving, particularly in America, out of a background which he calls tradition-direction and inner-direction, a new social character which he calls other-direction, one in which conformity is insured by sensitization to the expectations and preferences of others. People in the other-directed society have material abundance and ample leisure, but, says Riesman, the solution of the problems of scarcity and work does not mean that Utopia has arrived: "They pay for these changes however — here, as always, the solution of old problems gives rise to new ones — by finding themselves in a centralized and bureaucratized society and a world shrunken and agitated by the contact — accelerated by industrialization — of races, nations, and cultures. . . . Increasingly, other people are the problem, not the material environment."[5]

Economics is a science in which solutions are changing the nature of the problems raised. Concepts such as money and labor have historically been framed in the context of the general scarcity of things, but today in

---

[4] See W. Barton Leach, "Perpetuities in the Atomic Age: The Sperm Bank and the Fertile Decendent" [sic], American Bar Association Journal, Vol. 48, No. 10, October 1962, pp. 942–944.
[5] The Lonely Crowd, abridged edition (New Haven and London: Yale University Press, 1961), p. 18.

leading industrial nations automation is solving problems of production, and as a result an economy of abundance displaces an economy of scarcity. Money ceases to be a symbol of scarce goods; millions of people become permanently unemployable; poverty mounts in an affluent economy! Radically new hypotheses are urgently needed, yet this is an area where, as in religion, critical thinking is handicapped by notions of orthodoxy and heterodoxy. For example, when economists suggest that the United States consider extending the social security system into a non-job income so that each citizen has a constitutional right to receive a fixed income from the government, cries of "creeping socialism," "incipient communism," "welfarism," and "parasitic paternalism" cloud the issue and the problem is almost lost in the maelstrom of charges and countercharges.

Nevertheless, man is coming to the conclusion in this twentieth century that social, economic, and political problems cannot be separated from each other, and also that no nation can any longer solve its problems within its own boundaries in blissful neglect of relationships to other nations. Future historians may decide that the greatest discovery of the twentieth century was not the Theory of Relativity, nor the Dead Sea Scrolls, nor space exploration, nor the decipherment of the genetic code, but the realization that man has reached a stage in his development in which all problems and all solutions have global implications. Scientific inventions, technological improvements, and social revolutions soon become international problems. The future of man is a race between man's ability to develop the techniques of his own destruction and his ability to develop a climate of opinion which looks at problem solving on a world-wide scale.

3. *Nature of the conclusion*

In the preceding chapters we have used the terms "conclusion" and "solution" interchangeably, although in many cases it is apparent that conclusion has been used to refer to a statement which is a verbal answer to a problem, while solution has been used to refer to an active answer to a problem. A man may *conclude* that he will vote for the Democratic candidate for President, but if he does not actually vote on Election Day, he has not *solved* his problem. However, there is a more generic meaning of the term "conclusion" which we shall examine here. The conclusion to a problem is any means by which the problem ceases to be a problem. There are two ways in which a problem may be concluded: the problem may be solved, or the problem may be dissolved.

A solved problem is a problem that is met head on. The situation in which something needed changing and for which settled routines were not adequate to provide the needed change is now changed. If the problem was a headache, the taking of two aspirins and a glass of water may be the solution. A solution deals with the problem. There may be created a dozen other problems in the process of solving one, but that is quite another matter.

Sometimes the solution to a problem requires nothing more than the reaching of a verbal statement. If our problem is: What is the Tibetan name of Mount Everest? we turn to the gazetteer section in *Webster's New International Dictionary* and find that the Tibetan name of Mount Everest is "Chomo-lungma." That is all. We don't have to go to Tibet; we don't have to climb Everest; we don't even have to know what Chomo-lungma means. The word "Chomo-lungma" almost magically solves the problem. The problem is no more. Sometimes the solution of a problem requires much more than a mere verbal solution. If a young man's problem is: Whom shall I marry? and he tells himself that Judy Davis is the one whom he will marry, but does nothing about it, his problem is not solved! A marriage counselor would probably hold that if he concluded mentally that Judy was the woman he would marry, and then does nothing about it, Judy is not the woman for him. A verbal solution to such a problem is no solution. Another example is the decision of the United States Supreme Court in 1954 that in the field of public education there is no place for the doctrine of "separate but equal." The court stated that the lower courts of the land should demand "a prompt and reasonable start toward full compliance" and that solutions should be worked out to the ending of segregation of white and Negro children "with all deliberate speed." In 1963 the Supreme Court redefined "deliberate speed," stating that this term did not mean indefinite delay. The solution to this problem is not the decision of the Court, but the actual desegregation of the public schools.

Not all conclusions are solutions; some conclusions are dissolutions. A problem that is dissolved is eliminated as completely as a problem that is solved, but the means are different. A dissolved problem is one that is shown to be a pseudo-problem. It was a problem only because it was wrongly stated, or because it was based on false assumptions. We only imagined that there was a problem. One such problem, according to many philosophers, is the problem of the freedom of the human individual to act according to his own choices. It is commonly called the freewill problem, and it is often presented in terms of an alleged conflict between man's feeling of freedom and the conviction of the scientist that causal order holds throughout the universe. The argument that man is not free may be put in this fashion:

All things in the natural world are things whose behavior is caused.
Man is one of the things in the natural world.

Therefore, man is a thing whose behavior is caused.

Nothing can be both caused and free.
Man is a thing whose behavior is caused.

Therefore, man is not a thing whose behavior is free.

The deduction of this argument is impeccable. But the first premise in the second syllogism should be carefully examined. Is it true that nothing can be both caused and free? Does "caused" mean "non-free," and does "free" mean "non-caused"? They do, if they are contradictories. Many contemporary philosophers argue that "caused" means "predictable on the basis of natural laws," whereas "free" means "exempt from external compulsion." Is "predictable on the basis of natural laws" the contradictory of "exempt from external compulsion"? Of course not! Then the problem is solved, we might think — man is free. However, the philosophers add, "Not so fast! The problem is not solved! Man is free, as you say, but man is *also* caused. You see, the original problem was: Is man free or caused? What we claim is that man is *both* free and caused. The original problem was confusedly stated; in fact, the problem arose out of the way in which it was stated. There is no freewill problem in this sense. We have not *solved* the problem; we have shown that it was a false problem. The problem is *dissolved*."

There may be other problems which are neither solved nor dissolved. These would be genuine problems which lie beyond the ability of man to settle. Many philosophers regard the question of the existence of God as such a problem. The problem "Is there a God?" they contend, is a problem which the mind of man cannot resolve. There is not enough supporting evidence to conclude "Yes," and too much supporting evidence to conclude "No," and the problem is too important to conclude "Pseudoproblem." Therefore, some say, "Let your hopes help you make up your mind"; others say, "Start acting in the direction of your desires"; others say, "Try to forget it"; and still others say, "Admit you don't know."

4. *Application of the conclusion*

There is a story that one day in the John Dewey home, Mr. Dewey's son filled the bathtub with water in order to sail his toy boat. When Mr.

Dewey came home, he found the bathroom floor flooded and water pouring into the hall. The great philosopher of action stood dumbfounded in the doorway of the bathroom contemplating the mess, until he was accosted by his young son, "Well, don't just stand there! Get a mop!"

There is always the possibility that the person with a problem may carefully analyze his problem, form hypotheses, examine and test the hypotheses, draw a verbal conclusion, and then never apply the conclusion. A young man may seriously ask himself if he should go to college, may decide that he should, and yet never go. G. B. Shaw loved to take potshots at teachers as people who had somehow missed life. Teaching was a vocation for the impotent, he said. "Those who can, do; those who can't, teach." But this dichotomy is false. To divide men into men of ideas and men of action makes sense if it means that some men think and avoid acting, whereas other men act in the absence of thought; but the dichotomy is misleading and false, if it implies that thinking and acting exclude one another. The application is part of the total process of critical thinking. Intellectuals who are only intellectuals are not very intelligent!

5. Critical thinking and the good life

Is the good life the life with few problems? The ancient Epicurean philosophers thought so, and concluded that the best life was the one with no problems — the state of the dead. The Stoic philosophers faced problems squarely, though without enthusiasm, assuring themselves that the "backdoor of life" (suicide) is always open. Men of the twentieth century are sometimes oppressed with the realization that their lives are filled with many unsolved problems. Why should we in the twentieth century with all our know-how be so frustrated in the face of personal, local, national, international, and cosmic problems? they ask.

Part of our confusions can be located in the fact that we do not know where we are in the development of man. Time-binding animals though we be, we find difficulty in lifting our eyes and minds above the present. We fail to see that we are in this second half of the twentieth century in revolt against piecemeal philosophies such as Positivism, Marxism, Utopianism, and other early twentieth-century remnants of the Enlightenment. The optimism which once flowed so freely in high school and college graduation addresses, political campaign speeches, Fourth of July celebrations, and businessmen's luncheon clubs sounds today strangely anachronistic, almost an adolescent whistling in the dark. Existentialism, one of the philosophies of our revolt, attempts to establish subjectivism in Western thought — an ingredient that has been missing since the rise of modern science. It contends that man has over-intellectualized his thought and over-organized his life. Contemporary art joins Existentialism in pushing man into a Post-Enlightenment Period. While some think that our contemporary art is art that has lost its themes, others hold that the theme of contemporary art and Existentialism is the revelation to man of his estrangements from Nature, from other men, from the Source of Being, and from himself.

Is the defender of critical thinking in the contemporary world a voice crying in the wilderness? Is critical thinking a part of the lost worlds of Scholasticism, the Renaissance, and the Enlightenment; worlds which, though different in many ways, shared in the assumptions that the cosmos is rational and that man can understand it? Although contemporary man is confused, this is not conclusive evidence that the world is irrational, or that man is unable to cope with his problems. If a problem cannot be settled by critical thinking, then wisdom consists in identifying the problem. Semantics should teach one when to speak, and when to remain silent; logic should teach one when to reason, and when to forego reasoning. There is always the danger that logic with its rules and principles may restrain rather than enhance the thinking of men. The articles appearing in philosophical journals are not overwhelming evidence that logicians are putting their disciplined talents to work on the problems of men. Logic can be a pleasant parlor game, or a conversational piece. Logic can also be the examination of problems within its own tight little province. An editor of the *New York Times* may have had the latter sort of logician in mind when he wrote, "Of course there are some students who take logic too seriously. They are the purists with whom it is not possible to have a vague and inaccurate chat. 'Define your terms,' they interrupt, 'don't say all, say one or two,' and so on, until your mild generalization that people aren't the way they used to be has assumed an importance you know it does not deserve. The young logician is complacent at your retreat when you cannot actually prove to him that what you say is true, but in his passion for preciseness he does not realize he has just lost a friend — a friend indeed who has not really retreated but is even now muttering under his breath that all those people who study logic are dolts, especially the young ones."[6] We would be most unfair to philosophers if we were to leave the impression that only laymen are aware of the limitations of logic. Whitehead says, "Logic, conceived as an adequate analysis of the advance

---

[6] *New York Times,* June 14, 1957, p. 24.

of thought is a fake. It is a superb instrument, but it requires a background of common sense."[7]

We have been studying logic in this volume as neither a game nor a disinfectant, but as critical thinking, the technique of solving the problems of man in a real world. Our thesis has been that critical thinking is an art. Hence we have been careful not to guarantee automatic success to anyone who will follow the Fourteen Easy Steps to Critical Thinking! In critical thinking, as in all art, there is a hiatus between aspiration and achievement. Man's abilities are finite, and his problems are many; yet past successes warrant restrained hope for the future. The eighteenth-century philosopher, John Locke, using the language of another day, expresses the note of optimism with which we shall conclude this study of the art of critical thinking: "For though the comprehension of our understanding comes exceeding short of the vast extent of things, yet we shall have cause enough to magnify the bountiful Author of our being for that proportion and degree of knowledge he has bestowed on us, so far above all the rest of the inhabitants of this our mansion. . . . We shall not have much reason to complain of the narrowness of our minds, if we will but employ them about what may be of use to us; for of that they are very capable: and it will be an unpardonable as well as childish peevishness, if we undervalue the advantages of our knowledge, and neglect to improve it to the ends for which it was given us, because there are some things that are set out of the reach of it. It will be no excuse to an idle and untoward servant, who would not attend his business by candlelight, to plead that he had not broad sunshine. The candle that is set up in us shines bright enough for all our purposes. . . . If we will disbelieve every thing because we cannot certainly know all things, we shall do much-what as wisely as he who would not use his legs, but sit still and perish because he had no wings to fly. . . . Our business here is not to know all things, but those which concern our conduct. If we can find out those measures whereby a rational creature, put in that state which man is in this world, may and ought to govern his opinions and actions depending thereon, we need not be troubled that some other things escape our knowledge."[8]

---

[7] *The Philosophy of A. N. Whitehead*, ed. P. A. Schilpp (Evanston and Chicago: Northwestern University Press, 1941), p. 700.

[8] *Essay Concerning Human Understanding*, Bk. I, Chap. I, Secs. 5, 6.

INDEX

Alexander, S.: on assumptions, 113–114

Alternative statement, 147; relation to conditionals, 132–135; defined, 132, 134n; sign of, 132

Ames Demonstration, 71, 90

Analogy: in hypothesis formation, 92–94; defined, 92; as tools of explanation and as aids to hypothesis formation, 92–93; Russell's use of, 92–93; Hobbes' use of, 93; Darwin's use of, 93–94

Antecedent: meaning in a conditional statement, 126–127

Appearance: distinction between appearance and reality, 187–188

Argument: validity of, 108

Aristotle, 34, 96, 97; on origin of mathematics, 12; as an authority, 68, 201; and Bacon, 110; on Laws of Thought, 118; class inclusion in, 137; on induction, 150; experiment in, 200–201

Asher, Harry: experiment with LSD drugs, 196

Assumption: examination of, 109; locating of, 113–117; in Zen Buddhism, 113; S. Alexander on, 113–114; no philosophy without, 114; as starting point, 114; as primitive idea, 114; in Declaration of Independence, 114; kinds of, 114; expressed by enthymeme, 115; defined, 115; in Euclid, 115–116; in Lewis Carroll, 115–116; definition as type of, 115; difficulty in locating, 117; challenging of, 117–118

Asymmetry: defined, 137

Authority: as source of information, 66–69; defined, 67; uses of, 67–68

Axiom: as a kind of assumption, 114; defined, 114; and postulate distinguished, 115; in Euclid, 116

Bacon, Francis, 201, 203; Idols of the Mind, 110–113, 188; on fictions, 122; on relation of induction and deduction, 208

Baker, Ross A.: on scientific hunch, 94–96

Bancroft, W. D.: on classification of scientists, 89

Bergson, Henri, 118; on metaphys-